101 Stories to
Open the Heart and
Rekindle the Spirit

心灵鸡汤

——第一辑

CHICKEN SOUP FOR THE SOUL®

Jack Canfield and Mark Victor Hansen

安徽科学技术出版社

Health Communications, Inc.

[皖]版贸登记号:1200055
图书在版编目(CIP)数据

心灵鸡汤.第1辑:英文/(美)坎费尔德,(美)汉森著.—合肥:安徽科学技术出版社,2000.10
ISBN 7-5337-2046-6

Ⅰ.心… Ⅱ.①坎… ②汉… Ⅲ.英语-语言读物,文学 Ⅳ.H319.4:I

中国版本图书馆 CIP 数据核字(2000)第 48660 号

*
安徽科学技术出版社出版
(合肥市跃进路1号新闻出版大厦)
邮政编码:230063
电话号码:(0551)2833431
新华书店经销 合肥晓星印刷厂印刷
*
开本:889×1194 1/32 印张:9.625 字数:248千
2004年6月第10次印刷
印数:5 000
ISBN 7-5337-2046-6/H·309 定价:18.00元

If there is light in the soul,
There will be beauty in the person.
If there is beauty in the person,
There will be harmony in the house.
If there is harmony in the house,
There will be order in the nation.
If there is order in the nation,
There will be peace in the world.

Chinese Proverb

With love we dedicate this book to our wives,
Georgia and Patty, and our children,
Christopher, Oran, Kyle, Elisabeth and Melanie,
who are chicken soup for our souls.
You are constantly opening our hearts and
rekindling our spirits. We love you very much!

Contents

1. ON LOVE

2. LEARNING TO LOVE YOURSELF

3. ON PARENTING

4. ON LEARNING

5. LIVE YOUR DREAM

6. OVERCOMING OBSTACLES

7. ECLECTIC WISDOM

Acknowledgments

This book took almost two years from conception to completion. It was a labor of love and took the combined efforts of many people. We especially wish to acknowledge the following:

Patty Mitchell, who typed and retyped each of these stories at least five times. Her commitment to this project included many weekdays until 10:00 P.M. and lots of weekends. Thank you, Patty! We couldn't have done it without you.

Kim Wiele, for the monumental typing and retyping of many of the stories, handling much of the extensive research and coordinating all of the seemingly endless work to secure copyright permission of the stories we didn't write ourselves. She did a terrific job. Thanks, Kim.

Kate Driesen, who assisted with the typing, read and commented on each story and helped with much of the research. You were always there when there were deadlines. Thank you.

Wanda Pate, who contributed endlessly in helping with typing and research.

Cheryl Millikin, who kept the processing and flow of the material working all along.

Lisa Williams, for taking care of Mark's business so he

could be dedicated to this book.

Larry Price and Mark Powers, for keeping everything else going while this book was being written.

To the hundreds of people who listened, read and commented on these stories, poems and quotes.

To all of our friends at the National Speakers Association, who so generously gave of their own material to complete this book. We especially want to thank Dottie Walters for her continued encouragement and support.

To Frank Siccone, a dear friend, who contributed several of his stories and quotes.

To Jeff Herman, for being such an inspired literary agent and for believing in the book from the beginning. Jeff, we love working with you.

To Peter Vegso, Gary Seidler and Barbara Nichols at Health Communications for catching the vision of the book long before anyone else did. We appreciate your enthusiastic support.

To Cindy Spitzer, who wrote and edited several of the most important stories in this book. Cindy, your contribution was invaluable.

To Marie Stilkind, our editor at Health Communications, for her timeless efforts in bringing this book to its high state of excellence.

To Bob Proctor, who contributed several stories and anecdotes from his voluminous file of teaching stories. Thank you, Bob. You've been a good friend.

To Brandon Hall, who helped us with two stories.

We also want to thank the following people for giving us very valuable feedback on the first draft: Ellen Angelis, Kim Angelis, Jacob Blass, Rick Canfield, Dan Drubin, Kathy Fellows, Patty Hansen, Norman Howe, Ann Husch, Tomas

Nani, Dave Potter, Danielle Lee, Michele Martin, Georgia Noble, Lee Potts, Linda Price, Martin Rutte, Lou Tartaglia, Dottie Walters, Rebecca Weidekehr, Harold C. Wells.

Introduction

We know everything we need to know to end the needless emotional suffering that many people currently experience. High self-esteem and personal effectiveness are available to anyone willing to take the time to pursue them.

It is difficult to translate the spirit of a live presentation into the written word. Stories we tell every day have had to be rewritten five times to work as well in print as they do live. When you are reading these stories, please forget everything you ever learned in your speed-reading classes. Slow down. Listen to the words in your heart as well as in your mind. Savor each story. Let it touch you. Ask yourself, what does it awaken in me? What does it suggest for my life? What feeling or action does it call forth from my inner being? Let yourself have a personal relationship with each story.

Some stories will speak louder to you than others. Some will have deeper meaning. Some will make you cry. Some will make you laugh. Some will give you a warm feeling all over. Some may hit you right between the eyes. There is no right reaction. There is only *your* reaction. Let it happen and let it be.

Don't hurry through this book. Take your time. Enjoy

it. Savor it. Engage it with your whole being. It represents thousands of hours of culling the "best of the best"from our 40 years of combined experience.

One last thing:Reading a book like this is a little like sitting down to eat a meal of all desserts. It may be a little too rich. It is a meal with no vegetables,salad or bread. It is all essence with very little froth.

In our seminars and workshops we take more time to set up and discuss the implications of each story. There are more explanations and explorations of how to apply the lessons and principles to your everyday life. Don't just read these stories. Take the time to digest them and make them your own.

If you find yourself moved to share a story with others,do it. When a story makes you think of another person,call the person it brings to mind and share it. Engage these stories and let them move you to do whatever comes up for you. They are meant to inspire and motivate you.

For a lot of these stories we went back to the original source and asked them to write it or tell it in their own words. Many of the stories will be in their voice,not ours. We have attributed every story we could to the original source. For all of those that are from fellow speakers and trainers,we have included a contributors section in the back of the book where we have listed their name,address and phone number so you can contact them yourself if you wish.

We hope you will enjoy reading this book as much as we have enjoyed writing it.

1

ON LOVE

The day will come when, after harnessing space, the winds, the tides and gravitation, we shall harness for God the energies of love. And on that day, for the second time in the history of the world, we shall have discovered fire.

Teilhard de Chardin

Love: The One Creative Force

Spread love everywhere you go: first of all in your own house. Give love to your children, to your wife or husband, to a next door neighbor.... Let no one ever come to you without leaving better and happier. Be the living expression of God's kindness; kindness in your face, kindness in your eyes, kindness in your smile, kindness in your warm greeting.

Mother Teresa

A college professor had his sociology class go into the Baltimore slums to get case histories of 200 young boys. They were asked to write an evaluation of each boy's future. In every case the students wrote, "He hasn't got a chance." Twenty-five years later another sociology professor came across the earlier study. He had his students follow up on the project to see what had happened to these boys. With the exception of 20 boys who had moved away or died, the students learned that 176 of the remaining 180 had achieved more than ordinary success as lawyers, doctors and businessmen.

The professor was astounded and decided to pursue the matter further. Fortunately, all the men were in the area and he was able to ask each one, "How do you account for your success?" In each case the reply came with feeling, "There was a teacher."

The teacher was still alive, so he sought her out and asked the old but still alert lady what magic formula she had used to pull these boys out of the slums into successful achievement.

The teacher's eyes sparkled and her lips broke into a gentle smile. "It's really very simple," she said. "I loved those boys."

Eric Butterworth

All I Remember

When my father spoke to me, he always began the conversation with "Have I told you yet today how much I adore you?" The expression of love was reciprocated and, in his later years, as his life began to visibly ebb, we grew even closer... if that were possible.

At 82 he was ready to die, and I was ready to let him go so that his suffering would end. We laughed and cried and held hands and told each other of our love and agreed that it was time. I said, "Dad, after you've gone I want a sign from you that you're fine." He laughed at the absurdity of that; Dad didn't believe in reincarnation. I wasn't positive I did either, but I had had many experiences that convinced me I could get some signal "from the other side."

My father and I were so deeply connected I felt his heart attack in my chest at the moment he died. Later I mourned that the hospital, in their sterile wisdom, had not let me hold his hand as he had slipped away.

Day after day I prayed to hear from him, but nothing happened. Night after night I asked for a dream before I fell asleep. And yet four long months passed and I heard and felt nothing but grief at his loss. Mother had died five years before of Alzheimer's, and, though I had grown daughters of my own, I felt like a lost child.

One day, while I was lying on a massage table in a dark quiet room waiting for my appointment, a wave of longing for my father swept over me. I began to wonder if I had been too demanding in asking for a sign from him. I noticed that my mind was in a hyper-acute state. I experienced an unfamiliar clarity in which I could have added long columns of figures in my head. I checked to make sure I was awake and not dreaming, and I saw that I was as far removed from a dreamy state as one could possibly be. Each thought I had was like a drop of water disturbing a still pond, and I marveled at the peacefulness of each passing moment. Then I thought, "I've been trying to control the messages from the other side; I will stop that now."

Suddenly my mother's face appeared — my mother, as she had been before Alzheimer's disease had stripped her of her mind, her humanity and 50 pounds. Her magnificent silver hair crowned her sweet face. She was so real and so close I felt I could reach out and touch her. She looked as she had a dozen years ago, before the wasting away had begun. I even smelled the fragrance of Joy, her favorite perfume. She seemed to be waiting and did not speak. I wondered how it could happen that I was thinking of my father and my mother appeared, and I felt a little guilty that I had not asked for her as well.

I said, "Oh, Mother, I'm so sorry that you had to suffer with that horrible disease."

She tipped her head slightly to one side, as though to acknowledge what I had said about her suffering. Then she smiled — a beautiful smile — and said very distinctly, "But all I remember is love." And she disappeared.

I began to shiver in a room suddenly gone cold, and I knew in my bones that the love we give and receive is all that matters and all that is remembered. Suffering disappears; love remains.

Her words are the most important I have ever heard, and that moment is forever engraved on my heart.

I have not yet seen or heard from my father, but I have no doubts that someday, when I least expect it, he will appear and say, "Have I told you yet today that I love you?"

Bobbie Probstein

Heart Song

Once upon a time there was a great man who married the woman of his dreams. With their love, they created a little girl. She was a bright and cheerful little girl and the great man loved her very much.

When she was very little, he would pick her up, hum a tune and dance with her around the room, and he would tell her, "I love you, little girl."

When the little girl was growing up, the great man would hug her and tell her, "I love you, little girl." The little girl would pout and say, "I'm not a little girl anymore." Then the man would laugh and say, "But to me, you'll always be my little girl."

The little girl who-was-not-little-anymore left her home and went into the world. As she learned more about herself, she learned more about the man. She saw that he truly was great and strong, for now she recognized his strengths. One of his strengths was his ability to express his love to his family. It didn't matter where she went in the world, the man would call her and say, "I love you, little girl."

The day came when the little girl who-was-not-little-anymore received a phone call. The great man was damaged. He had had a stroke. He was aphasic, they explained to the girl. He couldn't talk anymore and they weren't sure that he could understand the words spoken to him. He could no longer smile, laugh, walk, hug, dance or tell the little girl who-was-not-little-anymore that he loved her.

And so she went to the side of the great man. When she walked into the room and saw him, he looked small and not strong at all. He looked at her and tried to speak, but he could not.

The little girl did the only thing she could do. She climbed up on the bed next to the great man. Tears ran from both of their eyes and she drew her arms around the useless shoulders of her father.

Her head on his chest, she thought of many things. She remembered the wonderful times together and how she had always felt protected and cherished by the great man. She felt grief for the loss she was to endure, the words of love that had comforted her.

And then she heard from within the man, the beat of his heart. The heart where the music and the words had always lived. The heart beat on, steadily unconcerned about the damage to the rest of the body. And while she rested there, the magic happened. She heard what she needed to hear.

His heart beat out the words that his mouth could no longer say. . .

I love you
I love you
I love you
Little girl
Little girl
Little girl
And she was comforted.

Patty Hansen

True Love

Moses Mendelssohn, the grandfather of the well-known German composer, was far from being handsome. Along with a rather short stature, he had a grotesque hunchback.

One day he visited a merchant in Hamburg who had a lovely daughter named Frumtje. Moses fell hopelessly in love with her. But Frumtje was repulsed by his misshapen appearance.

When it came time for him to leave, Moses gathered his courage and climbed the stairs to her room to take one last opportunity to speak with her. She was a vision of heavenly beauty, but caused him deep sadness by her refusal to look at him. After several attempts at conversation, Moses shyly asked, "Do you believe marriages are made in heaven?"

"Yes," She answered, still looking at the floor. "And do you?"

"Yes I do," He replied. "You see, in heaven at the birth of each boy, the Lord announces which girl he will marry. When I was born, my future bride was pointed out to me. Then The Lord added, 'But your wife will be humpbacked.'"

"Right then and there I called out, 'Oh Lord, a humpbacked woman would be a tragedy. Please, Lord, give me the hump and let her be beautiful.'"

Then Frumtje looked up into his eyes and was stirred by

some deep memory. She reached out and gave Mendelssohn her hand and later became his devoted wife.

Barry and Joyce Vissell

The Hugging Judge

Don't bug me! Hug me!

Bumper Sticker

Lee Shapiro is a retired judge. He is also one of the most genuinely loving people we know. At one point in his career, Lee realized that love is the greatest power there is. As a result, Lee became a hugger. He began offering everybody a hug. His colleagues dubbed him "the hugging judge" (as opposed to the hanging judge, we suppose). The bumper sticker on his car reads, "Don't bug me! Hug me!"

About six years age Lee created what he calls his Hugger Kit. On the outside it reads "A heart for a hug." The inside contains thirty little red embroidered hearts with stickums on the back. Lee will take out his Hugger Kit, go around to people and offer them a little red heart in exchange for a hug.

Lee has become so well known for this that he is often invited to keynote conferences and conventions, where he shares his message of unconditional love. At a conference in San Francisco, the local news media challenged him by saying. "It is easy to give out hugs here in the conference to people who self-selected to be here. But this would never work in the real world."

They challenged Lee to give away some hugs on the streets of San Francisco. Followed by a television crew from the local news station, Lee went out onto the street. First he approached a woman walking by. "Hi, I'm Lee Shapiro, the hugging judge. I'm giving out these hearts in exchange for a hug." "Sure," she replied. "Too easy," challenged the local commentator. Lee looked around. He saw a meter maid who was being given a hard time by the owner of a BMW to whom she was giving a ticket. He marched up to her, camera crew in tow, and said, "You look like you could use a hug. I'm the hugging judge and I'm offering you one." She accepted.

The television commentator threw down one final challenge. "Look, here comes a bus. San Francisco bus drivers are the toughest, crabbiest, meanest people in the whole town. Let's see you get him to hug you." Lee took the challenge.

As the bus pulled up to the curb. Lee said, "Hi, I'm Lee Shapiro, the hugging judge. This has got to be one of the most stressful jobs in the whole world. I'm offering hugs to people today to lighten the load a little. Would you like one?" The six-foot-two, 230-pound bus driver got out of his seat, stepped down and said, "Why not?"

Lee hugged him, gave him a heart and waved good-bye as the bus pulled out. The TV crew was speechless. Finally, the commentator said, "I have to admit, I'm very impressed."

One day Lee's friend Nancy Johnston showed up on his doorstep. Nancy is a professional clown and she was wearing her clown costume, makeup and all. "Lee, grab a bunch of your Hugger Kits and let's go out to the home for the disabled."

When they arrived at the home, they started giving out ballon hats, hearts and hugs to the patients. Lee was uncomfortable. He had never before hugged people who were terminally ill, severely retarded or quadriplegic. It was definitely a stretch. But after a while it became easier, with Nancy and Lee acquiring an entourage of doctors, nurses and orderlies who followed them from ward to ward.

After several hours they entered the last ward. These were 34 of the worst cases Lee had seen in his life. The feeling was so grim it took his heart away. But out of their commitment to share their love and to make a difference, Nancy and Lee started working their way around the room followed by the entourage of medical staff, all of whom by now had hearts on their collars and ballon hats on their heads.

Finally, Lee came to the last person, Leonard. Leonard was wearing a big white bib which he was drooling on. Lee looked at Leonard dribbling onto his bib and said, "Let's go, Nancy. There's no way we can get through to this person." Nancy replied, "C'mon, Lee. He's a fellow human being, too, isn't he?" Then she placed a funny balloon hat on his head. Lee took one of his little red hearts and placed it on Leonard's bib. He took a deep breath, leaned down and gave Leonard a hug.

All of a sudden Leonard began to squeal, "Eeeeehh! Eeeeeehh!" Some of the other patients in the room began to clang things together. Lee turned to the staff for some sort of explanation only to find that every doctor, nurse and orderly was crying. Lee asked the head nurse, "What's going on?"

Lee will never forget what she said: "This is the first time in 23 years we've ever seen Leonard smile."

How simple it is to make a difference in the lives of others.

Jack Canfield and Mark V. Hansen

© 1984 United Feature Syndicate, Inc.
5-12
YOU CAN ALWAYS TELL WHEN HE'S BEEN LISTENING TO LEO BUSCAGLIA TAPES..

It Can't Happen Here?

We need 4 hugs a day for survival. We need 8 hugs a day for maintenance. We need 12 hugs a day for growth.

Virginia Satir

We always teach people to hug each other in our work shops and seminars. Most people respond by saying, "You could never hug people where I work." Are you sure? Here is a letter from a graduate of one of our seminars.

Dear Jack,

I started out this day in rather a bleak mood. My friend Rosalind stopped over and asked me if I was giving hugs today. I just grumbled something but then I began to think about hugs and everything during the week. I would look at the sheet you gave us on How to Keep the Seminar Alive *and I would cringe when I got to the part about giving and getting hugs because I couldn't imagine giving hugs to the people at work.*

Well, I decided to make it "hugs day" and I started giving hugs to the customers who came to my counter. It was great to see how people just brightened up. An MBA student jumped up on top of the counter and did a dance. Some people actually came back and asked for more. These two Xerox repair guys, who were kind of just walking along not really talking to each other, were so surprised, they just woke up and suddenly were talking and laughing down the hall.

It feels like I hugged everybody in the Wharton Business School, plus whatever was wrong with me this morning, which included some physical pain, is all gone. I'm sorry that this letter is so long but I'm just really excited. The neatest thing was, at one point there were about 10 *people all hugging each other out in front of my counter. I couldn't believe this was happening.*

Love,
Pamela Rogers

P. S.: On the way home I hugged a policeman on 37th Street. He said, "Wow! Policemen never get hugs. Are you sure you don't want to throw something at me?"

Another seminar graduate sent us the following piece on hugging:

Hugging Is

Hugging is healthy. It helps the immune system, cures depression, reduces stress and induces sleep. It's invigo-

rating, rejuvenating and has no unpleasant side effects. Hugging is nothing less than a miracle drug.

Hugging is all natural. It is organic, naturally sweet, no artificial ingredients, nonpolluting, environmentally friendly and 100 *percent wholesome.*

Hugging is the ideal gift. Great for any occasion, fun to give and receive, shows you care, comes with its own wrapping and, of course, fully returnable.

Hugging is practically perfect. No batteries to wear out, inflation-proof, nonfattening, no monthly payments, theft-proof and nontaxable.

Hugging is an underutilized resource with magical powers. When we open our hearts and arms, we encourage others to do the same.

Think of the people in your life. Are there any words you'd like to say? Are there any hugs you'd want to share? Are you waiting and hoping someone else will ask first? Please don't wait! Initiate!

Charles Faraone

Jack Canfield

Who You Are Makes A Difference

A teacher in New York decided to honor each of her seniors in high school by telling them the difference they each made. Using a process developed by Helice Bridges of Del Mar, California, she called each student to the front of the class, one at a time. First she told them how the student made a difference to her and the class. Then she presented each of them with a blue ribbon imprinted with gold letters which read, "Who I Am Makes a Difference."

Afterwards the teacher decided to do a class project to see what kind of impact recognition would have on a community. She gave each of the students three more ribbons and instructed them to go out and spread this acknowledgment ceremony. Then they were to follow up on the results, see who honored whom and report back to the class in about a week.

One of the boys in the class went to a junior executive in a nearby company and honored him for helping him with his career planning. He gave him a blue ribbon and put it on his shirt. Then he gave him two extra ribbons, and said, "We're doing a class project on recognition, and we'd like you to go out, find somebody to honor, give them a blue ribbon, then give them the extra blue ribbon so they can acknowledge a third person to keep this acknowledgment ceremony going. Then please report back to me and tell me what happened."

Later that day the junior executive went in to see his boss, who had been noted, by the way, as being kind of a grouchy fellow. He sat his boss down and he told him that he deeply admired him for being a creative genius. The boss seemed very surprised. The junior executive asked him if he would accept the gift of the blue ribbon and would he give him permission to put it on him. His surprised boss said, "Well, sure."

The junior executive took the blue ribbon and placed it right on his boss's jacket above his heart. As he gave him the last extra ribbon, he said, "Would you do me a favor? Would you take this extra ribbon and pass it on by honoring somebody else? The young boy who first gave me the ribbons is doing a project in school and we want to keep this recognition ceremony going and find out how it affects people."

That night the boss came home to his 14-year-old son and sat him down. He said, "The most incredible thing happened to me today. I was in my office and one of the junior executives came in and told me he admired me and gave me a blue ribbon for being a creative genius. Imagine. He thinks I'm a creative genius. Then he put this blue ribbon that says 'Who I Am Makes A Difference' on my jacket above my heart. He gave me an extra ribbon and asked me to find somebody else to honor. As I was driving home tonight, I started thinking about whom I would honor with this ribbon and I thought about you. I want to honor you.

"My days are really hectic and when I come home I don't pay a lot of attention to you. Sometimes I scream at you for not getting good enough grades in school and for your bedroom being a mess, but somehow tonight, I just wanted to sit here and, well, just let you know that you do make a difference to me. Besides your mother, you are the most important person in my life. You're a great kid and I love you!"

The startled boy started to sob and sob, and he couldn't stop crying. His whole body shook. He looked up at his father and said through his tears, "I was planning on committing suicide tomorrow, Dad, because I didn't think you loved me. Now I don't need to."

Helice Bridges

You are invited to become a
Steward of the Dream

Who I Am Makes A Difference™

A Blue Ribbon
on every person in America
in the next five years ~ creating
the foundation for acknowledgment
for this generation and all generations to come.

Helice Bridges' dream is to have a blue ribbon pinned on every person in America by the year 2000. *To help make this dream come true, you can order "Who I Am Makes A Difference" blue ribbons by calling* [illegible] 1051 *or writing to HPC, P. O. Box* 2115, *Del Mar, California* 92014.

One At A Time

A friend of ours was walking down deserted Mexican beach at sunset. As he walked along, he began to see another man in the distance. As he grew nearer, he noticed that the local native kept leaning down, picking some thing up and throwing it out into the water. Time and again he kept hurling things out into the ocean.

As our friend approached even closer, he noticed that the man was picking up starfish that had been washed up on the beach and, one at a time, he was throwing them back into the water.

Our friend was puzzled. He approached the man and said, "Good evening, friend. I was wondering what you are doing."

"I'm throwing these starfish back into the ocean. You see, it's low tide right now and all of these starfish have been washed up onto the shore. If I don't throw them back into the sea, they'll die up here from lack of oxygen."

"I understand," my friend replied, "but there must be thousands of starfish on this beach. You can't possibly get to all of them. There are simply too many. And don't you realize this is probably happening on hundreds of beaches all up and down this coast. Can't you see that you can't possibly make a difference?"

The local native smiled, bent down and picked up yet another starfish, and as he threw it back into the sea, he replied, "Made a difference to that one!"

Jack Canfield and Mark V. Hansen

The Gift

Bennet Cerf relates this touching story about a bus that was bumping along a back road in the South.

In one seat a wispy old man sat holding a bunch of fresh flowers. Across the aisle was a young girl whose eyes came back again and again to the man's flowers. The time came for the old man to get off. Impulsively he thrust the flowers into the girl's lap. "I can see you love the flowers," he explained, "and I think my wife would like for you to have them. I'll tell her I gave them to you." The girl accepted the flowers, then watched the old man get off the bus and walk through the gate of a small cemetery.

Bannet Carf

A Brother Like That

A friend of mine named Paul received an automobile from his brother as a Christmas present. On Christmas Eve when Paul came out of his office, a street urchin was walking around the shiny new car, admiring it. "Is this your car, Mister?" he asked.

Paul nodded. "My brother gave it to me for Christmas." The boy was astounded. "You mean your brother gave it to you and it didn't cost you nothing? Boy, I wish ..." He hesitated.

Of course Paul knew what he was going to wish for. He was going to wish he had a brother like that. But what the lad said jarred Paul all the way down to his heels.

"I wish," the boy went on, "that I could be a brother like that."

Paul looked at the boy in astonishment, then impulsively he added, "Would you like to take a ride in my automobile?"

"Oh yes, I'd love that."

After a short ride, the boy turned and with his eyes aglow, said, "Mister, would you mind driving in front of my house?"

Paul smiled a little. He thought he knew what the lad wanted. He wanted to show his neighbors that he could ride home in a big automobile. But Paul was wrong again. "Will you stop where those two steps are?" the boy asked.

He ran up the steps. Then in a little while Paul heard him coming back, but he was not coming fast. He was carrying his little crippled brother. He sat him down on the bottom step, then sort of squeezed up against him and pointed to the car.

"There she is, Buddy, just like I told you upstairs. His brother gave it to him for Christmas and it didn't cost him a cent. And some day I'm gonna give you one just like it... then you can see for yourself all the pretty things in the Christmas windows that I've been trying to tell you about."

Paul got out and lifted the lad to the front seat of his car. The shining-eyed older brother climbed in beside him and the three of them began a memorable holiday ride.

That Christmas Eve, Paul learned what Jesus meant when he said: *"It is more blessed to give..."*

Dan Clark

On Courage

"So you think I'm courageous?" she asked.

"Yes, I do."

"Perhaps I am. But that's because I've had some inspiring teachers. I'll tell you about one of them. Many years ago, when I worked as a volunteer at Stanford Hospital, I got to know a little girl named Liza who was suffering from a rare and serious disease. Her only chance of recovery appeared to be a blood transfusion from her five-year-old brother, who had miraculously survived the same disease and had developed the antibodies needed to combat the illness. The doctor explained the situation to her little brother, and asked the boy if he would be willing to give his blood to his sister. I saw him hesitate for only a moment before taking a deep breath and saying, 'Yes, I'll do it if it will save Liza.'

"As the transfusion progressed, he lay in a bed next to his sister and smiled, as we all did, seeing the color returning to her cheeks, Then his face grew pale and his smile faded. He looked up at the doctor and asked with a trembling voice, 'Will I start to die right away?'

"Being young, the boy had misunderstood the doctor, he thought he was going to have to give her *all* his blood.

"Yes, I've learned courage," she added, "because I've had inspiring teachers."

Dan Millman

Big Ed

When I arrived in the city to present a seminar on Tough-Minded Management, a small group of people took me to dinner to brief me on the people I would talk to the next day.

The obvious leader of the group was Big Ed, a large burly man with a deep rumbling voice. At dinner he informed me that he was a troubleshooter for a huge international organization. His job was to go into certain divisions or subsidiaries to terminate the employment of the executive in charge.

"Joe," he said, "I'm really looking forward to tomorrow because all of the guys need to listen to a tough guy like you. They're gonna find out that my style is the right one." He grinned and winked.

I smiled. I knew the next day was going to be different from what he was anticipating.

The next day he sat impassively all through the seminar and left at the end without saying anything to me.

Three years later I returned to that city to present another management seminar to approximately the same group. Big Ed was there again. At about ten o'clock he suddenly stood up and asked loudly, "Joe, can I say something to these people?"

I grinned and said, "Sure. When anybody is as big as you

are, Ed, he can say anything he wants."

Big Ed went on to say, "All of you guys know me and some of you know what's happened to me. I want to share it, however, with all of you. Joe, I think you'll appreciate it by the time I've finished.

"When I heard you suggest that each of us, in order to become really tough-minded, needed to learn to tell those closest to us that we really loved them, I thought it was a bunch of sentimental garbage. I wondered what in the world that had to do with being tough. You had said toughness is like leather, and hardness is like granite, that the tough mind is open, resilient, disciplined and tenacious, But I couldn't see what love had to do with it.

"That night, as I sat across the living room from my wife, your words were still bugging me. What kind of courage would it take to tell my wife I loved her? Couldn't anybody do it? You had also said this should be in the daylight and not in the bedroom. I found myself clearing my throat and starting and then stopping. My wife looked up and asked me what I had said, and I answered, 'Oh nothing.' Then suddenly, I got up, walked across the room, nervously pushed her newspaper aside and said, 'Alice, I love you.' For a minute she looked startled. Then the tears came to her eyes and she said softly, 'Ed, I love you, too, but this is the first time in 25 years you've said it like that.'

"We talked a while about how love, if there's enough of it, can dissolve all kinds of tensions, and suddenly I decided on the spur of the moment to call my oldest son in New York. We have never really communicated well. When I got him on the phone, I blurted out, 'Son, you're liable to think I'm drunk, but I'm not. I just thought I'd call you and tell you I love you.'

"There was a pause at his end and then I heard him say quietly, 'Dad, I guess I've known that, but it's sure good to hear. I want you to know I love you, too.' We had a good chat and then I called my youngest son in San Francisco. We had been closer. I told him the same thing and this, too, led to a real fine talk like we'd never really had.

"As I lay in bed that night thinking, I realized that all the things you'd talked about that day — real management nuts and bolts — took on extra meaning, and I could get a handle on how to apply them if I really understood and practiced tough-minded love.

"As some of you guys here know, I really changed the way I work with people. I began to listen more and to really hear. I learned what it was like to try to get to know people's strengths rather than dwelling on their weaknesses. I began to discover the real pleasure of helping build their confidence. Maybe the most important thing of all was that I really began to understand that an excellent way to show love and respect for people was to expect them to use their strengths to meet objectives we had worked out together.

"Joe, this is my way of saying thanks. Incidentally, talk about practical! I'm now executive vice-president of the company and they call me a pivotal leader. Okay, you guys, now listen to this guy!"

Joe Batten

Love And The Cabbie

I was in New York the other day and rode with a friend in a taxi. When we got out, my friend said to the driver, "Thank you for the ride. You did a superb job of driving."

The taxi driver was stunned for a second. Then he said, "Are you a wise guy or something?"

"No, my dear man, and I'm not putting you on. I admire the way you keep cool in heavy traffic."

"Yeah," the driver said and drove off.

"What was that all about?" I asked.

"I am trying to bring love back to New York," he said. "I believe it's the only thing that can save the city."

"How can one man save New York?"

"It's not one man. I believe I have made that taxi driver's day. Suppose he has 20 fares. He's going to be nice to those 20 fares because someone was nice to him. Those fares in turn will be kinder to their employees or shopkeepers or waiters or even their own families. Eventually the goodwill could spread to at least 1,000 people. Now that isn't bad, is it?"

"But you're depending on that taxi driver to pass your goodwill to others."

"I'm not depending on it." my friend said. "I'm aware that the system isn't foolproof so I might deal with ten different people today. If out of ten I can make three happy, then eventually I can indirectly influence the attitudes of 3, 000 more."

"It sounds good on paper," I admitted, "but I'm not sure it works in practice."

"Nothing is lost if it doesn't. It didn't take any of my time to tell that man he was doing a good job. He neither received a larger tip nor a smaller tip. If it fell on deaf ears, so what? Tomorrow there will be another taxi driver I can try to make happy."

"You're some kind of a nut," I said.

"That shows how cynical you have become. I have made a study of this. The thing that seems to be lacking, besides money of course, for our postal employees, is that no one tells people who work for the post office what a good job they're doing."

"But they're not doing a good job."

"They're not doing a good job because they feel no one cares if they do or not. Why shouldn't someone say a kind word to them?"

We were walking past a structure in the process of being built and passed five workmen eating their lunch. My friend stopped. "That's a magnificent job you men have done. It must be difficult and dangerous work."

The workmen eyed my friend suspiciously.

"When will it be finished?"

"June," a man grunted.

"Ah. That really is impressive. You must all be very proud."

We walked away. I said to him, "I haven't seen anyone like you since *Man of La Mancha*."

"When those men digest my words, they will feel better

for it. Somehow the city will benefit from their happiness."

"But you can't do this all alone!" I protested. "You're just one man."

"The most important thing is not to get discouraged. Making people in the city become kind again is not an easy job, but if I can enlist other people in my campaign..."

"You just winked at a very plain-looking woman," I said.

"Yes, I know," he replied. "And if she's a schoolteacher, her class will be in for a fantastic day.

Art Buchwald

A Simple Gesture

Everybody can be great... because anybody can serve. You don't have to have a college degree to serve. You don't have to make your subject and verb agree to serve. You only need a heart full of grace. A soul generated by love.

Martin Luther King, Jr.

Mark was walking home from school one day when he noticed the boy ahead of him had tripped and dropped all of the books he was carrying, along with two sweaters, a baseball bat, a glove and a small tape recorder. Mark knelt down and helped the boy pick up the scattered articles. Since they were going the same way, he helped to carry part of the burden. As they walked Mark discovered the boy's name was Bill, that he loved video games, baseball and history, that he was having a lot of trouble with his other subjects and that he had just broken up with his girlfriend.

They arrived at Bill's home first and Mark was invited in for a Coke and to watch some television. The afternoon passed pleasantly with a few laughs and some shared small talk, then Mark went home. They continued to see each other around school, had lunch together once or twice, then both graduated from junior high school. They ended up in the same high school where they had brief contacts over the years. Finally the long awaited senior year came, and three weeks before graduation, Bill asked Mark if they could talk.

Bill reminded him of the day years ago when they had first met. "Do you ever wonder why I was carrying so many things home that day?" asked Bill. "You see, I cleaned out my locker because I didn't want to leave a mess for anyone else. I had stored away some of my mother's sleeping pills and I was going home to commit suicide. But after we spent some time together talking and laughing, I realized that if I had killed myself, I would have missed that time and so many others that might follow. So you see, Mark, when you picked up my books that day, you did a lot more. You saved my life."

John W. Schlatter

The Smile

Smile at each other, smile at your wife, smile at your husband, smile at your children, smile at each other — it doesn't matter who it is — and that will help you to grow up in greater love for each other.

Mother Teresa

Many Americans are familiar with *The Little Prince*, a wonderful book by Antoine de Saint-Exupery. This is a whimsical and fabulous book and works as a children's story as well as a thought-provoking adult fable. Far fewer are aware of Saint-Exupery's other writings, novels and short stories.

Saint-Exupery was a fighter pilot who fought against the Nazis and was killed in action. Before World War II, he fought in the Spanish Civil War against the fascists. He wrote a fascinating story based on that experience entitled *The Smile* (*Le Sourire*). It is this story which I'd like to share with you now. It isn't clear whether or not he meant this to be autobiographical or fiction. I choose to believe it is the former.

He said that he was captured by the enemy and thrown into a jail cell. He was sure that from the contemptuous looks and rough treatment he received from his jailers he would be executed the next day. From here, I'll tell the story as I remember it in my own words.

"I was sure that I was to be killed. I became terribly nervous and distraught. I fumbled in my pockets to see if there were any cigarettes which had escaped their search. I found one and because of my shaking hands, I could barely get it to my lips. But I had no matches, they had taken those.

"I looked through the bars at my jailer. He did not make eye contact with me. After all, one does not make eye contact with a thing, a corpse. I called out to him 'Have you got a light, *por favor*?' He looked at me, shrugged and came over to light my cigarette.

"As he came close and lit the match, his eyes inadvertently locked with mine. At that moment, I smiled. I don't know why I did that. Perhaps it was nervousness, perhaps it was because, when you get very close, one to another, it is very hard not to smile. In any case, I smiled. In that instant, it was as though a spark jumped across the gap between our two hearts, our two human souls. I know he didn't want to, but my smile leaped through the bars and generated a smile on his lips, too. He lit my cigarette but stayed near, looking at me directly in the eyes and continuing to smile.

"I kept smiling at him, now aware of him as a person and not just a jailer. And his looking at me seemed to have a new dimension, too. 'Do you have kids?' he asked.

" 'Yes, here, here.' I took out my wallet and nervously fumbled for the pictures of my family. He, too, took out the pictures of his *niños* and began to talk about his plans and hopes for them. My eyes filled with tears. I said that I feared that I'd never see my family again, never have the chance to see them grow up. Tears came to his eyes, too.

"Suddenly, without another word, he unlocked my cell and silently led me out. Out of the jail, quietly and by back routes, out of the town. There, at the edge of town, he released me. And without another word, he turned back toward the town.

"My life was saved by a smile."

Yes, the smile — the unaffected, unplanned, natural connection between people. I tell this story in my work because I'd like people to consider that underneath all the layers we construct to protect ourselves, our dignity, our titles, our degrees, our status and our need to be seen in certain ways — underneath all that, remains the authentic, essential self. I'm not afraid to call it *the soul.* I really believe that if that part of you and that part of me could recognize each other, we wouldn't be enemies. We couldn't have hate or envy or fear. I sadly conclude that all those other layers, which we so carefully construct through our lives, distance and insulate us from truly contacting others. Saint-Exupery's story speaks of that magic moment when two souls recognize each other.

I've had just a few moments like that. Falling in love is one example. And looking at a baby. Why do we smile when we see a baby? Perhaps it's because we see someone without all the defensive layers, someone whose smile for us we know to be fully genuine and without guile. And that baby-soul inside us smiles wistfully in recognition.

Hanoch McCarty

Amy Graham

After flying all night from Washington, D. C. I was tired as I arrived at the Mile High Church in Denver to conduct three services and hold a workshop on prosperity consciousness. As I entered the church, Dr. Fred Vogt asked me, "Do you know about the Make-A-Wish Foundation?"

"Yes," I replied.

"Well, Amy Graham has been diagnosed as having terminal leukemia. They gave her three days. Her dying wish was to attend your services."

I was shocked. I felt a combination of elation, awe and doubt. I couldn't believe it. I thought kids who were dying would want to go see Disneyland, meet Sylvester Stallone, Mr. "T" or Arnold Schwarzenegger. Surely they wouldn't want to spend their final days listening to Mark Victor Hansen. Why would a kid with only a few days to live want to come hear a motivational speaker? Suddenly my thoughts were interrupted...

"Here's Amy," Vogt said as he put her frail hand in mine. Before me stood a 17-year-old girl wearing a bright red and orange turban to cover her head, which was bald from all of the chemotherapy treatments. Her frail body was bent and weak. She said, "My two goals were to graduate from high school and to attend your sermon. My doctors didn't believe

I could do either. They didn't think I'd have enough energy. I got discharged into my parents care... This is my mom an dad."

Tears welled in my eyes; I was choked up. My equilibrium was being shaken. I was totally moved. I cleared my throat, smiled and said, "You and your folks are our guests. Thanks for wanting to come. We hugged, dabbed our eyes and separated.

I've attended many healing seminars in the United States, Canada, Malaysia, New Zealand and Australia. I've watched the best healers at work and I've studied, researched, listened, pondered and questioned what worked, why and how.

That Sunday afternoon I held a seminar that Amy and her parents attended. The audience was packed to overflowing with over a thousand attendees eager to learn, grow and become more fully human.

I humbly asked the audience if they wanted to learn a healing process that might serve them for life. From the stage it appeared that everyone's hand was raised high in the air. They unanimously wanted to learn.

I taught the audience how to vigorously rub their hands together, separate them by two inches and feel the healing energy. Then I paired them off with a partner to feel the healing energy emanating from themselves to another. I said, "If you need a healing, accept one here and now."

The audience was in alignment and it was an ecstatic feeling. I explained that everyone has healing energy and healing potential. Five percent of us have it so dramatically pouring forth from our hands that we could make it our profession. I said, "This morning I was introduced to Amy Graham, a 17-year-old, whose final wish was to be at this seminar. I want to bring her up here and let you all send healing life-force energy toward her. Perhaps we can help. She did not request it. I am just doing this spontaneously because it feels right."

The audience chanted, "Yes! Yes! Yes! Yes!"

Amy's dad led her up onto the stage. She looked frail from all of the chemotherapy, too much bed rest and an absolute lack of exercise. (The doctors hadn't let her walk for the two weeks prior to this seminar.)

I had the group warm up their hands and send her healing energy, after which they gave her a tearful standing ovation.

Two weeks later she called to say that her doctor had discharged her after a total remission. Two years later she called to say she was married.

I have learned never to underestimate the healing power we all have. It is always there to be used for the highest good. We just have to remember to use it.

Mark V. Hansen

A Story For Valentine's Day

Larry and Jo Ann were an ordinary couple. They lived in an ordinary house on an ordinary street. Like any other ordinary couple, they struggled to make ends meet and to do the right things for their children.

They were ordinary in yet another way — they had their squabbles. Much of their conversation concerned what was wrong in their marriage and who was to blame.

Until one day when a most extraordinary event took place.

"You know, Jo Ann, I've got a magic chest of drawers. Every time I open them, they're full of socks and underwear," Larry said. "I want to thank you for filling them all these years."

This wasn't the first time Larry had done something odd, so Jo Ann pushed the incident out of her mind until a few days later.

Jo Ann stared at her husband over the top of her glasses. "What do you want, Larry?"

"Nothing. I just want you to know I appreciate those magic drawers."

This wasn't the first time Larry had done something odd, so Jo Ann Pushed the incident out of her mind until a few days later.

"Jo Ann, thank you for recording so many correct check numbers in the ledger this month. You put down the right numbers 15 out of 16 times. That's a record."

Disbelieving what she had heard, Jo Ann looked up from her mending. "Larry, you're always complaining about my recording the wrong check numbers. Why stop now?"

"No reason. I just wanted you to know I appreciate the effort you're making."

Jo Ann shook her head and went back to her mending, "What's got into him?" she mumbled to herself.

Nevertheless, the nextday when Jo Ann wrote a check at the grocery store, she glanced at her checkbook to confirm that she had put down the right check number. "Why do I suddenly care about those dumb check numbers?"she asked herself.

She tried to disregard the incident, but Larry's strange behavior intensified.

"Jo Ann, that was a great dinner," he said one evening. "I appreciate all your effort. Why, in the past 15 years I'll bet you've fixed over 14, 000 meals for me and the kids."

Then "Gee, Jo Ann, the house looks spiffy. You've really worked hard to get it looking so good." And even "Thanks, Jo Ann, for just being you. I really enjoy your company."

Jo Ann was growing worried. "Where's the sarcasm, the criticism?" she wondered.

Her fears that something peculiar was happening to her husband were confirmed by 16-year-old Shelly, who complained, "Dad's gone bonkers, Mom. He just told meI looked nice. With all this makeup and these sloppy clothes, he still said it. That's not Dad, Mom. What's wrong with him?"

Whatever was wrong, Larry didn't get over it. Day in and

day out he continued focusing on the positive.

Over the weeks, Jo Ann grew more accustomed to her mate's unusual behavior and occasionally even gave him a grudging "Thank you." She prided herself on taking it all in stride, until one day something so peculiar happened, she became completely discombobulated:

"I want you to take a break," Larry said. "I am going to do the dishes. So please take your hands off that frying pan and leave the kitchen."

(Long, long pause.) "Thank you, Larry. Thank you very much!"

Jo Ann's step was now a little lighter, her self-confidence higher and once in a while she hummed. She didn't seem to have as many blue moods anymore. "I rather like Larry's new behavior, she thought.

That would be the end of the story except one day another most extraordinary event took place. This time it was Jo Ann who spoke.

"Larry," she said, "I want to thank you for going to work and providing for us all these years. I don't think I've ever told you how much I appreciate it."

Larry has never revealed the reason for his dramatic change of behavior no matter how hard Jo Ann has pushed for an answer, and so it will likely remain one of life's mysteries. But it's one I'm thankful to live with.

You see, I am Jo Ann.

Jo Ann Larsen
Deseret News

Carpe Diem!

One who stands as a shining example of courageous expression is John Keating, the transformative teacher portrayed by Robin Williams in *Dead Poets Society.* In this masterful motion picture, Keating takes a group of regimented, uptight and spiritually impotent students at a rigid boarding school and inspires them to make their lives extraordinary.

These young men, as Keating points out to them, have lost sight of their dreams and ambitions. They are automatically living out their parents' programs and expectations for them. They plan to become doctors, lawyers and bankers because that is what their parents have told them they are going to do. But these dry fellows have given hardly any thought to what their hearts are calling them to express.

An early scene in the movie shows Mr. Keating taking the boys down to the school lobby where a trophy case displays photos of earlier graduating classes. "Look at these pictures, boys," Keating tells the students. "The young men you behold had the same fire in their eyes that you do. They planned to take the world by storm and make something magnificent of their lives. That was 70 years ago. Now they are all pushing up daisies. How many of them really lived out their dreams? Did they do what they set out to accomplish?"Then Mr. Keating leans into the cluster of preppies and whispers audibly, "*Carpe diem*! Seize the day!"

At first the students do not know what to make of this strange teacher. But soon they ponder the importance of his words. They come to respect and revere Mr. Keating, who has given them a new vision — or returned their original ones.

All of us are walking around with some kind of birthday card we would like to give — some personal expression of joy, creativity or aliveness that we are hiding under our shirt.

One character in the movie, Knox Overstreet, has a terminal crush on a gorgeous girl. The only problem is that she is the girlfriend of a famous jock. Knox is infatuated with this lovely creature down to a cellular level but he lacks the confidence to approach her. Then he remembers Mr. Keating's advice: *Seize the day*! Knox realizes he cannot just go on dreaming — if he wants her, he is going to have to do something about it. And so he does. Boldly and poetically he declares to her his most sensitive feelings. In the process he gets turned away by her, punched in the nose by her boyfriend and faces embarrassing setbacks. But Knox is unwilling to forsake his dream, so he pursues his heart's desire. Ultimately she feels the genuineness of his caring and opens her heart to him. Although Knox is not especially good-looking or popular, the girl is won over by the power of his sincere intention. He has made his life extraordinary.

I had a chance to practice seizing the day myself. I developed a crush on a cute girl I met in a pet store. She was younger than I, she led a very different lifestyle and we did not have a great deal to talk about. But somehow none of this seemed to matter. I enjoyed being with her and I felt a sparkle in her presence. And it seemed to me she enjoyed my company as well.

When I learned her birthday was coming up, I decided to ask her out. On the threshold of calling her, I sat and looked at the phone for about half an hour. Then I dialed and hung up before it rang. I felt like a high school boy, bouncing between excited anticipation and fear of rejection. A voice from hell kept telling me that she would not like me and that I had a lot of nerve asking her out. But I felt too enthusiastic about being with her to let those fears stop me. Finally I got up the nerve to ask her. She thanked me for asking and told me she already had plans.

I felt shot down. The same voice that told me not to call advised me to give up before I was further embarrassed. But I was intent on seeing what this attraction was about. There was more inside of me that wanted to come to life. I had feelings for this woman, and I had to express them.

I went to the mall and got her a pretty birthday card on which I wrote a poetic note. I walked around the corner to the pet shop where I knew she was working. As I approached the door, that same disturbing voice cautioned me, "What if she doesn't like you? What if she rejects you?" Feeling vulnerable, I stuffed the card under my shirt. I decided that if she showed me signs of affection, I would give it to her; if she was cool to me, I would leave the card hidden. This way I would not be at risk and would avoid rejection or embarrassment.

We talked for a while and I did not get any signs one way or the other from her. Feeling ill-at-ease, I began to make my exit.

As I approached the door, however, another voice spoke to me. It came in a whisper, not unlike that of Mr. Keating. It prompted me, "Remember Knox Overstreet... *Carpe diem*!" Here I was confronted with my aspiration to fully express my heart and my resistance to face the insecurity of emotional nakedness. How can I go around telling other people to live their vision, I asked myself, when I am not living my own? Besides, what's the worst thing that could happen? Any woman would be delighted to receive a poetic birthday card. I decided to seize the day. As I made that choice I felt a surge of courage course through my veins. There was indeed power in intention.

I felt more satisfied and at peace with myself than I had in a long time... I needed to learn to open my heart and give love without requiring anything in return.

I took the card out from under my shirt, turned around, walked up to the counter and gave it to her. As I handed it to her I felt an incredible aliveness and excitement — plus fear. (Fritz Perls said that fear is "excitement without breath.") But I did it.

And do you know what? She was not particularly impressed. She said, "Thanks" and put the card aside without even opening it. My heart sank. I felt disappointed and rejected. Getting no response seemed even worse than a direct brush-off.

I offered a polite good-bye and walked out of the store. Then something amazing happened. I began to feel exhilarated. A huge rush of internal satisfaction welled up within me and surged through my whole being. I had expressed my heart and that felt fantastic! I had stretched beyond fear and gone out on the dance floor. Yes, I had been a little clumsy, but I did it. (Emmet Fox said, "Do it trembling if you must, but do it!") I had put my heart on the line without demanding a guarantee of the results. I did not give in order to get something back. I opened my feelings to her without an attachment to a particular response.

The dynamics that are required to make any relationship work: Just keep putting your love out there.

My exhilar ation deepened to a warm bliss. I felt more satisfied and at peace with myself than I had in a long time. I realized the purpose of the whole experience: I needed to learn to open my heart and give love without requiring anything in return. This experience was not about creating a relationship with this woman. It was about deepening my relationship with myself. And I did it. Mr. Keating would have been proud. But most of all, I was proud.

I have not seen the girl much since then, but that experience changed my life. Through that simple interaction I clearly saw the dynamics that are required to make any relationship and perhaps the whole world work: *Just keep putting your love out there.*

We believe that we are hurt when we don't receive love. But that is not what hurts us. Our pain comes when we do not *give* love. We were born to love. You might say that we are divinely created love machines. We function most powerfully when we are giving love. The world has led us to believe that our well-being is dependent on other people loving us. But this is the kind of upside-down thinking that has caused so many of our problems. The truth is that our well-being is dependent on our *giving* love. It is not about what comes back; it is about *what goes out*!

Alan Cohen

I Know You, You're Just Like Me!

One of our closest friends is Stan Dale. Stan teaches a seminar on love and relationships called Sex, Love and Intimacy. Several years ago, in an effort to learn what the people in the Soviet Union were really like, he took 29 people to the Soviet Union for two weeks. When he wrote about his experiences in his newsletter, we were deeply touched by the following anecdote.

While walking through a park in the industrial city of Kharkov, I spotted an old Russian veteran of World War II. They are easily identified by the medals and ribbons they still proudly display on their shirts and jackets. This is not an act of egotism. It is their country's way of honoring those who helped save Russia, even though 20 million Russians were killed by the Nazis. I went up to this old man sitting with his wife and said, "Druzhba i mir" (friendship and peace). The man looking at me as if in disbelief, took the button we had made for the trip and said "Friendship" in Russian and showed a map of the U. S. and the U. S. S. R. being held by loving hands, and said, "Americanski?" I replied, "Da, Americanski. Druzhba i mir." He clasped both my hands as if we were long lost brothers and repeated again, "Americanski!" This time there was recognition and love in his statement.

For the next few minutes he and his wife spoke in Russian as if I understood every word, and I spoke English as if I knew he would understand. You know what? Neither of us understood a word, but we surely understood each other. We hugged, and laughed and cried, all the while saying, "Druzhba i mir, Americanski." "I love you, I am proud to be in your country, we do not want war. *I love you!*"

After about five minutes we said good-bye, and the seven of us in our little group walked on. About 15 minutes later, some considerable distance on, this same old veteran caught up with us. He came up to me, took off his Order of Lenin medal (probably his most prized possession) and pinned it to my jacket. He then kissed me on the lips and gave me one of the warmest, most loving hugs I have ever received. Then we both cried, looked into each other's eyes for the longest time, and said, "Dossvedanya" (good-bye).

The above story is symbolic of our entire "Citizen Diplomacy" trip to the Soviet Union. Every day we met and touched hundreds of people in every possible and impossible setting. Neither the Russians nor ourselves will ever be the same. There are now hundreds of school children from the three schools we visited who will not be quite so ready to think of Americans as people who want to "nuke" them. We danced, sang and played with children of every age, and then we hugged, kissed and shared presents. They gave us flowers, cakes, buttons, paintings, dolls, but most importantly, their hearts and open minds.

More than once we were invited to be members of wedding parties, and no biological family member could have been more warmly accepted, greeted and feted than we were. We hugged, kissed, danced and drank champagne, schnapps and vodka with the bride and groom, as well as Momma and Poppa and the rest of the family.

In Kursk, we were hosted by seven Russian families who volunteered to take us in for a wonderful evening of food, drink and conversation. Four hours later, none of us wanted to part. Our group now has a complete new family in Russia.

The following night "our family" was feted by us at our hotel. The band played until almost midnight, and guess what? Once again we ate, drank, talked, danced and cried when it came time to say good-bye. We danced every dance as if we were passionate lovers, which is exactly what we were.

I could go on forever about our experiences, and yet there would be no way to convey to you exactly how we felt. How would you feel when you arrived at your hotel in Moscow, if there were a telephone message waiting for you, written in Russian, from Mikhail Gorbachev's office saying he regretted he could not meet with you that weekend because he would be out of town, but instead he had arranged for your entire group to meet for two hours in a round-table discussion with about a half-dozen members of the Central Committee? We had an extremely frank discussion about everything, including sex.

How would you feel if more than a dozen old ladies, wearing babushkas, came down from the steps of their apartment buildings and hugged and kissed you? How would you feel when your guides, Tanya and Natasha, told you and the whole group that they had never seen anyone like you? And when we left, all 30 of us cried because we had fallen in love with these fabulous women, and they with us. Yes, how would you feel? Probably just like us.

Each of us had our own experience, of course, but the collective experience bears out one thing for certain: The only way we are ever going to ensure peace on this planet is to adopt the entire world as "our family." We are going to have to hug them, and kiss them. And dance and play with them. And we are going to have to sit and talk and walk and cry with them. Because when we do, we'll be able to see that, indeed, everyone is beautiful, and we all complement each other so beautifully, and we would all be poorer without each other. Then the saying, "I know you, you're just like me!" will take on a mega-meaning of, "This is 'my family,' and I will stand by them no matter what!"

Stan Dale

Another Way

The train clanked and rattled through the suburbs of Tokyo on a drowsy spring afternoon. Our car was comparatively empty — a few housewives with their kids in tow, some old folks going shopping. I gazed absently at the drab houses and dusty hedgerows.

At one station the doors opened, and suddenly the afternoon quiet was shattered by a man bellowing violent, incomprehensible curses. The man staggered into our car. He wore laborer's clothing and was big, drunk and dirty. Screaming, he swung at a woman holding a baby. The blow sent her spinning into the laps of an elderly couple. It was a miracle that the baby was unharmed.

Terrified, the couple jumped up and scrambled toward the other end of the car. The laborer aimed a kick at the retreating back of the old woman but missed as she scuttled to safety. This so enraged the drunk that he grabbed the metal pole in the center of the car and tried to wrench it out of its stanchion. I could see that one of his hands was cut and bleeding. The train lurched ahead, the passengers frozen with fear. I stood up.

I was young then, some 20 years ago, and in pretty good shape. I'd been putting in a solid eight hours of Aikido training nearly every day for the past three years. I liked to throw and grapple. I thought I was tough. The trouble was, my martial skill was untested in actual combat. As students of Aikido, we were not allowed to fight.

"Aikido," my teacher had said again and again, "is the art of reconciliation. Whoever has the mind to fight has broken his connection with the universe. If you try to dominate people, you're already defeated. We study how to resolve conflict, not how to start it."

I listened to his words. I tried hard. I even went so far as to cross the street to avoid the "chimpira," the pinball punks who lounged around the train stations. My forbearance exalted me. I felt both tough and holy. In my heart, however, I wanted an absolutely legitimate opportunity whereby I might save the innocent by destroying the guilty.

"This is it!" I said to myself as I got to my feet. "People are in danger. If I don't do something fast, somebody will probably get hurt."

Seeing me stand up, the drunk recognized a chance to focus his rage. "Aha!" he roared. "A foreigner! You need a lesson in Japanese manners!"

I held on a lightly to the commuter strap overhead and gave him a slow look of disgust and dismissal. I planned to take this turkey apart, but he had to make the first move. I wanted him mad, so I pursed my lips and blew him an insolent kiss.

"All right!" he hollered. "You're gonna get a lesson!" He gathered himself for a rush at me.

A fraction of a second before he could move, someone shouted "Hey!" It was earsplitting. I remember the strangely joyous, lilting quality of it — as though you and a friend had been searching diligently for something, and he had suddenly stumbled upon it. "Hey!"

I wheeled to my left; the drunk spun to his right. We both stared down at a little old Japanese man. He must have been well into his seventies, this tiny gentleman, sitting there immaculate in his kimono. He took no notice of me, but beamed delightedly at the laborer, as though he had a most important, most welcome secret to share.

"C'mere," The old man said in an easy vernacular, beckoning to the drunk. "C'mere and talk with me." He waved his hands lightly.

The big man followed, as if on a string. He planted his feet belligerently in front of the old gentleman and roared above the clacking wheels, "Why the hell should I talk to you?" The drunk now had his back to me. If his elbow moved so much as a millimeter, I'd drop him in his socks.

The old man continued to beam at the laborer. "What'cha been drinkin'?" he asked, his eyes sparkling with interest. "I been drinkin's ake," the laborer bellowed back, "and it's none of your business!" Flecks of spittle spattered the old man.

"Oh, that's wonderful," the old man said, "absolutely wonderful! You see, I love sake, too. Every night, me and my wife (she's 76, you know), we warm up a little bottle of sake and take it out into the garden, and we sit on an old wooden bench. We watch the sun go down, and we look to see how our persimmon tree is doing. My greatgrandfather planted that tree, and we worry about whether it will recover from those ice storms we had last winter. Our tree has done better than I expected, though, especially when you consider the poor quality of the soil. It is gratifying to watch when we take our sake and go out to enjoy the evening — even when it rains!" He looked up at the laborer, eyes twinkling.

As he struggled to follow the old man, his face began to

soften. His fists slowly unclenched. "Yeah," he said. "I love persimmons, too..." His voice trailed off.

"Yes," said the old man, smiling, "and I'm sure you have a wonderful wife."

"No," replied the laborer. "My wife died." Very gently, swaying with the motion of the train, the big man began to sob. "I don't got no wife, I don't got no home, I don't got no job. I'm so ashamed of myself." Tears rolled down his cheeks, a spasm of despair rippled through his body.

As I stood there in my well-scrubbed youthful innocence, my make-this-world-safe-for-democracy righteousness, I felt dirtier than he was.

Then the train arrived at my stop. As the doors opened, I heard the old man cluck sympathetically. "My, my," he said, "that is a difficult predicament indeed. Sit down here and tell me about it."

I turned my head for one last look. The laborer was sprawled on the seat with his head in the old man's lap. The old man was softly stroking the filthy, matted hair.

As the train pulled away, I sat down on a bench in the station. What I had wanted to do with muscle had been accomplished with kind words. I had just seen Aikido in action, and the essence of it was love. I would have to practice the art with an entirely different spirit. It would be a long time before I could speak about the resolution of conflict.

Terry Dobson

The Gentlest Need

At least once a day our old black cat comes to one of us in a way that we've all come to see as a special request. It does not mean he wants to be fed or to be let out or anything of that sort. His need is for something very different.

If you have a lap handy, he'll jump into it; if you don't, he's likely to stand there looking wistful until you make him one. Once in it, he begins to vibrate almost before you stroke his back, scratch his chin and tell him over and over what a good kitty he is. Then his motor really revs up; he squirms to get comfortable; he "makes big hands." Every once in a while one of his purrs gets out of control and turns into a snort. He looks at you with wide open eyes of adoration, and he gives you the cat's long slow blink of ultimate trust.

After a while, little by little, he quiets down. If he senses that it's all right, he may stay in your lap for a cozy nap. But he is just as likely to hop down and stroll away about his business. Either way, he's all right.

Our daughter puts it simply: "Blackie needs to be purred."

In our household he isn't the only one who has that need: I share it and so does my wife. We know the need isn't exclusive to any one age group. Still, because I am a schoolman as well as a parent, I associate it especially with youngsters, with their quick, impulsive need for a hug, a warm lap, a hand held out, a coverlet tucked in, not because anything's wrong, not because anything needs doing, just because that's the way they are.

There are a lot of things I'd like to do for all children. If I could do just one, it would be this: to guarantee every child, everywhere, at least one good purring every day.

Kids, like cats, need time to purr.

Fred T. Wilhelms

Bopsy

The 26-year-old mother stared down at her son who was dying of terminal leukemia. Although her heart was filled with sadness, she also had a strong feeling of determination. Like any parent she wanted her son to grow up and fulfill all his dreams. Now that was no longer possible. The leukemia would see to that. But she still wanted her son's dreams to come true.

She took her son's hand and asked, "Bopsy, did you ever think about what you wanted to be when you grew up? Did you ever dream and wish about what you would do with your life?"

"Mommy, I always wanted to be a fireman when I grew up."

Mom smiled back and said, "Let's see if we can make your wish come true." Later that day she went to her local fire department in Phoenix Arizona, where she met Fireman Bob, who had a heart as big as Phoenix. She explained her son's finalwish and asked if it might be possible to give her six-year-old son a ride around the block on a fire engine.

Fireman Bob said, "Look, we can do better than that. If you'll have your son ready at seven o'clock Wednesday morning, we'll make him an honorary fireman for the whole day. He can come down to the fire station, eat with us, go out on all the fire calls, the whole nine yards! And, if you'll give us his sizes, we'll get a real fire uniform made for him, with a real fire hat — not a toy one — with the emblem of the Phoenix Fire Department on it, a yellow slicker like we wear and rubber boots. They're all manufactured right here in Phoenix, so we can get them fast."

Three days later Fireman Bob picked up Bopsy, dressed him in his fire uniform and escorted him from his hospital bed to the waiting hook and ladder truck. Bopsy got to sit up on the back of the truck and help steer it back to the fire station. He was in heaven.

There were three fire calls in Phoenix that day and Bopsy got to go out on all three calls. He rode in the different fire engines, the paramedics' van and even the fire chief's car. He was also videotaped for the local news program.

Having his dream come true, with all the love and attention that was lavished upon him, so deeply touched Bopsy that he lived three months longer than any doctor thought possible.

One night all of his vital signs began to drop dramatically and the head nurse, who believed in the Hospice concept that no one should die alone, began to call the family members to the hospital. Then she remembered the day Bopsy had spent as a fireman, so she called the fire chief and asked if it would be possible to send a fireman in uniform to the hospital to be with Bopsy as he made his transition. The chief replied, "We can do better than that. We'll be there in five minutes. Will you please do me a favor? When you hear the sirens screaming and see the lights flashing, will you announce over the PA system that there is not a fire? It's just the fire department coming to see one of its finest members one more time. And will you open the window to his room?

Thanks."

About five minutes later a hook and ladder truck arrived at the hospital, extended its ladder up to Bopsy's third flood open window and 14 firemen and two firewomen climbed up the ladder into Bopsy's room.

With his mother's permission, they hugged him and held him and told him how much they loved him. With his dying breath, Bopsy looked up at the fire chief and said, "Chief, am I really a fireman now?"

"Bopsy, you are," the chief said.

With those words, Bopsy smiled and closed his eyes for the last time.

Jack Canfield and Mark V. Hansen

REASSURANCE
50¢
TomWilson

Puppies For Sale

A store owner was tacking a sign above his door that read "Puppies For Sale." Signs like that have a way of attracting small children, and sure enough, a little boy appeared under the store owner's sign. "How much are you going to sell the puppies for?" he asked.

The store owner replied, "Anywhere from $30 to $50."

The little boy reached in his pocket and pulled out some change. "I have $2.37," he said. "Can I please look at them?"

The store owner smiled and whistled and out of the kennel came Lady, who ran down the aisle of his store followed by five teeny, tiny balls of fur. One puppy was lagging considerably behind. Immediately the little boy singled out the lagging, limping puppy and said, "What's wrong with that little dog?"

The store owner explained that the veterinarian had examined the little puppy and had discovered it didn't have a hip socket. It would always limp. It would always be lame. The little boy became excited. "That is the little puppy that I want to buy."

The store owner said, "No, you don't want to buy that little dog. If you really want him, I'll give him to you."

The little boy got quite upset. He looked straight into the

store owner's eyes, pointing his finger, and said, "I don't want you to give him to me. That little dog is worth every bit as much as all the other dogs and I'll pay full price. In fact, I'll give you $2. 37 now, and 50 cents a month until I have him paid for."

The store owner countered. "You really don't want to buy this little dog. He is never going to be able to run and jump and play with you like the other puppies."

To this, the little boy reached down and rolled up his pant lag to reveal a badly twisted. , crippled left leg supported by a big metal brace. He looked up at the store owner and softly replied, "Well, I don't run so well myself, and the little puppy will need someone who understands!"

Dan Clark

Weathering the Storm

2

LEARNING TO LOVE YOURSELF

Oliver Wendell Holmes once attended a meeting in which he was the shortest man present.

"Dr. Holmes," quipped a friend, "I should think you'd feel rather small among us big fellows."

"I do," retorted Holmes, "I feel like a dime among a lot of pennies."

The Golden Buddha

And now here is my secret, a very simple secret; it is only with the heart that one can see rightly, what is essential is invisible to the eye.

Antoine de Saint-Exupery

In the fall of 1988 my wife Georgia and I were invited to give a presentation on self-esteem and peak performance at a conference in Hong Kong. Since we had never been to the Far East before, we decided to extend our trip and visit Thailand.

When we arrived in Bangkok, we decided to take a tour of the city's most famous Buddhist temples. Along with our interpreter and driver, Georgia and I visited numerous Buddhist temples that day, but after a while they all began to blur in our memories.

However, there was one temple that left an indelible impression in our hearts and minds. It is called the Temple of the Golden Buddha. The temple itself is very small, probably no larger than thirty feet by thirty feet. But as we entered, we were stunned by the presence of a ten-and-a-half-foot tall, solid-gold Buddha. It weighs over two-and-a-half tons and is valued at approximately one hundred and ninety-six million dollars! It was quite an awesome sight — the kindly gentle, yet imposing solid-gold Buddha smiling down at us.

As we immersed ourselves in the normal sightseeing tasks (taking pictures while oohing and ahhing over the statue), I walked over to a glass case that contained a large piece of clay about eight inches thick and twelve inches wide. Next to the glass case was a typewritten page describing the history of this magnificent piece of art.

Back in 1957 a group of monks from a monastery had to relocate a clay Buddha from their temple to a new location. The monastery was to be relocated to make room for the development of a highway through Bangkok. When the crane began to lift the giant idol, the weight of it was so tremendous that it began to crack. What's more, rain began to fall. The head monk, who was concerned about damage to the sacred Buddha, decided to lower the statue back to the ground and cover it with a large canvas tarp to protect it from the rain.

Later that evening the head monk went to check on the Buddha. He shined his flashlight under the tarp to see if the Buddha was staying dry. As the light reached the crack, he noticed a little gleam shining back and thought it strange. As he took a closer look at this gleam of light, he wondered if there might be something underneath the clay. He went to fetch a chisel and hammer from the monastery and began to chip away at the clay. As he knocked off shards of clay, the little gleam grew brighter and bigger. Many hours of labor went by before the monk stood face to face with the extraordinary solid-gold Buddha.

Historians believe that several hundred years before the head monk's discovery, the Burmese army was about to invade Thailand (then called Siam). The Siamese monks, realizing that their country would soon be attacked, covered their precious golden Buddha with an outer covering of clay in order to keep their treasure from being looted by the Burmese. Unfortunately, it appears that the Burmese slaughtered all the Siamese monks, and the well-kept secret of the golden Buddha remained intact until that fateful day in 1957.

As we flew home on Cathay Pacific Airlines I began to think to myself, "We are all like the clay Buddha covered with a shell of hardness created out of fear, and yet underneath each of us is a 'golden Buddha,' a 'golden Christ' or a 'golden essence,' which is our real self. Somewhere along the way, between the ages of two and nine, we begin to cover up our 'golden essence,' our natural self. Much like the monk with the hammer and the chisel, our task now is to discover our true essence once again."

Jack Canfield

Start With Yourself

The following words were written on the tomb of an Anglican Bishop in the Crypts of Westminister Abbey:

> When I was young and free and my imagination had no limits, I dreamed of changing the world. As I grew older and wiser, I discovered the world would not change, so I shortened my sights somewhat and decided to change only my country.
>
> But it, too, seemed immovable.
>
> As I grew into my twilight years, in one last desperate attempt, I settled for changing only my family, those closest to me, but alas, they would have none of it.
>
> And now as I lie on my deathbed, I suddenly realize: *If I had only changed my self first*, then by example I would have changed my family.
>
> From their inspiration and encouragement, I would then have been able to better my country and, who knows, I may have even changed the world.

Anonymous

Nothing But The Truth!

David Casstevens of the *Dallas Morning News* tells a story about Frank Szymanski, a Notre Dame center in the 1940s, who had been called as a witness in a civil suit at South Bend.

"Are you on the Notre Dame football team this year?" the judge asked.

"Yes, Your Honor."

"What position?"

"Center, Your Honor."

"How good a center?"

Szymanski squirmed in his seat, but said firmly: "Sir, I'm the best center Notre Dame has ever had."

Coach Frank Leahy, who was in the courtroom, was surprised. Szymanski always had been modest and unassuming. So when the proceedings were over, he took Szymanski aside and asked why he had made such a statement. Szymanski blushed.

"I hated to do it, Coach," he said. "But, after all, I *was* under oath."

Dallas Morning News

Covering All The Bases

A little boy was overheard talking to himself as he strode through his backyard, baseball cap in place and toting ball and bat. "I'm the greatest baseball player in the world," he said proudly. Then he tossed the ball in the air, swung and missed. Undaunted, he picked up the ball, threw it into the air and said to himself, "I'm the greatest player ever!" He swung at the ball again, and again he missed. He paused a moment to examine bat and ball carefully. Then once again he threw the ball into the air and said, "I'm the greatest baseball player who ever lived." He swung the bat hard and again missed the ball.

"Wow!" he exclaimed. "What a pitcher!"

Source Unknown

After church one Sunday morning, my five-year-old granddaughter was intently drawing on a piece of paper. When asked what she was drawing, she replied that she was drawing God. "But no one knows what God looks like," I said.

"They will when I finish this picture!" she answered.

Jacque Hall

My Declaration Of Self-Esteem

What I am is good enough if I would only be it openly.

Carl Rogers

The following was written in answer to a 15-year-old girl's question, "How can I prepare myself for a fulfilling life?"

I am me.

In all the world, there is no one else exactly like me. There are people who have some parts like me but no one adds up exactly like me. Therefore, everything that comes out of me is authentically mine because I alone choose it.

I own everything about me — my body, including everything it does; my mind, including all my thoughts and ideas; my eyes, including the images of all they behold; my feelings, whatever they might be — anger, joy, frustration, love, disappointment, excitement; my mouth and all the words that come out of it — polite, sweet and rough, correct or incorrect; my voice, loud and soft; all my actions, whether they be to others or myself.

I own my fantasies, my dreams, my hopes, my fears. I own all my triumphs and successes, all my failures and mistakes.

Because I own all of me, I can become intimately acquainted with me. By so doing, I can love me and be friendly with me in all my parts. I can then make it possible for all of me to work in my best interests.

I know there are aspects about myself that puzzle me, and other aspects that I do not know. But as long as I am friendly and loving to myself, I can courageously and hopefully look for the solutions to the puzzles and for ways to find out more about me.

However I look and sound, whatever I say and do, and whatever I think and feel at a given moment in time is me. This is authentic and represents where I am at that moment in time.

When I review later how I looked and sounded, what I said and did, and how I thought and felt, some parts may turn out to be unfitting. I can discard that which is unfitting and keep that which proved fitting, and invent something new for that which I discarded.

I can see, hear, feel, think, say and do. I have the tools to survive, to be close to others, to be productive, to make sense and order out of the world of people and things outside of me.

I own me and therefore I can engineer me.

I am me and I am okay.

Virginia Satir

The Bag Lady

She used to sleep in the Fifth Street Post Office. I could smell her before I rounded the entrance to where she slept, standing up, by the public phones. I smelled the urine that seeped through the layers of her dirty clothing and the decay from her nearly toothless mouth. If she was not asleep, she mumbled incoherently.

Now they close the post office at six to keep the homeless out, so she curls up on the sidewalk, talking to herself, her mouth flapping open as though unhinged, her smells diminished by the soft breeze.

One Thanksgiving we had so much food left over, I packed it up, excused myself from the others and drove over to Fifth Street.

It was a frigid night. Leaves were swirling around the streets and hardly anyone was out, all but a few of the luckless in some warm home or shelter. But I knew I would find her.

She was dressed as she always was, even in summer: The warm woolly layers concealing her old, bent body. Her bony hands clutched the precious shopping cart. She was squatting against a wire fence in front of the playground next to the post office. "Why didn't she choose some place more protected from the wind?" I thought, and assumed she was so crazy she did not have the sense to huddle in a doorway.

I pulled my shiny car to the curb, rolled down the window and said, "Mother ... would you..." and was shocked at the word "Mother." But she was ... is ... in some way I cannot grasp.

I said, again, "Mother, I've brought you some food. Would you like some turkey and stuffing and apple pie?"

At this old woman looked at me and said quite clearly and distinctly, her two loose lower teeth wobbling as she spoke, "Oh, thank you very much, but I'm quite full now. Why don't you take it to someone who really needs it?" Her words were clear, her manners gracious. Then I was dismissed: Her head sank into her rags again.

Bobbie Probstein

Response/Ability

the game we play
is let's pretend
and pretend
we're not
pretending

we choose to
forget
who we are
and then forget
that we've
forgotten

who are we really?

the center
that watches
and runs the show
that can choose
which way

the I AM
consciousness
that powerful
loving perfect
reflection
of the cosmos

but in our attempt
to cope with
early situations
we chose or were
hypnotized into
a passive position

to avoid
punishment
or the loss of love
we chose to deny
our
response/ability

it will go
things just
happened
or that we were
being controlled
taken over
we put ourselves
down
and have become
used to this
masochistic
posture
this weakness
this indecisiveness
pretending that
but we are
in reality
free
a center
of cosmic energy
your will
is your power

don't pretend
you don't have it

or you won't

Bernard Gunther

The Rules For Being Human

1. **You will receive a body.**
   You may like it or hate it, but it will be yours for the entire period of this time around.
2. **You will learn lessons.**
   You are enrolled in a full-time informal school called Life. Each day in this school you will have the opportunity to learn lessons. You may like the lessons or think them irrelevant and stupid.
3. **There are no mistakes, only lessons.**
   Growth is a process of trial and error: Experimentation. The "failed" experiments are as much a part of the process as the experiment that ultimately "works."
4. **A lesson is repeated until learned.**
   A lesson will be presented to you in various forms until you have learned it. When you have learned it, you can then go on to the next lesson.
5. **Learning lessons does not end.**
   There is no part of life that does not contain its lessons. If you are alive, there are lessons to be learned.
6. **"There" is no better than "here."**
   When your "there" has become a "here," you will simply obtain another "there" that will again look better than "here."

7. **Others are merely mirrors of you.**
   You cannot love or hate something about another person unless it reflects something you love or hate about yourself.
8. **What you make of your life is up to you.**
   You have all the tools and resource
   you need. What you do with them is up to
   you. The choice is yours.
9. **Your answers lie inside you.**
   The answers to Life's questions lie inside you. All you need to do is look, listen and trust.
10. **You will forget all this.**

Chérie Carter-Scott

3

ON PARENTING

Perhaps the greatest social service that can be rendered by anybody to the country and to mankind is to bring up a family.

George Bernard Shaw

Children Learn What They Live

If children live with criticism,
they learn to condemn.
If children live with hostility,
they learn to fight.
If children live with fear,
they learn to be apprehensive.
If children live with pity,
they learn to feel sorry for themselves.
If children live with ridicule,
they learn to be shy.
If children live with jealousy,
they learn what envy is.
If children live with shame,
they learn to feel guilty.
If children live with tolerance,
they learn to be patient.
If children live with encouragement,
they learn to be confident.
If children live with praise,
they learn to appreciate.
If children live with approval,
they learn to like them selves.
If children live with acceptance,

they learn to find love in the world.
If children live with recognition,
they learn to have a goal.
If children live with sharing,
they learn to be generous.
If children live with honesty and fairness,
they learn what truth and justice are.
If children live with security,
they learn to have faith in themselves
and in those around them.
If children live with friendliness,
they learn that the world is a nice
place in which to live.
If children live with serenity,
they learn to have peace of mind.
With what are your children living?

Dorothy L. Nolte

Why I Chose My Father To Be My Dad

I grew up on a beautiful sprawling farm in Iowa, raised by parents who are often described as the "Salt of the earth and the backbone of the community." They were all the things we know good parents to be: loving, committed to the task of raising their children with high expectations and a positive sense of self-regard. They expected us to do morning and evening chores, get to school on time, get decent grades and be good people.

There are six children. Six children! It was never my idea that there should be so many of us, but then no one consulted me. To make matters worse, fate dropped me off in the middle of the American heartland in a most harsh and cold climate. Like all children, I thought that there had been a great universal mistake and I had been placed in the wrong family — most definitely in the wrong state. I disliked coping with the elements. The winters in Iowa are so freezing cold that you have to make rounds in the middle of the night to see that livestock aren't stranded in a place where they would freeze to death. Newborn animals had to be taken in the barn and sometimes warmed up in order to be kept alive. Winters are *that* cold in Iowa!

My dad, an incredibly handsome, strong, charismatic and energetic man was always in motion. My brothers and sisters and I were in awe of him. We honored him and held him in the highest esteem. Now I understand why. There were no inconsistencies in his life. He was an honorable man, highly principled. Farming, his chosen work, was his passion; he was the best. He was at home raising and caring for animals. He felt at one with the earth and took great pride in planting and harvesting the crops. He refused to hunt out of season, even though deer, pheasants, quail and other game roamed our farmlands in abundance. He refused to use soil additives or feed the animals anything other than natural grains. He taught us why he did this and why we must embrace the same ideals. Today I can see how conscientious he was because this was in the mid-1950s before there was an attempt at universal commitment to earth-wide environmental preservation.

Dad was also a very impatient man, but not in the middle of the night when he was checking his animals during these late night rounds. The relationship we developed from these times together was simply unforgettable. It made a compelling difference in my life. I learned so much about him. I often hear men and women say they spent so little time with their fathers. Indeed the heart of today's men's groups is about groping for a father they never really knew. I knew mine.

Back then I felt as if I was secretly his favorite child, although it's quite possible that each of us six children felt that way. Now that was both good news and bad. The bad news was that I was the one selected by Dad to go with him for these midnight and early morning barnyard checks, and I absolutely detested getting up and leaving a warm bed to go out into the frosty air. But my dad was at his best and most lovable during those times. He was most understanding, patient, gentle and was a good listener. His voice was gentle and his smile made me understand my mother's passion for him.

It was during these times when he was a model teacher — always focusing on the whys, the reasons for doing. He talked endlessly for the hour or hour-and-a-half that it took to make the rounds. He talked about his war experiences, the whys of the war he served in and about the region, its people, the effects of war and its aftermath. Again and again he told his story. In school I found history all the more exciting and familiar.

He talked about what he gained from his travels and why seeing the world was so important. He instilled a need and love of traveling. I had worked in or visited some 30 countries by the time I was 30 years old.

He talked about the need and love of learning and why a formal education is important, and he talked about the difference between intelligence and wisdom. He wanted so much for me to go beyond my high school degree. "You can do it," he'd say over and over. "You're a Burres. You are bright, you have a good mind and, remember, you're a Burres." There was no way I was going to let him down. I had more than enough confidence to tackle any course of study. Eventually I completed a Ph. D. and later earned a second doctorate. Though the first doctorate was for Dad and the second for me, there was definitely a sense of curiosity and quest that made both easy to attain.

He talked about standards and values, developing character and what it meant in the course of one's life. I write and teach on a similar theme. He talked about how to make and evaluate decisions, when to cut your losses and walk away and when to stick it out, even in the face of adversity. He talked about the concept of *being and becoming* and not just *having and getting*. I still use that phrase. "Never sell out on your heart," he said. He talked about gut instincts and how to decipher between those and emotional sells, and how to avoid being fooled by others. He said, "Always listen to your instincts and know that all the answers you'll ever need are within you. Take quiet time alone. Be still enough to find the answers within and then listen to them. Find something you love to do, then live a life that shows it. Your goals should stem from your values, and then your work will radiate your heart's desire. This will divert you from all silly distractions that will only serve to waste your time — your very life is about time — how much you can grow in whatever years you are given. Care about people," he said, "and always respect mother earth. Wherever you shall live, be sure you have full view of the trees, sky and land."

My father. When I reflect on how he loved and valued his children, I'm genuinely sorry for the youth who will never know their fathers in this way or will never feel the power of character, ethics, drive and sensitivity all in one person — as I do in mine. My dad modeled what he talked. And I always knew he was serious about me. I knew he felt me worthy, and he wanted me to see that worth.

Dad's message made sense to me because I never saw any conflict in the way he lived his life. He had thought about his life and he lived it daily. He bought and paid for several farms over time (he's as active today as he was then). He married and has loved the same woman for a lifetime. My mother and he, now married for nearly 50 years, are still inseparable sweethearts. They are the greatest lovers I've known. And he loved his family so much. I thought he was overly possessive and protective of his children, but now that I'm a parent I can understand those needs and see them for what they are. Though he thought he could save us from the measles and almost did, he vehemently refused to lose us to destructive vices. I also see how determined he was that we be caring and responsible adults.

To this day five of his children live within a few miles of him, and they have chosen a version of his lifestyle. They are devoted spouses and parents, and agriculture is their chosen work. They are without a doubt, the backbone of their community. There is a twist to all this, and I suspect it's because of his taking me on those midnight rounds. I took a different direction than did the other five children. I began a career as an educator, counselor and university professor, eventually writing several books for parents and children to share what I had learned about the importance of developing self-esteem in the childhood years. My messages to my daughter, while altered a bit, are the values that I learned from my father, tempered with my life experiences, of course. They continue to be passed on.

I should tell you a bit about my daughter. She's a tomboy, a beautiful 5 foot 9 athlete who letters in three sports each year, frets over the difference between an A and a B, and was just named a finalist in the Miss Teen California contest. But it's not her outward gifts and accomplishments that remind me of my parents. People always tell me that my daughter possesses a great kindness, a spirituality, a special fire deep inside that radiates outward. The essence of my parents is personified in their granddaughter.

The rewards of esteeming their children and being dedicated parents have had a most nourishing effect on the lives of my parents as well. As of this writing, my father is at the Mayo Clinic in Rochester, Minnesota, for a battery of tests, scheduled to take from six to eight days. It is December. Because of the harsh winter, he took a hotel room near the clinic (as an outpatient). Because of obligations at home, my mother was only able to stay with him for the first few days. So on Christmas Eve, they were apart.

That night I first called my dad in Rochester to say Merry Christmas. He sounded down and despondent. Then, I called my mother in Iowa. She was sad and morose. "This is the first time your father and I have ever spent the holidays apart," she lamented. "It's just not Christmas without him."

I had 14 dinner guests arriving, all ready for a festive evening. I returned to cooking, but not being able to get my parents' dilemma fully off my mind, I called my older sister. She called my brothers. We conferenced by phone. It was settled. Determined that our parents should not be without each other on Christmas Eve, my younger brother would drive the two hours to Rochester to pick up my father and bring him home without telling my mother. I called my father to tell him of the plans. "Oh, no," he said, "it's far too dangerous to come out on a night like this." My brother arrived in Rochester and knocked at my father's hotel door. He called me from Dad's room to tell me he wouldn't go. "You have to tell him, Bobbie. You're the only one he'll listen to."

"Go, Dad," I said gently.

He did. Tim and my dad started for Iowa. We kids kept track of their progress, the journey and the weather by talking with them on my brother's car phone. By now, all my guests had arrived and all were a part of this ordeal. Whenever the phone rang, we put it on the speaker phone so we could hear the latest! It was just past 9:00 when the phone rang and it was Dad on the car phone, "Bobbie, how can I possibly go home without a gift for your mom? It would be the first time in nearly 50 years I didn't get her perfume for Christmas!" By now my entire dinner party was engineering this plan. We called my sister to get the names of nearby open shopping centers so they could stop for the only gift my dad would consider giving Mom — the same brand of perfume he has given her every year at Christmas.

At 9:52 that evening, my brother and my dad left a little shopping mall in Minnesota for the trip home. At 11:50 they drove into the farmstead. My father, acting like a giggling school boy, stepped around the corner of the house and stood out of sight.

"Mom, I visited Dad today and he said to bring you his laundry," my brother said as he handed my mom the suitcases.

"Oh," she said softly and sadly, "I miss him so much, I might as well do these now."

Said my father coming out from his hiding, "You won't have time to do them tonight."

After my brother called me to relay this touching scene between our parents — these two friends and lovers — I phoned my mother. "Merry Christmas, Mother!"

"Oh, you kids...," she said in a crackling voice, choking back tears. She was unable to continue. My guests cheered.

Though I was 2,000 miles away from them, it was one of the most special Christmases I've shared with my parents. And, of course, to date my parents have not been apart on Christmas Eve. That's the strength of children who love and honor their parents and, of course, the committed and marvelous marriage my parents share.

"Good parents," Jonas Salk once told me, "give their children roots and wings. Roots to know where home is, wings to fly away and exercise what's been taught them. "If gaining the skills to lead one's life purposefully and having a safe nest and being welcomed back to it is the legacy of parents, then I believe I chose my parents well. It was this past Christmas that I most fully understood why it was necessary that these two people be my parents. Though wings have taken me around the globe, eventually to nest in lovely California, the roots my parents gave me will be an indelible foundation forever.

Bettie B. Youngs

The Animal School

Once upon a time, the animals decided they must do something heroic to meet the problems of "a new world." So they organized a school.

They adopted an activity curriculum consisting of running, climbing, swimming and flying. To make it easier to administer the curriculum, all the animals took all the subjects.

The duck was excellent in swimming, in fact better than his instructor, but he made only passing grades in flying and was very poor in running. Since he was slow in running, he had to stay after school and also drop swimming in order to practice running. This was kept up until his webbed feet were badly worn and he was only average in swimming. But average was acceptable in school, so nobody worried about that except the duck.

The rabbit started at the top of the class in running, but had a nervous breakdown because of so much make-up work in swimming.

The squirrel was excellent in climbing until he developed frustration in the flying class where his teacher made him start from the ground up instead of from the treetop down. He also developed a "charlie horse" from overexertion and then got a C in climbing and a D in running.

The eagle was a problem child and was disciplined severely. In the climbing class he beat all the others to the top of the tree, but insisted on using his own way to get there.

At the end of the year, an abnormal eel that could swim exceedingly well, and also run, climb and fly a little, had the highest average and was valedictorian.

The prairie dogs stayed out of school and fought the tax levy because the administration would not add digging and burrowing to the curriculum. They apprenticed their children to a badger and later joined the groundhogs and gophers to start a successful private school.

Does this fable have a moral?

George H. Reavis

Touched

She is my daughter and is immersed in the turbulence of her 16th year. Following a recent bout with illness, she learned her best friend would soon be moving away. School was not going as well as she had hoped, nor as well as her mother and I had hoped. She exuded sadness through a muffle of blankets as she huddled in bed, searching for comfort. I wanted to reach out to her and wrench away all the miseries that had taken root in her young spirit. Yet, even aware of how much I cared for her and wanted to remove her unhappiness, I knew the importance of proceeding with caution.

As a family therapist I've been well-educated about inappropriate expressions of intimacy between fathers and daughters, primarily by clients whose lives have been torn apart by sexual abuse. I'm also aware of how easily care and closeness can be sexualized, especially by men who find the emotional field foreign territory and who mistake any expression of affection for sexual invitation. How much easier it was to hold and comfort her when she was two or three or even seven. But now her body, our society and my manhood all seemed to conspire against my comforting my daughter. How could I console her while still respecting the necessary boundaries between a father and a teenage daughter? I settled for offering her a back rub. She consented.

I gently massaged her bony back and knotted shoulders as I apologized for my recent absence. I explained that I had just returned from the international back-rubbing finals, where I had placed fourth. I assured her that it's hard to beat the back rub of a concerned father, especially if he's a world class back rubbing concerned father. I told her all about the contest and the other contestants as my hands and fingers sought to loosen tightened muscles and unlock the tensions in her young life.

I told her about the shrunken antique Asian man who had placed third in the contest. After studying acupuncture and his entire life, he could focus all his energy into his fingers, elevating back rubbing to an art. "He poked and prodded with prestidigitatious precision," I explained, showing my daughter a sample of what I'd learned from the old man. She groaned, though I wasn't sure whether in response to my alliteration or my touch. Then I told her about the woman who had placed second. She was from Turkey and since her childhood had practiced the art of belly dancing, so she could make muscles move and ripple in fluid motion. With her back rub, her fingers awakened in tired muscles and weary bodies an urge to vibrate and quiver and dance. "She let her fingers do the walking and the muscles tagged along," I said, demonstrating.

"That's weird," emanated faintly from a face muffled by a pillow. Was it my one-liner or my touch?

Then I just rubbed my daughter's back and we settled into silence. After a time she asked, "So who got first place?"

"You'd never believe it!" I said. "It was baby!" And I explained how the soft, trusting touches of an infant exploring a world of skin and smells and tastes was like no other touch in the world. Softer than soft. Unpredictable, gentle, searching. Tiny hands saying more than words could ever express. About belonging. About trust. About innocent love. And then I gently and softly touched her as I had learned from the infant. I recalled vividly her own infancy — holding her, rocking her, watching her grope and grow into her world. I realized that she, in fact, was the infant who had taught me about the touch of the infant.

After another period of gentle back rubbing and silence, I said I was glad to have learned so much from the world's expert back rubbers. I explained how I had become an even better back rubber for a 16-year-old daughter painfully stretching herself into adult shape. I offered a silent prayer of thanks that such life had been placed in my hands and that I was blessed with the miracle of touching even a part of it.

Victor Nelson

I Love You, Son

Thoughts while driving my son to school: Morning, Kid. You look pretty sharp in your Cub Scout gear, not as fat as your old man when he was a Cub. I don't think my hair was ever as long until I went away to college, but I think I'd recognize you any way by what you are: a little shaggy around the ears, scuffed around the toes, wrinkled in the knees... We get used to one another...

Now that you're eight I notice I don't see a whole lot of you anymore. On Columbus Day you left at nine in the morning. I saw you for 42 seconds at lunch and you reappeared for supper at five. I miss you, but I know you've got serious business to take care of. Certainly as serious as, if not more important than, the things the other commuters on the road are doing.

You've got to grow up and out and that's more important than clipping coupons, arranging stock options or selling people short. You've got to learn what you are able to do and what you aren't — and you've got to learn how to deal with that. You've got to learn about people and how they behave when they don't feel good about themselves — like the bullies who hang out at the bike rack and hassle the smaller kids. Yeah, you'll even have to learn how to pretend that name-calling doesn't hurt. It'll always hurt, but you'll have to put up a front or they'll call you worse names next time. I only hope you remember how it feels — in case you ever decide to rank a kid who's smaller than you.

When was the last time I told you I was proud of you? I guess if I can't remember, I've got work to do. I remember the last time I yelled at you — told you we'd be late if you didn't hurry — but, on balance, as Nixon used to say, I haven't given you as many pats as yells. For the record, in case you read this, I am proud of you. I especially like your independence, the way you take care of yourself even when it frightens me just a little bit. You've never been much of a whiner and that makes you a superior kid in my book.

Why is it that fathers are so slow to realize that eight-year-olds need as many hugs as four-year-olds? If I don't watch out, pretty soon I'll be punching you on the arm and saying, "Whaddaya say, kid?!" instead of hugging you and telling you I love you. Life is too short to hide affection. Why is it that eight-year-olds are so slow to realize that 36-year-olds need as many hugs as four-year-olds?

Did I forget to tell you that I'm proud you went back to a box lunch after one week's worth of that indigestible hot lunch? I'm glad you value your body.

I wish the drive weren't so short... I want to talk about last night... When your younger brother was asleep and we let you stay up and watch the Yankees game. Those times are so special. There's no way you can plan them. Every time we try to plan something together, it's not as good or rich or warm. For a few all-too-short minutes it was as if you'd already grown up and we sat and talked without any words about "How are you doing in school, son?" I'd already checked your math homework the only way I could — with a calculator. You're better with numbers than I'll ever be.

So, we talked about the game and you knew more about the players than I did and I learned from you. And we were both happy when the Yankees won.

Well, there's the crossing guard. He'll probably outlive all of us. I wish you didn't have to go to school today. There are so many things I want to say.

Your exit from my car is so quick. I want to savor the moment and you've already spotted a couple of your friends.

I just wanted to say "I love you, son..."

Victor B. Miller

What You Are Is As Important As What You Do

Who you are speaks so loudly I can't hear what you're saying.

Ralph Waldo Emerson

It was a sunny Saturday afternoon in Oklahoma City. My friend and proud father Bobby Lewis was taking his two little boys to play miniature golf. He walked up to the fellow at the ticket counter and said, "How much is it to get in?"

The young man replied, "$3.00 for you and $3.00 for any kid who is older than six. We let them in free if they are six or younger. How old are they?"

Bobby replied, "The lawyer's three and the doctor is seven, so I guess I owe you $6.00."

The man at the ticket counter said, "Hey, Mister, did you just win the lottery or something? You could have saved yourself three bucks. You could have told me that the older one was six; I wouldn't have known the difference." Bobby replied, "Yes, that may be true, but the kids would have known the difference."

As Ralph Waldo Emerson said, "Who you are speaks so

loudly I can't hear what you're saying." In challenging times when ethics are more important than ever before, make sure you set a good example for everyone you work and live with.

Patricia Fripp

A Mom's Life

Take your plate into the kitchen, please.
Take it downstairs when you go.
Don't leave it there, take it upstairs.
Is that yours?
Don't hit your brother.
I'm talking to you.
Just a minute, please, can't you see I'm talking?
I said, Don't interrupt.
Did you brush your teeth?
What are you doing out of bed?
Go back to bed.
You can't watch in the afternoon.
What do you mean, there's nothing to do?
Go outside.
Read a book.
Turn it down.
Get off the phone.
Tell your friend you'll call her back. Right now!
Hello. No, she's not home.
She'll call you when she gets home.
Take a jacket. Take a sweater.
Take one anyway.
Someone left his shoes in front of the TV.

Get the toys out of the hall. Get the boys out of the bathtub. Get the toys off the stairs.
Do you realize that could kill someone?
Hurry up.
Hurry up. Everyone's waiting.
I'll count to ten and then we're going without you.
Did you go to the bathroom?
If you don't go, you're not going.
I mean it.
Why didn't you go before you left?
Can you hold it?
What's going on back there?
Stop it.
I said, Stop it!
I don't want to hear about it.
Stop it or I'm taking you home right now.
That's it. We're going home.
Give me a kiss.
I need a hug.
Make your bed.
Clean up your room.
Set the table.
I need you to set the table!
Don't tell me it's not your turn.
Please move your chair in to the table.
Sit up.
Just try a little. You don't have to eat the whole thing.
Stop playing and eat.
Would you watch what you're doing?
Move your glass. It's too close to the edge.
Watch it!
More, what?

More, please. That's better.
Just eat one bite of salad.
You don't always get what you want. That's life.
Don't argue with me. I'm not discussing this anymore.
Go to your room.
No, ten minutes are not up.
One more minute.
How many times have I told you, don't do that.
Where did the cookies go?
Eat the old fruit before you eat the new fruit.
I'm not giving you mushrooms. I've taken all the mushrooms out. See?
Is your homework done?
Stop yelling. If you want to ask me something, come here.
STOP YELLING. IF YOU WANT TO ASK ME SOMETHING, COME HERE.
I'll think about it.
Not now.
Ask your father.
We'll see.
Don't sit so close to the television, it's bad for your eyes.
Calm down.
Calm down and start over.
Is that the truth?
Fasten your seat belt.
Did everyone fasten their seat belts?
I'm sorry, that's the rule. I'm sorry, that's the rule. I'm sorry, that's the rule.

Delia Ephron

The Perfect American Family

It is 10: 30 on a perfect Saturday morning and we are, for the moment, the perfect American family. My wife has taken our six-year-old to his first piano lesson. Our 14-year-old has not yet roused from his slumber. The four-year-old watches tiny, anthropomorphic beings hurl one another from cliffs in the other room. I sit at the kitchen table reading the newspaper.

Aaron Malachi, thee four-year-old, apparently bored by the cartoon carnage and the considerable personal power obtained by holding the television's remote control, enters my space.

"I'm hungry," he says.

"Want some more cereal?"

"No."

"Want some yogurt?"

"No."

"Want some eggs?"

"No, Can I have some ice cream?"

"No."

For all I know, ice cream may be far more nourishing than processed cereal or antibiotic-laden eggs but, according to my cultural values, it is wrong to have ice cream at 10: 45 on a Saturday morning.

Silence. About four seconds. "Daddy, we have very much of life left, don't we?"

"Yes, we have lots of life left, Aaron."

"Me and you and Mommy?"

"That's right."

"And Isaac?"

"Yes."

"And Ben?"

"Yes. You and me and Mommy and Isaac and Ben."

"We have very much of life left. Until all the people die."

"What do you mean?"

"Until all the people die and the dinosaurs come back."

Aaron sits down on the table, cross-legged like a Buddha, in the center of my newspaper.

"What do you mean, Aaron, 'until all the people die'?"

"You said everybody dies. When everybody dies, then the dinosaurs will come back. The cavemen lived in caves, dinosaur caves. Then the dinosaurs came back and squished 'em."

I realize that already for Aaron life is a limited economy, a resource with a beginning and an end. He envisions himself and us somewhere along that trajectory, a trajectory that ends in uncertainty and loss.

I am faced with an ethical decision. What should I do now? Should I attempt to give him God, salvation, eternity? Should I toss him some spiel like, "Your body is just a shell and after you die, we will all be together in spirit forever"?

Or should I leave him with his uncertainty and his anxiety because I think it's real? Should I try to make him an anxious existentialist or should I try to make him feel better?

I don't know. I stare at the newspaper. The Celtics are consistently losing on Friday nights. Larry Bird is angry at somebody, but I can's see who, because Aaron's foot is in the way. I don't know but my neurotic, addictive, middle-class sensibility is telling me that this is a very important moment, a moment when Aaron's ways of constructing his world are being formed. Or maybe my neurotic, addictive, middle-class sensibility is just making me think that. If life and death are an illusion, then why should I trifle with how someone else understands them?

On the table Aaron plays with an "army guy," raising his arms and balancing him on his shaky legs. It was Kevin McHale that Larry Bird was angry at. No, not Kevin McHale, it was Jerry Sichting. But Jerry Sichting is no longer with the Celtics. Whatever happened to Jerry Sichting? Everything dies, everything comes to an end. Jerry Sichting is playing for Sacramento or Orlando or he has disappeared.

I should not trifle with how Aaron understands life and death because I want him to have a solid sense of structure, a sense of the permanence of things. It's obvious what a good job the nuns and priests did with me. It was agony or bliss. Heaven and hell were not connected by long distance service. You were on God's team or you were in the soup, and the soup was hot. I don't want Aaron to get burned, but I want him to have a strong frame. The neurotic but unavoidable anxiety can come later.

Is that possible? It is possible to have a sense that God, spirit, karma, Y*H*W*H, something — is transcendent, without traumatizing the presentness of a person, without beating it into them? Can we have our cake and eat it too, ontologically speaking? Or is their fragile sensibility, their "there-ness," sundered by such an act?

Sensing a slight increase in agitation on the table, I know

that Aaron is becoming bored with his guy. With an attitude of drama benefiting the moment, I clear my throat and begin with a professional tone.

"Aaron, death is something that some people believe . . ."

"Dad," Aaron interrupts, "could we play a video game? It's not a very violent game," he explains, hands gesticulating. "It's not like a killing game. The guys just kind of flop over."

"Yes," I say with some relief, "let's play video games. But first there's something else we have to do."

"What?" Aaron stops and turns from where he has run, already halfway to the arcade.

"First, let's have some ice cream."

Another perfect Saturday for a perfect family. For now.

Michael Murphy

The trouble with you, Sheldon, is
you lack self-confidence.

Just Say It!

If you were going to die soon and had only one phone call you could make, who would you call and what would you say? And why are you waiting?

Stephen Levine

One night, after reading one of the hundreds of parenting books I've read, I was feeling a little guilty because the book had described some parenting strategies I hadn't used in a while. The main strategy was to talk with your child and use those three magic words: "I love you." It had stressed over and over that children need to know that unconditionally and unequivocally that you really love them.

I went upstairs to my son's bedroom and knocked on the door. As I knocked, all I could hear were his drums. I knew he was there but he wasn't answering. So I opened the door and, sure enough, there he was sitting with his earphones on, listening to a tape and playing his drums. After I leaned over to get his attention, I said to him, "Tim, have you got a second?"

He said, "Oh sure, Dad. I'm always good for one." We proceeded to sit down and after about 15 minutes and a lot of small talk and stuttering, I just looked at him and said, "Tim, I really love the way you play drums."

He said, "Oh, thanks, Dad, I appreciate it."

I walked out of the door and said, "See you later!" As I was walking downstairs, it dawned on me that I went up there with a certain message and had not delivered it. I felt it was really important to get back up there and have another chance to say those three magic words.

Again I climbed the stairs, knocked on the door and opened it. "You got a second, Tim?"

"Sure, Dad. I'm always good for a second or two. What do you need?"

"Son, the first time I came up here to share a message with you, something else came out. It really wasn't what I wanted to share with you. Tim, do you remember when you were learning how to drive, it caused me a lot of problems? I wrote three words and slipped them under your pillow in hopes that would take care of it. I'd done my part as a parent and expressed my love to my son." Finally after a little small talk, I looked at Tim and said, "What I want you to know is that we love you."

He looked at me and said, "Oh, thanks, Dad. That's you and Mom?"

I said, "Yeah, that's both of us, we just don't express it enough."

He said, "Thanks, that means a lot. I know you do."

I turned around and walked out the door. As I was walking downstairs, I started thinking, "I can't believe this. I've already been up there twice — I know what the message is and yet something else comes out of my mouth."

I decided I'm going back there now and let Tim know exactly how I feel. He's going to hear it directly from me. I don't care if he is six feet tall! So back I go, knock on the door and he yells "Wait a minute. Don't tell me who it is. Could that be you, Dad?"

I said, "How'd you know that?" and he responded. "I've known you ever since you were a parent, Dad."

Then I said "Son, have you got just one more second?"

"You know I'm good for one, so come on in. I suppose you didn't tell me what you wanted to tell me?"

I said, "How'd you know that?"

"I've known you ever since I was in diapers."

I said, "Well, here it is, Tim, what I've been holding back on. I just want to express to you how special you are to our family. It's not what you do, and it's not what you've done, like all the things you're doing with the junior high kids in town. It's who you are as a person. I love you and I just wanted you to know I love you, and I don't know why I hold back on something so important."

He looked at me and he said, "Hey, Dad, I know you do and it's really special hearing you say it to me. Thanks so much for your thoughts, as well as the intent."As I was walking out the door, he said, "Oh, hey, Dad. Have you got another second?"

I started thinking, "Oh no. What's he going to say to me?" I said, "Oh sure. I'm always good for one."

I don't know where kids get this — I'm sure it couldn't be from their parents, but he said, "Dad, I just want to ask you one question."

I said, "What's that?"

He looked at me and said,"Dad, have you been to a workshop or something like that?"

I'm thinking, "Oh no, like any other 18-year-old, he's got any number," and I said, "No, I was reading a book, and it said how important it is to tell your kids how you really feel about them."

"Hey, thanks for taking the time. Talk to you later, Dad."

I think what Tim taught me, more than anything else that night is that the only way you can understand the real meaning and purpose of love is to be willing to pay the price. You have to go out there and risk sharing it.

Gene Bedley

A Legacy Of Love

As a young man, Al was a skilled artist, a potter. He had a wife and two fine sons. One night, his oldest son developed a severe stomachache. Thinking it was only some common intestinal disorder, neither Al nor his wife took the condition very seriously. But the malady was actually acute appendicitis, and the boy died suddenly that night.

Knowing the death could have been prevented if he had only realized the seriousness of the situation, Al's emotional health deteriorated under the enormous burden of his guilt. To make matters worse his wife left him a short time later, leaving him alone with his six-year-old younger son. The hurt and pain of the two situations were more than Al could handle, and he turned to alcohol to help him cope. In time Al became an alcoholic.

As the alcoholism progressed, Al began to lose everything he possessed — his home, his land, his art objects, everything. Eventually Al died alone in a San Francisco motel room.

When I heard of Al's death, I reacted with the same disdain the world shows for one who ends his life with nothing material to show for it. "What a complete failure!" I thought. "What a totally wasted life!"

As time went by, I began to re-evaluate my earlier harsh

judgment. You see, I knew Al's now adult son, Ernie. He is one of the kindest, most caring, most loving men I have ever known. I watched Ernie with his children and saw the free flow of love between them. I knew that kindness and caring had to come from somewhere.

I hadn't heard Ernie talk much about his father. It is so hard to defend an alcoholic. One day I worked up my courage to ask him. "I'm really puzzled by something," I said. "I know your father was basically the only one to raise you. What on earth did he do that you became such a special person?"

Ernie sat quietly and reflected for a few moments. Then he said, "From my earliest memories as a child until I left home at 18, Al came into my room every night, gave me a kiss and said, 'love you, son.'"

Tears came to my eyes as I realized what a fool I had been to judge Al as a failure. He had not left any material possessions behind. But he had been a kind loving father, and he left behind one of the finest, most giving men I have ever known.

Bobbie Gee
Winning The Image Game

On Parenting

Your children are not your children.
They are the sons and daughters of Life's longing for itself.
They come through you but not from you,
And though they are with you, yet they belong not to you.
You may give them your love but not your thoughts,
For they have their own thoughts.
You may house their bodies but not their souls,
For their souls dwell in the house of tomorrow, which you cannot visit, not even in your dreams.
You may strive to be like them, but seek not to make them like you,
For life goes not backward nor tarries with yesterday.
You are the bows from which your children as living arrows are sent forth.
The archer sees the mark upon the path of the infinite, and He bends you with His might that His arrows might go swift and far.
Let your bending in the archer's hand be for gladness;
For even as He loves the arrow that flies, so He loves also the bow that is stable.

Kahlil Gibran

4

ON LEARNING

Learning is finding out
what you already know.
Doing is demonstrating
that you know it.
Teaching is reminding
others that they know it
just as well as you.
You are all learners,
doers, teachers.

Richard Bach

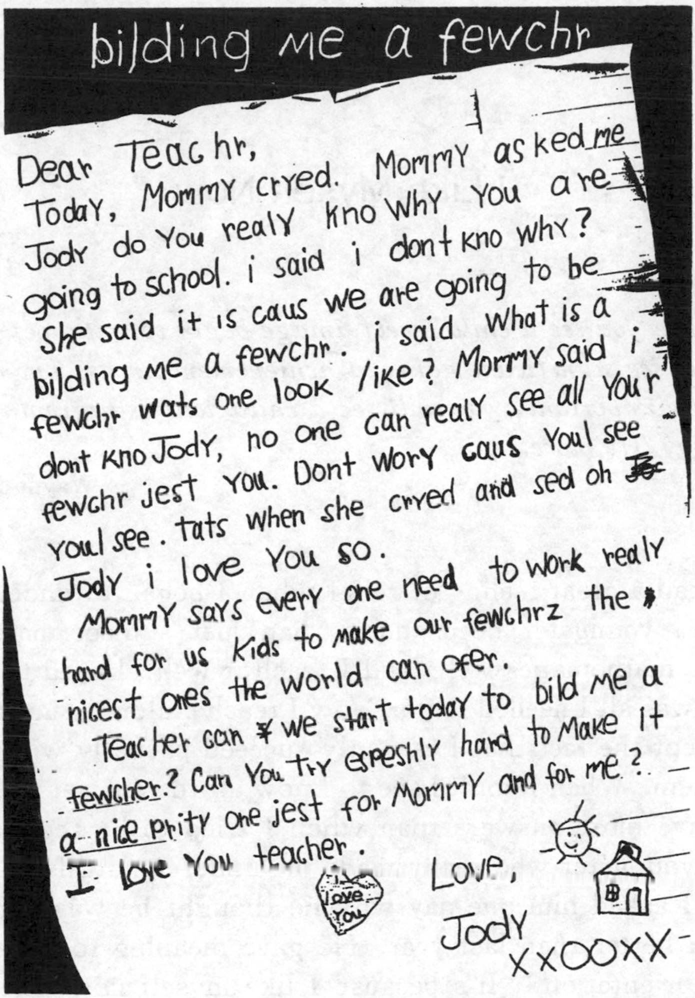

bilding me a fewchr

Dear Teachr,

Today, Mommy cryed. Mommy asked me Jody do You realy kno Why You are going to school. i said i dont kno why? She said it is caus we are going to be bilding me a fewchr. i said What is a fewchr wats one look like? Mommy said i dont kno Jody, no one can realy see all Your fewchr jest You. Dont wory caus Youl see Youl see. tats when she cryed and sed oh Jody i love You so.

Mommy says every one need to work realy hard for us kids to make our fewchrz the nicest ones the world can ofer.

Teacher can we start today to bild me a fewcher? Can You try espeshly hard to make it a nice prity one jest for Mommy and for me?

I love You teacher.

I love You

Love,
Jody
XXOOXX

Authored by Frank Trujillo

I Like Myself Now

Once you see a child's self-image begin to improve, you will see significant gains in achievement areas, but even more important, you will see a child who is beginning to enjoy life more.

Wayne Dyer

I had a great feeling of relief when I began to understand that a youngster needs more than just subject matter. I know mathematics well, and I teach it well. I used to think that was all I needed to do. Now I teach children, not math. I accept the fact that I can only succeed partially with some of them. When I don't have to know all the answers, I seem to have more answers than when I tried to be the expert. The youngster who really made me understand this was Eddie. I asked him one day why he thought he was doing so much better than last year. He gave meaning to my whole new orientation. "It's because I like myself now when I'm with you," he said.

A teacher quoted by Everett Shostrum in
Man, The Manipulator

All The Good Things

He was in the third grade class I taught at Saint Mary's School in Morris, Minnesota. All 34 of my students were dear to me, but Mark Eklund was one in a million. Very neat in appearance, he had that happy-to-be-alive attitude that made even his occasional mischievousness delightful.

Mark also talked incessantly. I tried to remind him again and again that talking without permission was not acceptable. What impressed me so much, though, was the sincere response every time I had to correct him for misbehaving. "Thank you for correcting me, Sister!" I didn't know what to make of it at first but before long I became accustomed to hearing it many times a day.

One morning my patience was growing thin when Mark talked once too often. I made a novice-teacher's mistake. I looked at Mark and said, "If you say one more word, I am going to tape your mouth shut!"

It wasn't ten seconds later when Chuck blurted out, "Mark is talking again." I hadn't asked any of the students to help me watch Mark, but since I had stated the punishment in front of the class, I had to act on it.

I remember the scene as if it had occurred this morning. I walked to my desk, very deliberately opened the drawer and took out a roll of masking tape. Without saying a word, I proceeded to Mark's desk, tore off two pieces of tape and made a big X with them over his mouth. I then returned to the front of the room.

As I glanced at Mark to see how he was doing, he winked at me. That did it! I started laughing. The entire class cheered as I walked back to Mark's desk, removed the tape and shrugged my shoulders. His first words were, "Thank you for correcting me, Sister."

At the end of the year I was asked to teach junior high math. The years flew by, and before I knew it Mark was in my classroom again. He was more handsome than ever and just as polite. Since he had to listen carefully to my instruction in the "new math," he did not talk as much in ninth grade.

One Friday things just didn't feel right. We had worked hard on a new concept all week, and I sensed that the students were growing frustrated with themselves — and edgy with one another. I had to stop this crankiness before it got out of hand. So I asked them to list the names of the other students in the room on two sheets of paper, leaving a space between each name. Then I told them to think of the nicest thing they could say about each of their classmates and write it down.

It took the remainder of the class period to finish the assignment, but as the students left the room, each one handed me their paper. Chuck smiled. Mark said, "Thank you for teaching me, Sister. Have a good weekend."

That Saturday, I wrote down the name of each student on a separate sheet of paper, and I listed what everyone else had said about that individual. On Monday I gave each student his or her list. Som of them ran two pages. Before long, the entire class was smiling. "Really?" I heard whispered. "I never knew that meant anything to anyone!" "I didn't know others liked me so much!"

No one ever mentioned those papers in class again. I never knew if they discussed them after class or with their parents, but it didn't matter. The exercise had accomplished its purpose. The students were happy with themselves and one another again.

That group of students moved on. Several years later, after I had returned from a vacation, my parents met me at the airport. As we were driving home, Mother asked the usual questions about the trip: How the weather was, my experiences in general. There was a slight lull in the conversation. Mother gave Dad a sideways glance and simply said, "Dad?" My father cleared his throat. "The Eklunds called last night," he began.

"Really?" I said. "I haven't heard from them for several years. I wonder how Mark is."

Dad responded quietly. "Mark was killed in Vietnam," He said. "The funeral is tomorrow, and his parents would like it if you could attend." To this day I can still point to the exact spot on I-494 where Dad told me about Mark.

I had never seen a serviceman in a military coffin before. Mark looked so handsome, so mature. All I could think at that moment was, *Mark, I would give all the masking tape in the world if only you could talk to me.*

The church was packed with Mark's friends. Chuck's sister sang "The Battle Hymn of the Republic." Why did it have to rain on the day of the funeral? It was difficult enough at the graveside. The pastor said the usual prayers and the bugler played taps. One by one those who loved Mark took a last walk by the coffin and sprinkled it with holy water.

I was the last one to bless the coffin. As I stood there, one of the soldiers who had acted as a pallbearer came up to me. "Were you Mark's math teacher?" he asked. I nodded as I continued to stare at the coffin. "Mark talked about you a lot," he said.

After the funeral most of Mark's former classmates headed to Chuck's farmhouse for lunch. Mark's mother and father were there, obviously waiting for me. "We want to show you something," his father said, taking a wallet out of his pocket. "They found this on Mark when he was killed. We thought you might recognize it."

Opening the billfold, he carefully removed two worn pieces of notebook paper that had obviously been taped, folded and refolded many times. I knew without looking that the papers were the ones on which I had listed all the good things each of Mark's classmates had said about him. "Thank you so much for doing that," Mark's mother said. "As you can see, Mark treasured it."

Mark's classmates started to gather around us. Chuck smiled rather sheepishly and said, "I still have my list. It's in the top drawer of my desk at home." John's wife said, "John asked me to put his in our wedding album." "I have mine, too," Marilyn said. "It's in my diary." Then Vicki, another classmate, reached into her pocketbook, took out her wallet and showed her worn and frazzled list to the group. "I carry this with me at all times," Vicki said without batting an eyelash. "I think we all save our lists."

That's when I finally sat down and cried. I cried for Mark and for all his friends who would never see him again.

Helen P. Mrosla

You Are A Marvel

Each second we live is a new and unique moment of the universe, a moment that will never be again... And what do we teach our children? We teach them that two and two make four, and that Paris is the capital of France.

When will we also teach them what they are?

We should say to each of them: Do you know what you are? You are a marvel. You are unique. In all the years that have passed, there has never been another child like you. Your legs, your arms, your clever fingers, the way you move.

You may become a Shakespeare, a Michelangelo, a Beethoven. You have the capacity for anything. Yes, you are a marvel. And when you grow up, can you then have another who is, like you, a marvel?

You must work — we must all work — to make the world worthy of its children.

Pablo Casals

All I Ever Really Needed To Know I Learned In Kindergarten

Most of what I really need to know about how to live and what to do and how to be, I learned in kindergarten. Wisdom was not at the top of the graduate mountain, but there in the sandbox at nursery school.

These are the things I learned: Share everything. Play fair. Don't hit people. Put things back where you found them. Clean up your own mess. Don't take things that aren't yours. Say you're sorry when you hurt somebody. Wash your hands before you eat. Flush. Warm cookies and cold milk are good for you. Live a balanced life. Learn some and think some and draw and paint and sing and dance and play and work every day some.

Take a nap every afternoon. When you go out into the world, watch for traffic, hold hands and stick together. Be aware of wonder. Remember the little seed in the plastic cup. The roots go down and the plant goes up and nobody really knows how or why, but we are all like that.

Goldfish and hamsters and white mice and even the little seed in the plastic cup — they all die. So do we.

And then remember the book about Dick and Jane and the first word you learned, the biggest word of all: LOOK. Everything you need to know is in there somewhere. The Golden Rule and love and basic sanitation. Ecology and politics and sane living.

Think of what a better world it would be if we all — he whole world — had cookies and milk about 3 o'clock every afternoon and then lay down with our blankets for a nap. Or if we had a basic policy in our nations to always put things back where we found them and clean up our own messes. And it is still true, no matter how old you are, when you go out into the world, it is better to hold hands and stick together.

Robert Fulghum

We Learn By Doing

Not many years ago I began to play the cello. Most people would say that what I am doing is "learning to play" the cello. But these words carry in to our minds the strange idea that there exists two very different processes: (1) learning to play the cello; and (2) playing the cello. They imply that I will do the first until I have completed it, at which point I will stop the first process and begin the second. In short, I will go on "learning to play" until I have "learned to play" and then I will begin to play. Of course, this is nonsense. There are not two processes, but one. We learn to do something by doing it. There is no other way.

John Holt

The Hand

A Thanksgiving Day editorial in the newspaper told of a school teacher who asked her class of first graders to draw a picture of something they were thankful for. She thought of how little these children from poor neighborhoods actually had to be thankful for. But she knew that most of them would draw pictures of turkeys or tables with food. The teacher was taken aback with the picture Douglas handed in. . . a simple childishly drawn hand.

But whose hand? The class was captivated by the abstract image. "I think it must be the hand of God that brings us food," said one child. "A farmer," said another, "because he grows the turkeys." Finally when the others were at work, the teacher bent over Douglas's desk and asked whose hand it was. "It's your hand, Teacher," he mumbled.

She recalled that frequently at recess she had taken Douglas, a scrubby forlorn child by the hand. She often did that with the children. But it meant so much to Douglas. Perhaps this was everyone's Thanksgiving, not for the material things given to us but for the chance, in whatever small way, to give to others.

Source Unknown

The Royal Knights Of Harlem

Within walking distance of my Manhattan apartment, but also light-years away, there is a part of New York called Spanish Harlem. In many ways it is a Third World country. Infant and maternal mortality rates are about the same as in say, Bangladesh, and average male life expectancy is even shorter. These facts it shares with the rest of Harlem, yet here many people are also separated from the more affluent parts of the city by language. When all this is combined with invisibility in the media, the condescension of many teachers and police who work in this Third World country but wouldn't dream of living there, and textbooks that have little to do with their lives, the lesson for kids is clear: They are "less than" people who live only a few blocks away.

At a junior high that rises from a barren patch of concrete playgrounds and metal fences on East 101st Street, Bill Hall teaches the usual English courses, plus English as a second language to students who arrive directly from Puerto Rico, Central and South America, even Pakistan and Hong Kong. Those kids are faced with a new culture, strange rules, a tough neighborhood and parents who may be feeling just as lost as they are. Bill Hall is faced with them.

While looking for an interest to bind one such group together and help them to learn English at the same time, Bill noticed someone in the neighborhood carrying a chessboard. As a chess player himself, he knew this game crossed many cultural boundaries, so he got permission from a very skeptical principal to start a chess club after school.

Few of the girls came. Never having seen women playing chess, they assumed this game wasn't for them, and without even a female teacher as a role model, those few who did come gradually dropped out. Some of the boys stayed away, too — chess wasn't the kind of game that made you popular in this neighborhood — but about a dozen remained to learn the basics. Their friends made fun of them for staying after school, and some parents felt that chess was a waste of time since it wouldn't help them get a job, but still, they kept coming. Bill was giving these boys something rare in their lives: the wholehearted attention of someone who believed in them.

Gradually, their skills at both chess and English improved. As they got more expert at the game, Bill took them to chess matches in schools outside Spanish Harlem. Because he paid for their subway fares and pizza dinners, no small thing on his teacher's salary, the boys knew he cared. They began to trust this middle-aged white man a little more.

To help them become more independent, Bill asked each boy to captain one event, and to handle all travel and preparation for it. Gradually, even when Bill wasn't around, the boys began to assume responsibility for each other: to coach those who were lagging behind, to share personal problems and to explain to each other's parents why chess wasn't such a waste of time after all. Gradually, too, this new sense of competence carried over into their classrooms and their grades began to improve.

As they became better students and chess players, Bill Hall's dreams for them grew. With a little money supplied by the Manhattan Chess Club, he took them to the State Finals in Syracuse.

What had been twelve disparate, isolated, often passive, shutdown kids had now become a team with their own chosen name: The Royal Knights. After finishing third in their own state, they were eligible for the Junior High School Finals in California.

By now, however, even Bill's own colleagues were giving him reasons why he shouldn't be spending so much time and effort. In real life, these ghetto kids would never "get past New Jersey," as one teacher put it. Why raise funds to fly them across the country and make them more dissatisfied with their lives? Nonetheless, Bill raised money for tickets to California. In that national competition, they finished seventeenth out of 109 teams.

By now chess had become a subject of school interest — if only because it led to trips. On one of their days at a New York chess club, the team members met a young girl from the Soviet Union who was the Women's World Champion. Even Bill was floored by the idea that two of his kids came up with: If this girl could come all the way from Russia, why couldn't The Royal Knights go there? After all, it was the chess capital of the world, and the Scholastic Chess Friendship Games were coming up.

Though no U. S. players their age had ever entered these games, officials in Bill's school district rallied round the idea. So did a couple of the corporations he approached for travel money. Of course, no one thought his team could win, but that wasn't the goal. The trip itself would widen the boys horizons, Bill argued. When Pepsi-Cola came up with a $20, 000 check, Bill began to realize that this crazy dream was going to come true.

They boarded the plane for the first leg of their trip to Russia as official representatives of the country from which they had felt so estranged only a few months before. But as veterans of Spanish Harlem, they also made very clear that they were representing their own neighborhood. On the back of their satin athletic jackets was emblazoned not "U. S. A.," but "The Royal Knights."

Once they were in Moscow, however, their confidence began to falter badly. The experience and deliberate style of their Soviet opponents were something they had never previously encountered. Finally one of the Knights broke the spell by playing a Soviet Grand master in his 30s to a draw in a simulation match. The Russians weren't invincible after all; just people like them. After that, the Knights won about half their matches, and even discovered a homegrown advantage in the special event of speed chess. Unlike the Soviet players, who had been taught that slowness and deliberation were virtues, the Knights had a street-smart style that made them both fast and accurate.

By the time Bill and his team got to Leningrad to take on the toughest part of their competition, the boys were feeling good again. Though they had been selected at random for their need to learn English, not for any talent at chess, and though they had been playing for only a few months, they won one match and achieved a draw in another.

When the Knights got back to New York, they were convinced they could do anything.

It was a conviction they would need. A few months later when I went to their junior high school club room, Bill Hall, a big gentle man who rarely gets angry, was furious about a recent confrontation between one of the Puerto Rican team members and a white teacher. As Bill urged the boy to explain to me, he had done so well on a test that the teacher, thinking he had cheated, made him take it over. When the boy did well a second time, the teacher seemed less pleased than annoyed to have been proven wrong. "If this had been a school in a different neighborhood," said Bill, "none of this would have happened."

It was the kind of classroom bias that these boys had been internalizing — but now had the self-esteem to resist. "Maybe the teacher was just jealous," the boy said cheerfully. "I mean, we put this school on the map."

And so they had. Their dingy junior high auditorium had just been chosen by a Soviet dance troupe as the site of a New York performance. Every principal in the school district was asking for a chess program, and local television and newspapers had interviewed The Royal Knights. Now that their junior high graduation was just weeks away, bids from various high schools with programs for "gifted" kids were flooding in, even one from a high school in California. Though all the boys were worried about their upcoming separation, it was the other team members who persuaded the boy who got that invitation to accept it.

"We told him to go for it," as one said. "We promised to write him every week," said another. "Actually," said a third, "We all plan to stay in touch for life."

With career plans that include law, accounting, teaching computer sciences — futures they wouldn't have thought possible before — there was no telling what continuing surprises they might share at reunions of this team that had become its own support group and family.

What were they doing, I asked, before Bill Hall and chess

playing came into their lives? There was a very long silence.

"Hanging out in the street and feeling like shit," said one boy, who now wants to become a lawyer.

"Taking lunch money from younger kids and a few drugs now and then," admitted another.

"Just lying on my bed, reading comics, and getting yelled at by my father for being lazy," said a third.

Was there anything in their schoolbooks that made a difference?

"Not until Mr. Hall thought we were smart," explained one to the nods of the others, "and then we were."

Gloria Steinem

The Little Boy

Once a little boy went to school.
He was quite a little boy.
And it was quite a big school.
But when the little boy
Found that he could go to his room
By walking right in from the door outside,
He was happy. And the school did not seem
Quite so big any more.

One morning,
When the little boy had been in school a while,
The teacher said:
"Today we are going to make a picture."
And the very first day He was there, the teacher said, "Today we are going to make a picture."
"Good!" thought the little boy. He liked to make pictures.
He could make all kinds:
Lions and tigers,
Chickens and cows,
Trains and boats —
And he took out his box of crayons
And began to draw.
But the teacher said:

"Wait! It is not time to begin!"
And she waited until everyone looked ready.

"Now," said the teacher.
"We are going to make flowers."
"Good!" thought the little boy,
He liked to make flowers,
And he began to make beautiful ones
With his pink and orange and blue crayons.

But the teacher said,
"Wait! And I will show you how."
And she drew a flower on the blackboard.
It was red, with a green stem.
"There," said the teacher.
"Now you may begin."

The little boy looked at the teacher's flower.
Then he looked at his own flower,
He liked his flower better than the teacher's.
But he did not say this,
He just turned his paper over
And made a flower like the teacher's.
It was red, with a green stem.

On another day,
When the little boy had opened
The door from the outside all by himself,
The teacher said,
"Today we are going to make something with clay."
"Good!" thought the little boy.
He liked clay.

He could make all kinds of things with clay:
Snakes and snowmen,
Elephants and mice,
Cars and trucks —
And he began to pull and pinch
His ball of clay.

But the teacher said,
"Wait! It is not time to begin!"
And she waited until everyone looked ready.

"Now," said the teacher,
"We are going to make a dish."
"Good!" thought the little boy,
He liked to make dishes,
And he began to make some
That were all shapes and sizes.

But the teacher said,
"Wait! And I will show you how."
And she showed everyone how to make
One deep dish.
"There," said the teacher,
"Now you may begin."

The little boy looked at the teacher's dish
Then he looked at his own.
He liked his dishes better than the teacher's
But he did not say this,
He just rolled his clay into a big ball again,
And made a dish like the teacher's.

It was a deep dish.

And pretty soon
The little boy learned to wait
And to watch,
And to make things just like the teacher.
And pretty soon
He didn't make things of his own anymore.

Then it happened
That the little boy and his family
Moved to another house,
In another city,
Any the little boy
Had to go to another school.

This school was even Bigger
Than the other one,
And there was no door from the outside
Into his room.
He had to go up some big steps,
And walk down a long hall
To get to his room.
And the very first day
He was there, the teacher said,
"Today we are going to make a picture."

"Good!" thought the little boy,
And he waited for the teacher
To tell him what to do
But the teacher didn't say anything.
She just walked around the room.

When she came to the little boy,
She said, "Don't you want to make a picture?"
"Yes," said the little boy.
"What are we going to make?"
"I don't know until you make it," said the teacher.
"How shall I make it?" asked the little boy.
"Why, any way you like," said the teacher.
"Any any color?" asked the little boy.
"Any color," said the teacher,
"If everyone made the same picture,
And used the same colors,
How would I know who made what,
And which was which?"
"I don't know," said the little boy.
And he began to make pink and orange
and blue flowers.

He liked his new school,
Even if it didn't have a door
Right in from the outside!

Helen E. Buckley

I Am A Teacher

I am a Teacher.

I was born the first moment that a question leaped from the mouth of a child.

I have been many people in many places.

I am Socrates exciting the youth of Athens to discover new ideas through the use of questions.

I am Anne Sullivan tapping out the secrets of the universe into the outstretched hand of Helen Keller.

I am Aesop and Hans Christian Andersen revealing truth through countless stories.

I am Marva Collins fighting for every child's right to an education.

I am Mary McCleod Bethune building a great college for my people, using orange crates for desks.

And I am Bel Kaufman struggling to go *Up The Down Staircase.*

The names of those who have practiced my profession ring like a hall of fame for humanity. . . Booker T. Washington, Buddha, Confucius, Ralph Waldo Emerson, Leo Buscaglia, Moses and Jesus.

I am also those whose names and faces have long been forgotten but whose lessons and character will always be remembered in the accomplishments of their students.

I have wept for joy at the weddings of former students, laughed with glee at the birth of their children and stood with head bowed in grief and confusion by graves dug too soon for bodies far too young.

Throughout the course of a day I have been called upon to be an actor, friend, nurse and doctor, coach, finder of lost articles, money lender, taxi driver, psychologist, substitute parent, salesman, politician and a keeper of the faith.

Despite the maps, charts, formulas, verbs, stories and books, I have really had nothing to teach, for my students really have only themselves to learn, and I know it takes the whole world to tell you who you are.

I am a paradox. I speak loudest when I listen the most. My greatest gifts are in what I am willing to appreciatively receive from my students.

Material wealth is not one of my goals, but I am a full-time treasure seeker in my quest for new opportunities for my students to use their talents and in my constant search for those talents that sometimes lie buried in self-defeat.

I am the most fortunate of all who labor.

A doctor is allowed to usher life into the world in one magic moment. I am allowed to see that life is reborn each day with new questions, ideas and friendships.

An architect knows that if he builds with care, his structure may stand for centuries. A teacher knows that if he builds with love and truth, what he builds will last forever.

I am a warrior, daily doing battle against peer pressure, negativity, fear, conformity, prejudice, ignorance and apathy. But I have great allies: Intelligence, Curiosity, Parental Support, Individuality, Creativity, Faith, Love and Laughter all rush to my banner with indomitable support.

And who do I have to thank for this wonderful life I am so fortunate to experience, but you the public, the parents. For you have done me the great honor to entrust to me your greatest contribution to eternity, your children.

And so I have a past that is rich in memories. I have a present that is challenging, adventurous and fun because I am allowed to spend my days with the future.

I am a teacher . . . and I thank God for it every day.

John W. Schlatter

5

LIVE YOUR DREAM

People who say it cannot be done should not interrupt those who are doing it.

Teilhard de Chardin

Make It Come True

In 1957 a ten-year-old boy in California set a goal. At the time Jim Brown was the greatest running back ever to play pro football and this tall, skinny boy wanted his autograph. In order to accomplish his goal, the young boy had to overcome some obstacles.

He grew up in the ghetto, where he never got enough to eat. Malnutrition took its toll, and a disease called rickets forced him to wear steel splints to support his skinny, bowed-out legs. He had no money to buy a ticket to get into the game, so he waited patiently near the locker room until the game ended and Jim Brown left the field. He politely asked Brown for his autograph. As Brown signed, the boy explained, "Mr. Brown, I have your picture on my wall. I know you hold all the records. You've my idol."

Brown smiled and began to leave, but the young boy wasn't finished. He proclaimed, "Mr. Brown, one day I'm going to break every record you hold!" Brown was impressed and asked, "What is your name, son?"

The boy replied, "Orenthal James. My friends call me O. J."

O.J. Simpson went on to break all but three of the rushing records held by Jim Brown before injuries shortened his football career. Goal setting is the strongest force for human motivation. Set a goal and make it come true.

Dan Clark

I Think I Can!

Whether you think you can or think you can't, you're right.

Henry Ford

Rocky Lyons, the son of New York Jets defensive end Marty Lyons, was five years old when he was driving through rural Alabama with his mother, Kelly. He was asleep on the front seat of their pickup truck, with his feet resting on her lap.

As his mom drove carefully down the winding two lane country road, she turned onto a narrow bridge. As she did, the truck hit a pothole and slid off the road, and the right front wheel got stuck in a rut. Fearing the truck would tip over, she attempted to jerk it back up onto the road by pressing hard on the gas pedal and spinning the steering wheel to the left. But Rocky's foot got caught between her leg and the steering wheel and she lost control of the pickup truck.

The truck flipped over and over down a 20-foot ravine. When it hit bottom, Rocky woke up. "What happened, Mama?" he asked. "Our wheels are pointing toward the sky."

Kelly was blinded by blood. The gearshift had jammed into her face, ripping it open from lip to forehead. Her gums were torn out, her cheeks pulverized, her shoulders crushed. With one shattered bone sticking out of her armpit, she was pinned against the crushed door.

"I'll get you out, Mama," announced Rocky, who had miraculously escaped injury. He slithered out from under Kelly, slid through the open window and tried to yank his mother out. But she didn't move. "Just let me sleep," begged Kelly, who was drifting in and out of consciousness. "No, Mama," Rocky insisted. "You can't go to sleep."

Rocky wriggled back into the truck and managed to push Kelly out of the wreckage. He then told her he'd climb up to the road and stop a car to get help. Fearing that no one would be able to see her little boy in the dark, Kelly refused to let him go alone. Instead they slowly crept up the embankment, with Rocky using his meager 40-pound frame to push his 104-pound mother. They crawled inches at a time. The pain was so great that Kelly wanted to give up, but Rocky wouldn't let her.

To urge his mother on, Rocky told her to think "about that little train," the one in the classic children's story, *The Little Engine That Could*, which managed to get up a steep mountain. To remind her, Rocky kept repeating his version of the story's inspirational phrase: "I know you can, I know you can."

When they finally reached the road, Rocky was able to see his mother's torn face clearly for the first time. He broke into tears. Waving his arms and pleading, "Stop! Please stop!" the boy hailed a truck. "Get my mama to a hospital," he implored the driver.

It took 8 hours and 344 stitches to rebuild Kelly's face. She looks quite different today — "I used to have a straight long nose, thin lips and high cheekbones; now I've got a pug nose, flat cheeks and much bigger lips" — but she has few visible scars and has recovered from her injuries.

Rocky's heroics were big news. But the spunky youngster insists he didn't do anything extraordinary. "It's not like I wanted it to happen," he explains. "I just did what anyone would have done." Says his mother, "If it weren't for Rocky, I'd have bled to death."

First heard from Michele Borba

Rest In Peace: The "I Can't" Funeral

Donna's fourth-grade classroom looked like many others I had seen in the past. Students sat in five rows of six desks. The teacher's desk was in the front and faced the students. The bulletin board featured student work. In most respects it appeared to be a typically traditional elementary classroom. Yet something seemed different that day I entered it for the first time. There seemed to be an undercurrent of excitement.

Donna was a veteran small-town Michigan school-teacher only two years away from retirement. In addition she was a volunteer participant in a county-wide staff development project I had organized and facilitated. The training focused on language arts ideas that would empower students to feel good about themselves and take charge of their lives. Donna's job was to attend training sessions and implement the concepts being presented. My job was to make classroom visitations and encourage implementation.

I took an empty seat in the back of the room and watched. All the students were working on a task, filling a sheet of notebook paper with thoughts and ideas. The ten-year-old student closest to me was filling her page with "I Can'ts."

"I can't kick the soccer ball past second base."

"I can't do long division with more than three numerals."

"I can't get Debbie to like me."

Her page was half full and she showed no signs of letting up. She worked on with determination and persistence.

I walked down the row glancing at students' papers. Everyone was writing sentences, describing things they couldn't do.

"I can't do ten push-ups."

"I can't hit one over the left-field fence."

"I can't eat only one cookie."

By this time, the activity engaged my curiosity, so I decided to check with the teacher to see what was going on. As I approached her, I noticed that she too was busy writing. I felt it best not to interrupt.

"I can't get John's mother to come in for a teacher conference."

"I can't get my daughter to put gas in the car."

"I can't get Alan to use words instead of fists."

Thwarted in my efforts to determine why students and teacher were dwelling on the negative instead of writing the more positive "I Can" statements, I returned to my seat and continued my observations. Students wrote for another ten minutes. Most filled their page. Some started another.

"Finish the one you're on and don't start a new one," were the instructions Donna used to signal the end of the activity. Students were then instructed to fold their papers in half and bring them to the front. When students reached the teacher's desk, they placed their "I Can't" statements into an empty shoe box.

When all of the student papers were collected, Donna added hers. She put the lid on the box, tucked it under her arm and headed out the door and down the hall. Students followed the teacher. I followed the students.

Halfway down the hall the procession stopped. Donna entered the custodian's room, rummaged around and came out with a shovel. Shovel in one hand, shoe box in the other, Donna marched the students out of the school to the farthest corner of the playground. There they began to dig.

They were going to bury their "I Can'ts"! The digging took over ten minutes because most of the fourth-graders wanted a turn. When the hole approached three-feet deep, the digging ended. The box of "I Can'ts" was placed in position at the bottom of the hole and quickly covered with dirt.

Thirty-one 10- and 11-year-olds stood around the freshly dug grave site. Each had at least one page full of "I Can'ts" in the shoe box, four-feet under. So did their teacher.

At this point Donna announced, "Boys and girls, please join hands and bow your heads." The students complied. They quickly formed a circle around the grave, creating a bond with their hands. They lowered their heads and waited. Donna delivered the eulogy.

"Friends, we gather today to honor the memory of 'I Can't.' While he was with us on earth, he touched the lives of everyone, some more than others. His name, unfortunately, has been spoken in every public building — schools, city halls, state capitols and yes, even The White House.

"We have provided 'I Can't' with a final resting place and a headstone that contains his epitaph. He is survived by his brothers and sister, 'I Can', 'I Will' and 'I'm Going to Right Away.' They are not as well known as their famous relative and are certainly not as strong and powerful yet. Perhaps some day, with your help, they will make an even bigger mark on the world.

"May 'I Can't' rest in peace and may everyone present

pick up their lives and move forward in his absence. Amen."

As I listened to the eulogy I realized that these students would never forget this day. The activity was symbolic, a metaphor for life. It was a right-brain experience that would stick in the unconscious and conscious mind forever.

Writing "I Can'ts," burying them and hearing the eulogy. That was a major effort on the part of this teacher. And she wasn't done yet. At the conclusion of the eulogy she turned the students around, marched them back into the classroom and held a wake.

They celebrated the passing of "I Can't" with cookies, popcorn and fruit juices. As part of the celebration, Donna cut out a large tombstone from butcher paper. She wrote the words "I Can't" at the top and put RIP in the middle. The date was added at the bottom.

The paper tombstone hung in Donna's classroom for the remainder of the year. On those rare occasions when a student forgot and said, "I Can't," Donna simply pointed to the RIP sign. The student then remembered that "I Can't" was dead and chose to rephrase the statement.

I wasn't one of Donna's students. She was one of mine. Yet that day I learned an enduring lesson from her.

Now, years later, whenever I hear the phrase, "I Can't," I see images of that fourth-grade funeral. Like the students, I remember that "I Can't" is dead.

Chick Moorman

The 333 Story

I was doing a weekend seminar at the Deerhurst Lodge, north of Toronto. On Friday night a tornado swept through a town north of us called Barrie, killing several people and doing millions of dollars worth of damage. Sunday night, as I was coming home, I stopped the car when I got to Barrie. I got out on the side of the highway and looked around. It was a mess. Everywhere I looked there were smashed houses and cars turned upside down.

That same night Bob Templeton was driving down the same highway. He stopped to look at the disaster just as I had, only his thoughts were different than my own. Bob was the vice president of Telemedia Communications, which owns a string of radio stations in Ontario and Quebec. He thought there must be something we could do for these people with the radio stations they had.

The following night I was doing another seminar in Toronto. Bob Templeton and Bob Johnson, another vice president from Telemedia, came in and stood in the back of the room. They shared their conviction that there had to be something they could do for the people in Barrie. After the seminar we went back to Bob's office. He was now committed to the idea of helping the people who had been caught in the tornado.

The following Friday he called all the executives at Telemedia into his office. At the top of a flip chart he wrote three 3s. He said to his executives "How would you like to raise 3 million dollars 3 days from now in just 3 hours and give the money to the people in Barrie?" There was nothing but silence in the room.

Finally someone said, "Templeton, you're crazy. There is no way we could do that."

Bob said, "Wait a minute. I didn't ask you if we *could or* even if we *should*. I just asked you if you'd *like* to."

They all said, "Sure, we'd like to." He then drew a large T underneath the 333. On one side he wrote, "Why we can't." On the other side he wrote, "How we can."

"I'm going to put a big X on the 'Why we can't side.' We're not going to spend any time on the ideas of why we can't. That's of no value. On the other side we're going to write down every idea that we can come up with on how we can. We're not going to leave the room until we figure it out." There was silence again.

Finally, someone said, "We could do a radio show across Canada."

Bob said, "That's a great idea," and wrote it down.

Before he had it written, someone said, "You can't do a radio show across Canada. We don't have radio stations across Canada." That was a pretty valid objection. They only had stations in Ontario and Quebec.

Templeton replied, "That's why we can. That stays." But this was a really strong objection because radio stations are very competitive. They usually don't work together and to get them to do so would be virtually impossible according to the standard way of thinking.

All of a sudden someone suggested, "You could get Harvey Kirk and Lloyd Robertson, the biggest names in Canadian broadcasting to anchor the show." (That would be like getting Tom Brokaw and Sam Donaldson to anchor the show. They are anchors on national TV. They are not going to go on radio.) At that point it was absolutely amazing how fast and furious the creative ideas began to flow.

That was on a Friday. The following Tuesday they had a radiothon. They had 50 radio stations all across the country that agreed to broadcast it. It didn't matter who got the credit as long as the people in Barrie got the money. Harvey Kirk and Lloyd Robertson anchored the show and they succeeded in raising 3 million dollars in 3 hours within 3 business days!

You see you can do anything if you put your focus on how to do it rather than on why you can't.

Bob Proctor

There Are No Vans

I remember one Thanksgiving when our family had no money and no food, and someone came knocking on our door. A man was standing there with a huge box of food, a giant turkey and even some pans to cook it in. I couldn't believe it. My dad demanded, "Who are you? Where are you from?"

The stranger announced, "I'm here because a friend of yours knows you're in need and that you wouldn't accept direct help, so I've brought this for you. Have a great Thanksgiving."

My father said, "No, no, we can't accept this." The stranger replied "You don't have a choice," closed the door and left.

Obviously that experience had a profound impact on my life. I promised myself that someday I would do well enough financially so that I could do the same thing for other people. By the time I was 18 I had created my Thanksgiving ritual. I like to do things spontaneously, so I would go out shopping and buy enough food for one or two families. Then I would dress like a delivery boy, go to the poorest neighborhood and just knock on a door. I always included a note that explained my Thanksgiving experience as a kid. The note concluded, "All that I ask in return is that you take good enough care of yourself so that someday you can do the same thing for someone else. "I have received more from this annual ritual than I have from any amount of money I've ever earned.

Several years ago I was in New York City with my new wife during Thanksgiving. She was sad because we were not with our family. Normally she would be home decorating the house for Christmas, but we were stuck here in a hotel room.

I said, "Honey, look, why don't we decorate some lives today instead of some old trees?" When I told her what I always do on Thanksgiving, she got excited. I said, "Let's go someplace where we can really appreciate who we are, what we are capable of and what we can really give. Let's go to Harlem!" She and several of my business partners who were with us weren't really enthusiastic about the idea. I urged them: "C'mon, let's go to Harlem and feed some people in need. We won't be the people who are giving it because that would be insulting. We'll just be the delivery people. We'll go buy enough food for six or seven families for 30 days. We've got enough. Let's just go do it! That's what Thanksgiving really is: Giving good thanks, not eating turkey. C'mon. Let's go do it!"

Because I had to do a radio interview first, I asked my partners to get us started by getting a van. When I returned from the interview, they said "We just can't do it. There are no vans in all of New York. The rent-a-car places are all out of vans. They're just not available."

I said, "Look, the bottom line is that if we want something, we can make it happen! All we have to do is take action. There are plenty of vans here in New York City. We just don't have one. Let's go get one."

They insisted, "We've called everywhere. There aren't any."

I said, "Look down at the street. Look down there. Do you see all those vans?" They said, "Yeah, we see them."

"Let's go get one," I said. First I tried walking out in front of vans as they were driving down the street. I learned something about New York drivers that day: They don't stop; they speed up.

Then we tried waiting by the light. We'd go over and knock on the window and the driver would roll it down, looking at us kind of leery, and I'd say "Hi. Since today is Thanksgiving, We'd like to know if you would be willing to drive us to Harlem so we can feed some people." Every time the driver would look away quickly, furiously roll up the window and pull away without saying anything.

Eventually we got better at asking. We'd knock on the window, they'd roll it down and we'd say, "Today is Thanksgiving. We'd like to help some underprivileged people, and we're curious if you'd be willing to drive us to an underprivileged area that we have in mind here in New York City." That seemed slightly more effective but still didn't work. Then we started offering people $100 to drive us. That got us even closer, but when we told them to take us to Harlem, they said no and drove off.

We had talked to about two dozen people who all said no. My partners were ready to give up on the project, but I said, "It's the law of averages: somebody is going to say *yes*." Sure enough, the perfect van drove up. It was perfect because it was extra big and would accommodate all of us. We went up, knocked on the window and we asked the driver, "Could you take us to a disadvantaged area? We'll pay you a hundred dollars."

The driver said, "You don't have to pay me. I'd be happy to take you. In fact, I'll take you to some of the most difficult spots in the whole city." Then he reached over on the seat and grabbed his hat. As he put it on, I noticed that it said, "Salvation Army." The man's name was Captain John Rondon and he was the head of the Salvation Army in the South Bronx.

We climbed into the van in absolute ecstasy. He said, "I'll take you place you never even thought of going. But tell me something. Why do you people want to do this?" I told him my story and that I wanted to show gratitude for all that I had by giving something back.

Captain Rondon took us into parts of the South Bronx that make Harlem look like Beverly Hills. When we arrived, we went into a store where we bought a lot of food and some baskets. We packed enough for seven families for 30 days. Then we went out to start feeding people. We went to buildings where there were half a dozen people living in one room: "squatters" with no electricity and no heat in the dead of winter surrounded by rats, cockroaches and the smell of urine. It was both an astonishing realization that people lived this way and a truly fulfilling experience to make even a small difference.

You see, you can make anything happen if you commit to it and take action. Miracles like this happen every day — even in a city where "there are no vans."

Anthony Robbins

Ask, Ask, Ask

The greatest saleswoman in the world today doesn't mind if you call her a girl. That's because Markita Andrews has generated more than eighty thousand dollars selling Girl Scout cookies since she was seven years old.

Going door-to-door after school, the painfully shy Markita transformed herself into a cookie-selling dynamo when she discovered, at age 13, the secret of selling.

It starts with desire. Burning, white-hot desire.

For Markita and her mother, who worked as a waitress in New York after her husband left them when Markita was eight years old, their dream was to travel the globe. "I'll work hard to make enough money to send you to college," her mother said one day. "You'll go to college and when you graduate, you'll make enough money to take you and me around the world. Okay?"

So at age 13 when Markita read in her Girl Scout magazine that the Scout who sold the most cookies would win an all-expenses-paid trip for two around the world, she decided to sell all the Girl Scout cookies she could — more Girl Scout cookies than anyone in the world, ever.

But desire alone is not enough. To make her dream come true, Markita knew she needed a plan. "Always wear your right outfit, your professional garb," her aunt advised.

"When you are doing business, dress like you are doing business. Wear your Girl Scout uniform. When you go up to people in their tenement buildings at 4:30 or 6:30 and especially on Friday night, ask for a big order. Always smile, whether they buy or not, always be nice. And don't ask them to buy your cookies; ask them to invest."

Lots of other Scouts may have wanted that trip around the world. Lots of other Scouts may have had a plan. But only Markita went off in her uniform each day after school, ready to ask — and keep asking — folks to invest in her dream. "Hi. I have a dream. I'm earning a trip around the world for me and my mom by merchandising Girl Scout cookies," She'd say at the door. "Would you like to invest in one dozen or two dozen boxes of cookies?"

Markita sold 3,526 boxes of Girl Scout cookies that year and won her trip around the world. Since then, she has sold more than 42,000 boxes of Girl Scout cookies, spoken at sales conventions across the country, starred in a Disney movie about her adventure and has coauthored the best-seller, *How to Sell More Cookies, Condos, Cadillacs, Computers... And Everything Else*.

Markita is no smarter and no more extroverted than thousands of other people, young and old, with dreams of their own. The difference is Markita has discovered the secret of selling: Ask, Ask, Ask! Many people fail before they even begin because they fail to *ask* for what they want. The fear of rejection leads many of us to reject ourselves and our dreams long before anyone else ever has the chance — no matter what we're selling.

And everyone is selling something. "You're selling yourself everyday — in school, to your boss, to new people you meet," said Markita at 14. "My mother is a waitress: she sells the daily special. Mayors and presidents trying to get votes are selling... One of my favorite teachers was Mrs. Chapin. She made geography interesting, and that's really selling... I see selling everywhere I look. Selling is part of the whole world."

It takes courage to ask for what you want. Courage is not the absence of fear. It's doing what it takes despite one's fear. And, as Markita has discovered, the more you ask, the easier (and more fun) it gets.

Once, on live TV, the producer decided to give Markita her toughest selling challenge. Markita was asked to sell Girl Scout cookies to another guest on the show. "Would you like to invest in one dozen or two dozen boxes of Girl Scout cookies?" she asked.

"Girl Scout cookies?! I don't buy any Girl Scout cookies!" he replied. "I'm a Federal Penitentiary warden. I put 2,000 rapists, robbers, criminals, muggers and child abusers to bed every night."

Unruffled, Markita quickly countered, "Mister, if you take some of these cookies, maybe you won't be so mean and angry and evil. And, Mister, I think it would be a good idea for you to take some of these cookies back for every one of your 2,000 prisoners, too."

Markita asked.

The warden wrote a check.

Jack Canfield and Mark V. Hansen

Did The Earth Move For You?

Eleven-year-old Angela was stricken with a debilitating disease involving her nervous system. She was unable to walk and her movement was restricted in other ways as well. The doctors did not hold out much hope of her ever recovering from this illness. They predicted she'd spend the rest of her life in a wheelchair. They said that few, if any, were able to come back to normal after contracting this disease. The little girl was undaunted. There, lying in her hospital bed, she would vow to anyone who'd listen that she was definitely going to be walking again someday.

She was transferred to a specialized rehabilitation hospital in the San Francisco Bay area. Whatever therapies could be applied to her case were used. The therapists were charmed by her undefeatable spirit. They taught her about *imaging* — about seeing herself walking. If it would do nothing else, it would at least give her hope and something positive to do in the long waking hours in her bed. Angela would work as hard as possible in physical therapy, in whirlpools and in exercise sessions. But she worked just as hard lying there faithfully doing her imaging, visualizing herself moving, moving, moving!

One day, as she was straining with all her might to imagine her legs moving again, it seemed as though a miracle happened: The bed moved! It began to move around the room! She screamed out, "Look what I'm doing! Look! Look! I can do it! I moved, I *moved*!"

Of course, at this very moment everyone else in the hospital was screaming, too, and running for cover. People were screaming, equipment was falling and glass was breaking. You see, it was the recent San Francisco earthquake. But don't tell that to Angela. She's convinced that she did it. And now only a few years later, she's back in school. On her own two legs. No crutches, no wheelchair. You see, anyone who can shake the earth between San Francisco and Oakland can conquer a piddling little disease, can't they?

Hanoch McCarty

Tommy's Bumper Sticker

A little kid down at our church in Huntington Beach came up to me after he heard me talk about the Children's Bank. He shook my hand and said, "My name is Tommy Tighe, I'm six years old and I want to borrow money from your Children's Bank."

I said, "Tommy, that's one of my goals, to loan money to kids. And so far all the kids have paid it back. What do you want to do?"

He said, "Ever since I was four I had a vision that I could cause peace in the world. I want to make a bumper sticker that says, 'PEACE, PLEASE! DO IT FOR US KIDS,' signed 'Tommy'."

"I can get behind that," I said. He needed $454 to produce 1,000 bumper stickers. The Mark Victor Hansen Children's Free Enterprise Fund wrote a check to the printer who was printing the bumper stickers.

Tommy's dad whispered in my ear, "If he doesn't pay the loan back, are you going to foreclose on his bicycle?"

I said, "No, knock on wood, every kid is born with honesty, morality and ethics. They have to be taught something else. I believe he'll pay us back." If you have a child who is over nine, let them w-o-r-k for m-o-n-e-y for someone honest, moral and ethical so they learn the principle early.

We gave Tommy a copy of all of my tapes and he listened to them 21 times each and took ownership of the material. It says, "Always start selling at the top." Tommy convinced his dad to drive him up to Ronald Reagan's home. Tommy rang the bell and the gatekeeper came out. Tommy gave a two-minute, irresistible sales presentation on his bumper sticker. The gatekeeper reached in his pocket, gave Tommy $1.50 and said, "Here, I want one of those. Hold on and I'll get the former President."

I asked, "Why did you ask him to buy?" He said, "You said in the tapes to ask everyone to buy." I said, "I did. I did. I'm guilty."

He sent a bumper sticker to Mikhail Gorbachev with a bill for $1.50 in U.S. funds. Gorbachev sent him back $1.50 and a picture that said, "Go for peace, Tommy," and signed it, "Mikhail Gorbachev, President."

Since I collect autographs, I told Tommy, "I'll give you $500.00 for Gorbachev's autograph."

He said, "No thanks, Mark."

I said, "Tommy, I own several companies. When you get older, I'd like to hire you."

"Are you kidding?" He answered. "When I get older, I'm going to hire you."

The Sunday edition of the *Orange County Register* did a feature section on Tommy's story, the Children's Free Enterprise Bank and me. Marty Shaw, the journalist, interviewed Tommy for six hours and wrote a phenomenal interview. Marty asked Tommy what he thought his impact would be on world peace. Tommy said, "I don't think I am old enough yet; I think you have to be eight or nine to stop all the wars in the world."

Marty asked, "Who are your heroes?"

He said, "My dad, George Burns, Wally Joiner and Mark Victor Hansen." Tommy has good taste in role models.

Three days later, I got a call from the Hallmark Greeting Card Company. A Hallmark franchisee had faxed a copy of the *Register* article. They were having a convention in San Francisco and wanted Tommy to speak. After all, they saw that Tommy had nine goals for himself:

1. Call about cost (baseball card collateral).
2. Have bumper sticker printed.
3. Make a plan for a loan.
4. Find out how to tell people.
5. Get address of leaders.
6. Write a letter to all of the presidents and leaders of other countries and send them all a free bumper sticker.
7. Talk to everyone about peace.
8. Call the newspaper stand and talk about my business.
9. Have a talk with school.

Hallmark wanted my company, Look Who's Talking, to book Tommy to speak. While the talk did not happen because the two-week lead time was too short, the negotiation between Hallmark, myself and Tommy was fun, uplifting and powerful.

Joan Rivers called Tommy Tighe to be on her syndicated television show. Someone had also faxed her a copy of the *Register* interview on Tommy.

"Tommy," Joan said, "this is Joan Rivers and I want you on my TV show which is viewed by millions."

"Great!" said Tommy. He didn't know her from a bottle of Vicks.

"I'll pay you $300," said Joan.

"Great!" said Tommy. Having listened repeatedly to and

mastered my *Sell Yourself Rich* tapes, Tommy continued selling Joan by saying: "I am only eight years old, so I can't come alone. You can afford to pay for my mom, too, can't you, Joan?"

"Yes!" Joan replied.

"By the way, I just watched a *Lifestyles of the Rich and Famous* show and it said to stay at the Trump Plaza when you're in New York. You can make that happen, can't you, Joan?"

"Yes," she answered.

"The show also said when in New York, you ought to visit the Empire State Building and the Statue of Liberty. You can get us tickets, can't you?"

"Yes..."

"Great. Did I tell you my mom doesn't drive? So we can use your limo, can't we?"

"Sure," said Joan.

Tommy went on *The Joan Rivers Show* and wowed Joan, the camera crew, the live and television audiences. He was so handsome, interesting, authentic and such a great self-starter. He told such captivating and persuasive stories that the audience was found pulling money out of their wallets to buy a bumper sticker on the spot.

At the end of the show, Joan leaned in and asked, "Tommy, do you really think your bumper sticker will cause peace in the world?"

Tommy, enthusiastically and with a radiant smile, said, "So far I've had it out two years and got the Berlin Wall down. I'm doing pretty good, don't you think?"

Mark V. Hansen

PEACE PLEASE!
DO IT FOR US KIDS
Tommy

*To date Tommy has sold over 2,500 of his bumper stickers and has repaid his $454 loan to Mark Victor Hansen's Children's Free Enterprise Bank. If you'd like to order one of Tommy's bumper stickers, send $3.00 to Tommy Tighe, 17283 Ward Street, Fountain Valley, CA 92708.

If You Don't Ask, You Don't Get —But If You Do, You Do

My wife Linda and I live in Miami, Florida. When we had just started our self-esteem training program called Little A-corns to teach children how to say no to drugs, sexual promiscuity and other self-destructive behavior, we received a brochure for and educational conference in San Diego. As we read the brochure and realized that everybody who is anybody was going to be there, we realized we had to go. But we didn't see how. We were just getting started, we were working out of our home and had just about exhausted our personal savings with the early stages of the work. There was no way we could afford the airline tickets or any of the other expenses. But we knew we had to be there, so we started asking.

The first thing I did was to call the conference coordinators in San Diego, explain why we just had to be there and ask them if they would give us two complimentary admissions to the conference. When I explained our situation, what we were doing and why we had to be there, they said yes. So now we had the tickets.

I told Linda we had the tickets and we could get into the conference. She said, "Great! But we're in Miami and the conference is in San Diego. What do we do next?"

So I said, "We've got to get transportation." I called an airline I knew was doing well at the time, Northeast Airlines. The woman who answered happened to be the secretary to the president so I told her what I needed. She put me directly through to the president, Steve Quinto. I explained to him that I had just talked to the conference people in San Diego, they had given us free tickets to the conference but we were stuck on how to get there and would he please donate two roundtrip tickets from Miami to San Diego. He said, "Of course I will," just like that. It was that fast and the next thing he said really floored me. He said, "Thank you for asking."

I said, "Pardon me?"

He said, "I don't often have the opportunity to do the best thing that I can for the world unless someone asks me to. The best thing I can ever do is to give of myself and you've asked me to do that. That's a nice opportunity and I want to thank you for that opportunity." I was blown away, but I thanked him and hung up the phone. I looked at my wife and said, "Honey, we got the plane tickets." She said, "Great! Where do we stay?"

Next I called the Holiday Inn Downtown Miami and asked, "Where is your headquarters?" They told me it was in Memphis, Tennessee, so I called Tennessee and they patched me through to the person I needed to talk to. It was a guy in San Francisco. He controlled all of the Holiday Inns in California. I then explained to him that we had obtained our plane tickets through the airlines and asked if there were some way he could help us with the lodging for the three days. He asked if it would be okay if he put us up in their new hotel in downtown San Diego as his guest. I said, "Yes, that would be fine."

He then said, "Wait a minute. I need to caution you that the hotel is about a 35-mile drive from the campus where the conference is being held and you'll have to find out how to get there."

I said, "I'll figure it out if I need to buy a horse." I thanked him and I said to Linda, "Well, honey, we've got the admission, we've got the plane tickets and we've got a place to stay. What we need now is a way to get back and forth from the hotel to the campus twice a day."

Next I called National Car Rental, told them the story and asked if they could help me out. They said, "Would a new Olds 88 be okay?" I said it would be.

In one day we had put the whole thing together.

We did wind up buying our own meals for part of the time but before the conference was over, I stood up, told this story at one of the general assemblies and said, "Anyone who wants to volunteer to take us to lunch now and again would be graciously thanked." About fifty people jumped up and volunteered so we wound up having some of the meals thrown in as well.

We had a marvelous time, learned a lot and connected with people like Jack Canfield who is still on our advisory board. When we returned, we launched the program and it's been growing about 100 percent a year. This last June we graduated our 2,250th family from the Little Acorn training. We've also held two major conferences for educators called *Making The World Safe For Children*, to which we've invited people from all over the world. Thousands of educators have come to get ideas on how to do self-esteem training in their classrooms while they're still teaching the three *Rs*.

The last time we sponsored the conference we invited educators from 81 nations to come. Seventeen nations sent representatives including some ministers of education. Out of that has grown invitations for us to take our program to the following places: Russia, Ukraine, Byelorussia, Gelaruth, Kazakhstan, Mongolia, Taiwan, the Cook Islands and New Zealand.

So you see you can get anything you want if you just ask enough people.

Rick Gelinas

Rick Little's Quest

At 5 A. M. Rick Little fell asleep at the wheel of his car, hurtled over a ten-foot embankment and crashed into a tree. He spent the next six months in traction with a broken back. Rick found himself with a lot of time to think deeply about his life-something for which the thirteen years of his education had not prepared him. Only two weeks after he was dismissed from the hospital, he returned home one afternoon to find his mother lying semiconscious on the floor from an overdose of sleeping pills. Rick confronted once again the inadequacy of his formal education in preparing him to deal with the social and emotional issues of his life.

During the following months Rick began to formulate an idea — the development of a course that would equip students with high self-esteem, relationship skills and conflict management skills. As Rick began to research what such a course should contain, he ran across a study by the National Institute of Education in which 1,000 30-year-olds had been asked if they felt their high school education had equipped them with the skills they needed for the real world. Over 80 percent responded, "Absolutely not."

These 30-year-olds were also asked what skills they now wish they had been taught. The top answers were relationship skills: How to get along better with the people you live with. How to find and keep a job. How to handle conflict. How to be a good parent. How to understand the normal development of a child. How to handle financial management. And how to intuit the meaning of life.

Inspired by his vision of creating a class that might teach these things, Rick dropped out of college and set across the country to interview high school students. In his quest for information on what should be included in the course, he asked over 2,000 students in 120 high schools the same two questions:

1. If you were to develop a program for your high school to help you cope with what you're meeting now and what you think you'll be meeting in the future, what would that program include?
2. List the top ten problems in your life that you wish were dealt with better at home and in school.

Whether the students were from wealthy private schools or inner city ghettos, rural or suburban, the answers were surprisingly the same. Loneliness and not not liking themselves topped the list of problems. In addition, they had the same list of skills they wished they were taught as the ones compiled by the 30-year-olds.

Rick slept in his car for two months, living on a total of $60.00. Most days he ate peanut butter on crackers. Some days he didn't eat at all. Rick had few resources but he was committed to his dream.

His next step was to make a list of the nation's top educators and leaders in counseling and psychology. He set out to visit everyone on his list to ask for their expertise and support. While they were impressed with his approach—asking students directly what they wanted to learn — they offered little help. "You're too young. Go back to college. Get your degree. Go to graduate school, then you can pursue this." They were less than encouraging.

Yet Rick persisted. By the time he turned 20, he had sold his car, his clothes, had borrowed from friends and was $ 32,000 in debt. Someone suggested he go to a foundation and ask for money.

His first appointment at a local foundation was a huge disappointment. As he walked into the office, Rick was literally shaking with fear. The vice president of the foundation was a huge dark-haired man with a cold stern face. For a half hour he sat without uttering a word while Rick poured his heart out about his mother, the two thousand kids and plans for a new kind of course for high school kids.

When he was through, the vice-president pushed up a stack of folders. "Son," he said, "I've been here nearly 20 years. We've funded all these education programs. And they all failed. Yours will, too. The reasons? They're obvious. You're 20 years old, you have no experience, no money, no college degree. Nothing!"

As he left the foundation office, Rick vowed to prove this man wrong. Rick began a study of which foundations were interested in funding projects for teenagers. He then spent months writing grant proposals — working from early morning until late at night. Rick worked for over a year laboriously writing grant proposals, each one carefully tailored to the interests and requirements of the individual foundations. Each one went out with high hopes and each one came back — rejected.

Proposal after proposal was sent out and rejected. Finally, after the 155th grant proposal had been turned down, all of Rick's support began to crumble.

Rick's parents were begging him to go back to college and Ken Greene, an educator who had left his job to help Rick write proposals, said, "Rick, I have no money left and I have a wife and kids to support. I'll wait for one more proposal. But if it's a turndown, I'll have to go back to Toledo and to teaching."

Rick had one last chance. Activated by desperation and conviction, he managed to talk himself past several secretaries and he secured a lunch date with Dr. Russ Mawby, President of the Kellogg Foundation. On their way to lunch they passed an ice cream stand. "Would you like one?" Mawby asked. Rick nodded. But his anxiety got the better of him. He crushed the cone in his hand and, with chocolate ice cream running between his fingers, he made a surreptitious but frantic effort to shake it loose before Dr. Mawby could note what had happened. But Mawby did see it, and bursting into laughter, he went back to the vendor and brought Rick a bunch of paper napkins.

The young man climbed into the car, red-faced and miserable. How could he request funding for a new educational program when he couldn't even handle an ice cream cone?

Two weeks later Mawby phoned. "You asked for $55,000. We're sorry, but the trustees voted against it." Rick felt tears pressing behind his eyes. For two years he had been working for a dream; which would now go down the drain.

"However," said Mawby, "the trustees did vote unanimously to give you $130, 000."

The tears came then. Rick could hardly even stammer out a thank you.

Since that time Rick Little has raised over $100,000,000

to fund his dream. The Quest Skills Programs are currently taught in over 30,000 schools in all 50 states and 32 countries. Three million kids per year are being taught important life skills because one 19-year-old refused to take "no" for an answer.

In 1989, because of the incredible success of Quest, Rick Little expanded his dream and was granted $65,000,000, the second largest grant ever given in U.S. history, to create The International Youth Foundation. The purpose of this foundation is to identify and expand successful youth programs all over the world.

Rick Little's life is a testament to the power of commitment to a high vision, coupled with a willingness to keep on asking until one manifests the dream.

Adapted from Peggy Mann

The Magic Of Believing

I'm not old enough to play baseball or football. I'm not eight yet. My mom told me when you start baseball, you aren't going to be able to run that fast because you had an operation. I told Mom I wouldn't need to run that fast. When I play baseball, I'll just hit them out of the park. Then I'll be able to walk.

Edward J. McGrath, Jr.
"An Exceptional View of Life"

Glenna's Goal Book

In 1977 I was a single mother with three young daughters, a house payment, a car payment and a need to rekindle some dreams.

One evening I attended a seminar and heard a man speak on the I x V = R Principle. (*Imagination mixed with Vividness becomes Reality.*) The speaker pointed out that the mind thinks in pictures, not in words. And as we vividly picture in our mind what we desire, it will become a reality.

This concept struck a chord of creativity in my heart. I knew the Biblical truth that the Lord gives us "the desires of our heart" (Psalms 37: 4) and that "as a man thinketh in his heart, so is he" (Proverbs 23: 7). I was determined to take my written prayer list and turn it into pictures. I began cutting up old magazines and gathering pictures that depicted the "desires of my heart." I arranged them in an expensive photo album and waited expectantly.

I was very specific with my pictures. They included:

1. A good-looking man
2. A woman in a wedding gown and a man in a tuxedo
3. Bouquets of flowers (I'm a romantic)
4. Beautiful diamond jewelry (I rationalized that God loved David and Solomon and they were two of the

richest men who ever lived)
5. An island in the sparkling blue Caribbean
6. A lovely home
7. New furniture
8. A woman who had recently become vice president of a large corporation. (I was working for a company that had no female officers. I wanted to be the first woman vice president in that company.)

About eight weeks later, I was driving down a California freeway, minding my own business at 10:30 in the morning. Suddenly a gorgeous red-and-white Cadillac passed me. I looked at the car because it was a beautiful car. And the driver looked at me and smiled, and I smiled back because I always smile. Now I was in deep trouble. Have you ever done that? I tried to pretend that I hadn't looked. "Who me? I didn't look at you!" He followed me for the next 15 miles. Scared me to death! I drove a few miles, he drove a few miles. I parked, he parked... and eventually I married him!

On the first day after our first date, Jim sent me a dozen roses. Then I found out that he had a hobby. His hobby was collecting diamonds. Big ones! And he was looking for somebody to decorate. I volunteered! We dated for about two years and every Monday morning I received a long-stemmed red rose and a love note from him.

About three months before we were getting married, Jim said to me, "I have found the perfect place to go on our honeymoon. We will go to St. John's Island down in the Caribbean." I laughingly said, "I never would have thought of that!"

I did not confess the truth about my picture book until Jim and I had been married for almost a year. It was then that we were moving into our gorgeous new home and furnishing it with the elegant furniture that I had pictured. (Jim turned out to be the West Coast wholesale distributor for one of the finest eastern furniture manufacturers.)

By the way, the wedding was in Laguna Beach, California, and included the gown and tuxedo as realities. Eight months after I created my dream book, I became the vice president of human resources in the company where I worked.

In some sense this sounds like a fairy tale, but it is absolutely true. Jim and I have made many "picture books" since we have been married. God has filled our lives with the demonstration of these powerful principles of faith at work.

Decide what it is that you want in every area of your life. Imagine it vividly. Then act on your desires by actually constructing your personal goal book. Convert your ideas into concrete realities through this simple exercise. There are no impossible dreams. And, remember, God has promised to give His children the desires of their heart.

Glenna Salsbury

Another Check Mark On The List

One rainy afternoon an inspired 15-year-old boy named John Goddard sat down at his kitchen table in Los Angeles and wrote three words at the top of a yellow pad, "My Life List." Under that heading he wrote down 127 goals. Since then he has completed 108 of those goals. Look at the list of Goddard's goals which appears below. These are not simple or easy goals. They include climbing the world's major mountains, exploring vast waterways, running a mile in five minutes, reading the complete works of Shakespeare and reading the entire *Encyclopedia Britannica*.

Explore:

✓ 1. Nile River
✓ 2. Amazon River
✓ 3. Congo River
✓ 4. Colorado River
5. Yangtze River, China
6. Niger River
7. Orinoco River, Venezuela
✓ 8. Rio Coco, Nicaragua

Study Primitive Cultures In:

✓ 9. The Congo
✓ 10. New Guinea
✓ 11. Brazil
✓ 12. Borneo
✓ 13. The Sudan John was nearly buried alive in a sandstorm.)
✓ 14. Australia
✓ 15. Kenya
✓ 16. The Philippines

✓ 17. Tanganyika (now Tanzania)
✓ 18. Ethiopia
✓ 19. Nigeria
✓ 20. Alaska

Climb:

21. Mount Everest
22. Mount Aconcagua, Argentina
23. Mount McKinley
✓ 24. Mount Huascaran, Peru
✓ 25. Mount Kilimanjaro
✓ 26. Mount Ararat, Turkey
✓ 27. Mount Kenya
28. Mount Cook, New Zealand
✓ 29. Mount Popocatepetl, Mexico
✓ 30. The Matterhorn
✓ 31. Mount Rainer
✓ 32. Mount Fuji
✓ 33. Mount Vesuvius
✓ 34. Mount Bromo, Java
✓ 35. Grand Tetons
✓ 36. Mount Baldy, California
✓ 37. Carry out careers in medicine and exploration (Studied pre-med and treats illnesses among primitive tribes)
38. Visit every country in the world (30 to go)
✓ 39. Study Navaho and Hopi Indians
✓ 40. Learn to fly a plane
✓ 41. Ride horse in Rose Parade

Photograph:

✓ 42. Iguacu Falls, Brazil
✓ 43. Victoria Falls, Rhodesia (Chased by a warthog in the process)
✓ 44. Sutherland Falls, New Zealand
✓ 45. Yosemite Falls
✓ 46. Niagara Falls
✓ 47. Retrace travels of Marco Polo and Alexander the Great

Explore Underwater:

✓ 48. Coral reefs of Florida
✓ 49. Great Barrier Reef, Australia (Photographed a 300-pound clam)
✓ 50. Red Sea

✓ 51. Fiji Islands
✓ 52. The Bahamas
✓ 53. Explore Okefenokee Swamp and the Everglades

Visit:
✓ 54. North and South Poles
✓ 55. Great Wall of China
✓ 56. Panama and Suez Canals
✓ 57. Easter Island
✓ 58. The Galapagos Islands
✓ 59. Vatican City (Saw the pope)
✓ 60. The Taj Mahal
✓ 61. The Eiffel Tower
✓ 62. The Blue Grotto
✓ 63. The Tower of London
✓ 64. The Leaning Tower of Pisa
✓ 65. The Sacred Well of Chichen-Itza, Mexico
✓ 66. Climb Ayers Rock in Australia,
67. Follow River Jordan from Sea of Galilee to Dead Sea 3

Swim In:
✓ 68. Lake Victoria
✓ 69. Lake Superior
✓ 70. Lake Tanganyika
✓ 71. Lake Titicaca, South America
✓ 72. Lake Nicaragua

Accomplish:
✓ 73. Become an Eagle Scout
✓ 74. Dive in a submarine
✓ 75. Land on and take off from an aircraft carrier
✓ 76. Fly in a blimp, hot air balloon and glider
✓ 77. Ride an elephant, camel, ostrich and bronco
✓ 78. Skin dive to 40 feet and hold breath two and a half minutes underwater
✓ 79. Catch a ten-pound lobster and a ten-inch abalone
✓ 80. Play flute and violin
✓ 81. Type 50 words a minute
✓ 82. Take a parachute jump
✓ 83. Learn water and snow skiing

✓ 84. Go on a church mission
✓ 85. Follow the John Muir Trail
✓ 86. Study native medicines and bring back useful ones
✓ 87. Bag camera trophies of elephant, lion, rhino, cheetah, cape buffalo and whale
✓ 88. Learn to fence
✓ 89. Learn jujitsu
✓ 90. Teach a college course
91. Watch a cremation ceremony in Bali
✓ 92. Explore depths of the sea
93. Appear in a Tarzan movie (He now considers this an irrelevant boyhood dream)
94. Own a horse, chimpanzee, cheetah, ocelot and coyote (Yet to own a chimp or cheetah)
95. Become a ham radio operator
✓ 96. Build own telescope
✓ 97. Write a book (On Nile trip)
✓ 98. Publish an article in *National Geographic* Magazine
✓ 99. High jump five feet
✓ 100. Broad jump 15 feet
✓ 101. Run a mile in five minutes
✓ 102. Weigh 175 pounds stripped (still does)
✓ 103. Perform 200 sit-ups and 20 pull-ups
✓ 104. Learn French, Spanish and Arabic
105. Study dragon lizards on Komodo Island (Boat broke down within 20 miles of island)
✓ 106. Visit birthplace of Grandfather Sorenson in Denmark
✓ 107. Visit birthplace of Grandfather Goddard in England
✓ 108. Ship aboard a freighter as a seaman
109. Read the entire *Encyclopedia Britannica* (Has read extensive

parts in each volume)

√110. Read the Bible from cover to cover

√111. Read the works of Shakespeare, Plato, Aristotle, Dickens, Thoreau, Poe, Rousseau, Bacon, Hemingway, Twain, Burroughs, Conrad, Talmage, Tolstoi, Longfellow, Keats, Whittier and Emerson (Not every work of each)

√112. Become familiar with the compositions of Bach, Beethoven, Debussy, Ibert, Mendelssohn, Lalo, Rimski-Korsakov, Respighi, Liszt, Rachmaninoff, Stravinsky, Toch, Tschaikovsky, Verdi

√113. Become proficient in the use of a plane, motorcycle, tractor, surfboard, rifle, pistol, canoe, microscope, football basketball, bow and arrow, lariat and boomerang

√114. Compose music

√115. Play *Clair de Lune* on the piano

√116. Watch fire-walking ceremony (In Bali and Surinam)

√117. Milk a poisonous snake (Bitten by a diamond back during a photo session)

√118. Light a match with a 22 rifle

√119. Visit a movie studio

√120. Climb Cheops' pyramid

√121. Become a member of the Explorers' Club and the Adventurers' Club

√122. Learn to play polo

√123. Travel through the Grand Canyon on foot and by boat

√124. Circumnavigate the globe (four times)

125. Visit the moon ("Some day if God wills")

✓126. Marry and have children (Has five children)

127. Live to see the 21st Century (He will be 75)

John Goddard

Look Out, Baby, I'm Your Love Man!

It is better to be prepared for an opportunity and not have one than to have an opportunity and not be prepared.

Whitney Young, Jr.

Les Brown and his twin brother were adopted by Mamie Brown, a kitchen worker and maid, shortly after their birth in a poverty-stricken Miami neighborhood.

Because of his hyperactivity and nonstop jabber, Les was placed in special education classes for the learning disabled in grade school and throughout high school. Upon graduation, he became a city sanitation worker in Miami Beach. But he had a dream of being a disc jockey.

At night he would take a transistor radio to bed where he listened to the local jive-talking deejays. He created an imaginary radio station in his tiny room with its torn vinyl flooring. A hairbrush served as his microphone as he practiced his patter, introducing records to his ghost listeners.

His mother and brother could hear him through the thin walls and would shout at him to quit flapping his jaws and go to sleep. But Les didn't listen to them. He was wrapped up in his own world, living a dream.

One day Les boldly went to the local radio station during his lunch break from mowing grass for the city. He got into the station manager's office and told him he wanted to be a disc jockey.

The manager eyed this disheveled young man in overalls and a straw hat and inquired, "Do you have any background in broadcasting?"

Les replied, "No, sir, I don't."

"Well, son, I'm afraid we don't have a job for you then."

Les thanked him politely and left. The station manager assumed that he had seen the last of this young man. But he underestimated the depth of Les Brown's commitment to his goal. You see, Les had a higher purpose than simply wanting to be a disc jockey. He wanted to buy a nicer house for his adoptive mother, whom he loved deeply. The disc jockey job was merely a step toward his goal.

Mamie Brown had taught Les to pursue his dreams, so he felt sure that he would get a job at that radio station in spite of what the station manager had said.

And so Les returned to the station every day for a week, asking if there were any job openings. Finally the station manager gave in and took him on as an errand boy — at no pay. At first, he fetched coffee or picked up lunches and dinner for the deejays who could not leave the studio. Eventually his enthusiasm for their work won him the confidence of the disc jockeys who would send him in their Cadillacs to pick up visiting celebrities such as the Temptations and Diana Ross and the Supremes. Little did any of them know that young Les did not have a driver's license.

Les did whatever was asked of him at the station — and

more. While hanging out with the deejays, he taught himself their hand movements on the control panel. He stayed in the control rooms and soaked up whatever he could until they asked him to leave. Then, back in his bedroom at night, he practiced and prepared himself for the opportunity that he knew would present itself.

One Saturday afternoon while Les was at the station, a deejay named Rock was drinking while on the air. Les was the only other person in the building, and he realized that Rock was drinking himself toward trouble. Les stayed close. He walked back and forth in front of the window in Rock's booth. As he prowled, he said to himself. "Drink, Rock, drink!"

Les was hungry, and he was ready. He would have run down the street for more booze if Rock had asked. When the phone rang, Les pounced on it. It was that station manager, as he knew it would be.

"Les, this is Mr. Klein."

"Yes," said Les. "I know."

"Les, I don't think Rock can finish his program."

"Yes sir, I know."

"Would you call one of the other deejays to come in and take over?"

"Yes, sir. I sure will."

But when Les hung up the telephone, he said to himself, "Now, he must think I'm crazy."

Les did dial the telephone, but it wasn't to call in another deejay. He called his mother first, and then his girlfriend. "You all go out on the front porch and turn up the radio because I'm about to come on the air!" he said.

He waited about 15 minutes before he called the general manager. "Mr. Klein, I can't find nobody," Les said.

Mr. Klein then asked, "Young man, do you know how to work the controls in the studio?"

"Yes sir," replied Les.

Les darted into the booth, gently moved Rock aside and sat down at the turntable. He was ready. And he was hungry. He flipped on the microphone switch and said, "Look out! This is me, LB, triple P — Les Brown, Your Platter Playing Poppa. There were none before me and there will be none after me. Therefore, that makes me the one and only. Young and single and love to mingle. Certified, bona fide, indubitably qualified to bring you satisfaction, a whole lot of action. Look out, baby, I'm your lo-o-ove man!"

Because of his preparation, Les was ready. He wowed the audience and his general manager. From that fateful beginning. Les went on to a successful career in broadcasting, politics, public speaking and television.

Jack Canfield

Willing To Pay The Price

When my wife Maryanne and I were building our Greenspoint Mall hair salon 13 years ago, a Vietnamese fellow would stop by each day to sell us doughnuts. He spoke hardly any English, but he was always friendly and through smiles and sign language, we got to know each other. His name was Le Van Vu.

During the day Le worked in a bakery and at night he and his wife listened to audio tapes to learn English. I later learned that they slept on sacks full of sawdust on the floor of the back room of the bakery.

In Vietnam the Van Vu family was one of the wealthiest in Southeast Asia. They owned almost one-third of North Vietnam, including huge holdings in industry and real estate. However, after his father was brutally murdered, Le moved to South Vietnam with his mother, where he went to school and eventually became a lawyer.

Like his father before him, Le prospered. He saw an opportunity to construct buildings to accommodate the ever-expanding American presence in South Vietnam and soon became one of the most successful builders in the country.

On a trip to the North, however, Le was captured by the North Vietnamese and thrown into prison for three years. He escaped by killing five soldiers and made his way back to

South Vietnam where he was arrested again. The South Vietnamese government had assumed he was a "plant" from the North.

After serving time in prison, Le got out and started a fishing company, eventually becoming the largest canner in South Vietnam.

When Le learned that the U. S. troops and embassy personnel were about to pull out of his country, he made a life-changing decision.

He took all of the gold he had hoarded, loaded it aboard one of his fishing vessels and sailed with his wife out to the American ships in the harbor. He then exchanged all his riches for safe passage out of Vietnam to the Philippines, where he and his wife were taken into a refugee camp.

After gaining access to the president of the Philippines, Le convinced him to make one of his boats available for fishing and Le was back in business again. Before he left the Philippines two years later en route for America (his ultimate dream), Le had successfully developed the entire fishing industry in the Philippines.

But en route to America, Le became distraught and depressed about having to start over again with nothing. His wife tells of how she found him near the railing of the ship, about to jump overboard.

"Le," she told him, "if you do jump, whatever will become of me? We've been together for so long and through so much. We can do this together." It was all the encouragement that Le Van Vu needed.

When he and his wife arrived in Houston in 1972, they were flat broke and spoke no English. In Vietnam, family takes care of family, and Le and his wife found themselves ensconced in the back room of his cousin's bakery in the

Greenspoint Mall. We were building our salon just a couple of hundred feet away.

Now, as they say, here comes the "message" part of this story:

Le's cousin offered both Le and his wife jobs in the bakery. After taxes, Le would take home $175 per week, his wife $125. Their total annual income, in other words, was $15,600. Further, his cousin offered to sell them the bakery whenever they could come up with a $30,000 down payment. The cousin would finance the remainder with a note for $90,000.

Here's what Le and his wife did:

Even with a weekly income of $300, they decided to continue to live in the back room. They kept clean by taking sponge baths for two years in the mall's restrooms. For two years their diet consisted almost entirely of bakery goods. Each year, for two years, they lived on a total, that's right, a total of $600, saving $30,000 for the down payment.

Le later explained his reasoning, "If we got ourselves an apartment, which we could afford on $300 per week, we'd have to pay the rent. Then, of course, we'd have to buy furniture. Then we'd have to have transportation to and from work, so that meant we'd have to buy a car. Then we'd have to buy gasoline for the car as well as insurance. Then we'd probably want to go places in the car, so that meant we'd need to buy clothes and toiletries. So I knew that if we got that apartment, we'd never get our $30,000 together."

Now, if you think you've heard everything about Le, let me tell you, there's more: After he and his wife had saved the $30,000 and bought the bakery, Le once again sat down with his wife for a serious chat. They still owed $90,000 to his cousin, he said, and as difficult as the past two years had been, they had to remain living in that back room for one more year.

I'm proud to tell you that in one year, my friend and mentor Le Van Vu and his wife, saving virtually every nickel of profit from the business, paid off the $90,000 note, and in just three years, owned an extremely profitable business free and clear.

Then, and only then, the Van Vus went out and got their first apartment. To this day, they continue to save on a regular basis, live on an extremely small percentage of their income, and, of course, always pay cash for any of their purchases.

Do you think that Le Van Vu is a millionaire today? I am happy to tell you, many times over.

John McCormack

Everybody Has A Dream

Some years ago I took on an assignment in a southern county to work with people on public welfare. What I wanted to do was show that everybody has the capacity to be self-sufficient and all we have to do is to activate them. I asked the county to pick a group of people who were on public welfare, people from different racial groups and different family constellations. I would then see them as a group for three hours every Friday. I also asked for a little petty cash to work with as I needed it.

The first thing I said after I shook hands with everybody was, "I would like to know what your dreams are." Everyone looked at me as if I were kind of wacky.

"Dreams? We don't have dreams."

I said, "Well, when you were a kid what happened? Wasn't there something you wanted to do?"

One woman said to me, "I don't know what you can do with dreams. The rats are eating up my kids."

"Oh," I said. "That's terrible. No, of course, you are very much involved with the rats and your kids. How can that be helped?"

"Well, I could use a new screen door because there are holes in my screen door."

I asked, "Is there anybody around here who knows how to

fix a screen door?"

There was a man in the group, and he said, "A long time ago I used to do things like that but now I have a terribly bad back, but I'll try."

I told him I had some money if he would go to the store and buy some screening and go and fix the lady's screen door. "Do you think you can do that?"

"Yes, I'll try."

The next week, when the group was seated, I said to the woman, "Well, is your screen door fixed?"

"Oh, yes," she said.

"Then we can start dreaming, can't we?"She sort of smiled at me.

I said to the man who did the work, "How do you feel?"

He said, "Well, you know, it's a very funny thing. I'm beginning to feel a lot better."

That helped the group to begin to dream. These seemingly small successes allowed the group t see that dreams were not insane. These small steps began that dreams were not insane. These small steps began to get people to see and feel that something really could happen.

I began to ask other people about their dreams. One woman shared that she always wanted to be a secretary. I said, "Well, what stands in your way?" (That's always my next question.)

She said, "I have six kids, and I don't have anyone to take care of them while I'm away."

"Let's find out," I said. "Is there anybody in this group who would take care of six kids for a day or two a week while this woman gets some training here at the community college?"

One woman said "I got kids, too, but I could do that."

"Let's do it," I said. So a plan was created and the woman went to school.

Everyone found something. The man who put in the screen door became a handyman. The woman who took in the children became a licensed foster care person. In 12 weeks I had all these people off public welfare. I've not only done that once, I've done it many times.

Virginia Satir

Follow Your Dream

I have a friend named Monty Roberts who owns a horse ranch in San Ysidro. He has let me use his house to put on fund-raising events to raise money for youth at risk programs.

The last time I was there he introduced me by saying, "I want to tell you why I let Jack use my house. It all goes back to a story about a young man who was the son of an itinerant horse trainer who would go from stable to stable, race track to race track, farm to farm and ranch to ranch, training horses. As a result, the boy's high school career was continually interrupted. When he was a senior, he was asked to write a paper about what he wanted to be and do when he grew up.

"That night he wrote a seven-page paper describing his goal of someday owning a horse ranch. He wrote about his dream in great detail and he even drew a diagram of a 200-acre ranch, showing the location of all the buildings, the stables and the track. Then he drew a detailed floor plan for a 4,000-square-foot house that would sit on the 200-acre dream ranch.

"He put a great deal of his heart into the project and the next day he handed it in to his teacher. Two days later he received his paper back. On the front page was a large red F with a note that read, 'See me after class.'

"The boy with the dream went to see the teacher after class and asked, 'Why did I receive an F?'

"The teacher said, 'This is an unrealistic dream for a young boy like you. You have no money. You come from an itinerant family. You have no resources. Owning a horse ranch requires a lot of money. You have to buy the land. You have to pay for the original breeding stock and later you'll have to pay large stud fees. There's no way you could ever do it.' Then the teacher added, 'If you will rewrite this paper with a more realistic goal, I will reconsider your grade.'"

"The boy went home and thought about it long and hard. He asked his father what he should do. His father said, 'Look, son, you have to make up your own mind on this. However, I think it is a very important decision for you.'

"Finally, after sitting with it for a week, the boy turned in the same paper, making no changes at all. He stated, 'You can keep the F and I'll keep my dream.'"

Monty then turned to the assembled group and said, "I tell you this story because you are sitting in my 4,000-square-foot house in the middle of my 200-acre horse ranch. I still have that school paper framed over the fireplace." He added, "The best part of the story is that two summers ago that same schoolteacher brought 30 kids to camp out on my ranch for a week. When the teacher was leaving, he said, 'Look, Monty, I can tell you this now. When I was your teacher, I was something of a dream stealer. During those years I stole a lot of kids' dreams. Fortunately you had enough gumption not to give up on yours.'"

Don't let anyone steal your dreams. Follow your heart, no matter what.

Jack Canfield

The Box

When I was a senior in college, I came home for Christmas vacation and anticipated a fun-filled fortnight with my two brothers. We were so excited to be together, we volunteered to watch the store so that my mother and father could take their first day off in years. The day before my parents went to Boston, my father took me quietly aside to the little den behind the store. The room was so small that it held only a piano and a hide-a-bed couch. In fact, when you pulled the bed out, it filled the room and you could sit on the foot of it and play the piano. Father reached behind the old upright and pulled out a cigar box. He opened it and showed me a little pile of newspaper articles. I had read so many Nancy Drew detective stories that I was excited and wide-eyed over the hidden box of clippings.

"What are they?" I asked.

Father replied seriously, "These are articles I've written and some letters to the editor that have been published."

As I began to read, I saw at the bottom of each neatly clipped article the name Walter Chapman, Esq. "Why didn't you tell me you'd done this?" I asked.

"Because I didn't want your mother to know. She has always told me that since I didn't have much education, I shouldn't try to write. I wanted to run for some political office also, but she told me I shouldn't try. I guess she was afraid she'd be embarrassed if I lost. I just wanted to try for the fun of it. I figured I could write without her knowing it, and so I did. When each item would be printed, I'd cut it out and hide it in this box. I knew someday I'd show the box to someone, and it's you."

He watched me as I read over a few of the articles and when I looked up, his big blue eyes were moist. "I guess I tried for something too big this last time," he added.

"Did you write something else?"

"Yes, I sent some suggestions in to our denominational magazine on how the national nominating committee could be selected more fairly. It's been three months since I sent it in. I guess I tried for something too big."

This was such a new side to my fun-loving father that I didn't quite know what to say, so I tried, "Maybe it'll still come."

"Maybe, but don't hold your breath." Father gave me a little smile and a wink and then closed the cigar box and tucked it into the space behind the piano.

The next morning our parents left on the bus to the Haverhill Depot where they took a train to Boston. Jim, Ron and I ran the store and I thought about the box. I'd never known my father liked to write. I didn't tell my brothers; it was a secret between Father and me. The Mystery of the Hidden Box.

Early that evening I looked out the store window and saw my mother get off the bus — alone. She crossed the Square and walked briskly through the store.

"Where's Dad?" we asked together.

"Your father's dead," she said without a tear.

In disbelief we followed her to the kitchen where she told

us they had been walking through the Park Street Subway Station in the midst of crowds of people when Father had fallen to the floor. A nurse bent over him, looked up at Mother and said simply, "He's dead."

Mother had stood by him stunned, not knowing what to do as people tripped over him in their rush through the subway. A priest said, "I'll call the police," and disappeared. Mother straddled Dad's body for about an hour. Finally an ambulance came and took them both to the only morgue where Mother had to go through his pockets and remove his watch. She'd come back on the train alone and then home on the local bus. Mother told us the shocking tale without shedding a tear. Not showing emotion had always been a matter of discipline and pride for her. We didn't cry either and we took turns waiting on the customers.

One steady patron asked, "Where's the old man tonight?"

"He's dead," I replied.

"Oh, too bad," and he left.

I'd not thought of him as the old man, and I was mad at the question, but he was 70 and Mother was only 60. He'd always been healthy and happy and he'd cared for frail mother without complaining and now he was gone. No more whistling, no more singing hymns while stocking shelves. The "Old man" was gone.

On the morning of the funeral, I sat at the table in the store opening sympathy cards and pasting them in a scrapbook when I noticed the church magazine in the pile. Normally I would never have opened what I viewed as a dull religious publication, but just maybe that sacred article might be there — and it was.

I took the magazine to the little den, shut the door, and burst into tears. I'd been brave, but seeing Dad's bold recommendations to the national convention in print was more than I could bear. I read and cried and then I read again. I pulled out the box from behind the piano and under the clippings I found a two-page letter to my father from Henry Cabot Lodge, Sr., thanking him for his campaign suggestions.

I didn't tell anyone about my box. It remained a secret.

Florence Littauer

Encouragement

Some of the greatest success stories of history have followed a word of encouragement or an act of confidence by a loved one or a trusted friend. Had it not been for a confident wife, Sophia, we might not have listed among the great names of literature the name of Nathaniel Hawthorne. When Nathaniel, a heartbroken man, went home to tell his wife that he was a failure and had been fired from his job in a customhouse, she surprised him with an exclamation of joy.

"Now," she said triumphantly, "You can write your book!"

"Yes," replied the man, with sagging confidence, "and what shall we live on while I am writing it?"

To his amazement, she opened a drawer and pulled out a substantial amount of money.

"Where on earth did you get that?" he exclaimed.

"I have always known you were a man of genius," she told him. "I knew that someday you would write a masterpiece. So every week, out of the money you gave me for housekeeping, I saved a little bit. So here is enough to last us for one whole year."

From her trust and confidence came one of the greatest novels of American literature, *The Scarlet Letter*.

Nido Qubein

Walt Jones

The big question is whether you are going to be able to say a hearty yes to your adventure.

Joseph Campbell

No one epitomizes the fact that success is a journey and not a destination than the many green and growing "human becomings" who do not allow age to be a deterrent to accomplishment. Florence Brooks joined the Peace Corps when she was 64 years of age. Gladys Clappison was living in the dormitory at the University of Iowa working on her Ph. D. in history at age 82. Then there was Ed Stitt, who at age 87, was working on his community college degree program in New Jersey. Ed said it kept him from getting "old-timers' disease" and kept his brain alive.

Probably no one person has stirred my imagination over the years more than Walt Jones of Tacoma, Washington. Walt outlived his third wife to whom he was married for 52 years. When she died, someone said to Walt that it must be sad losing such a long-time friend. His response was, "Well, of course it was, but then again it may be for the best."

"Why was that?"

"I don't want to be negative or say anything to defame her wonderful character, but she kind of petered out on me in the last decade."

When asked to explain, he went on to add, "She just never wanted to do nothin', just kind of became a stick-in-the-mud. Ten years ago when I was 94, I told my wife we ain't never seen nothin' except the beautiful Pacific Northwest. She asked me what was on my mind, and I told her I was thinkin' about buying a motor home and maybe we could visit all 48 of the contiguous states. 'What do you think of that?'

"She said, 'I think you're out of your mind, Walt.'

" 'Whydya say that?' I asked.

" 'We'd get mugged out there. We'd die and there wouldn't be a funeral parlor.' Then she asked me, 'Who's going to drive, Walter?' and I said, 'I am, Lambie.' 'You'll kill us!' she said.

"I'd like to make footprints in the sands of time before I check out, but you can't make footprints in the sands of time if you're sitting on your butt... unless your intent is to make buttprints in the sands of time."

"So now that she's gone, Walt, what do you intend to do?"

"What do I intend to do? I buried the old gal and bought me a motor home. This is 1976, and I intend to visit all 48 of the states to celebrate our bicentennial."

Walt got to 43 of the states that year selling curios and souvenirs. When asked if he ever picked up hitchhikers, he said, "No way. Too many of them will club you over the head for four bits or sue you for whiplash if you get into an accident."

Walt hadn't had his motor home but a few months and his wife had only been buried for six months when he was seen driving down the street with a rather attractive 62-year-old woman at his side.

"Walt?" he was asked.

"Yeah," he replied.

"Who was the woman sitting by your side? Who's your new lady friend, Walt?"

To which he replied, "Yes, she is."

"Yes she is what?"

"My lady friend."

"Lady friend? Walt, you've been married three times, you're 104 years of age. This woman must be four decades younger than you."

"Well," he responded, "I quickly discovered that man cannot live in a motor home alone."

"I can understand that, Walt. You probably miss having someone to talk to after having had a companion all these years."

Without hesitation Walt replied, "You know, I miss that, too."

"Too? Are you inferring that you have a romantic interest?"

"I just might."

"Walt..."

"What?" he said.

"There comes a time in a person's life when you knock that stuff off."

"Sex?" he replied.

"Yes."

"Why?" he asked.

"Well, because that kind of physical exertion could be hazardous to a person's health."

Walt considered the question and said, "Well, if she dies,

she dies."

In 1978 with double digit inflation heating up in our country, Walt was a major investor in a condominium development. When asked why he was taking his money out of a secure bank account and putting it into a condo development, he said, "Ain't you heard? These are inflationary times. You've got to put your money into real property so it will appreciate and be around for your later years when you really need it." How's that for positive thinking?

In 1980 he sold off a lot of his property in and around Pierce County, Washington. Many people thought Walt was cashing in his chips. He assembled his friends and quickly made it clear that he was not cashing in his chips, but he had sold off the property for cash flow. "I took a small down and a 30-year contract. I got four grand a month comin' in until I'm 138."

He celebrated his 110th birthday on the Johnny Carson Show. He walked out resplendent in his white beard and black hat looking a little like the late Colonel Sanders, and Johnny says, "It's good to have you here, Walt."

"It's good to be anywhere at 110, Johnny."

"110?"

"110."

"1-1-0?"

"What's the matter, Carson, you losin' your hearin'? That's what I said. That's what I am. What's the big deal?"

"The big deal is you're within three days of being twice as old as I am."

That would get your attention, wouldn't it? One hundred and ten years of age — a green, growing human becoming. Walt picked up the opening and quickly alluded to Johnny.

"How old would you be if you didn't know the date you

were born and there weren't no durned calendar to semidepress you once a year? Ever heard of people getting depressed because of a calendar date? Oh, Lordy, I hit my 30th birthday. I'm so depressed, I'm over the hill. Oh, no, I hit my 40th birthday.

Everybody in my work team dressed in black and sent a hearse to pick me up. Oh, no I'm 50 years old. Half a century old. They sent me dead roses with cobwebs. Johnny, who says you're supposed to roll over and die when you're 65? I have friends more prosperous since they were 75 than they were before. And as a result of a little condominium investment I made a few years ago, I've made more bucks since I was 105 than I did before. Can I give you my definition of depression, Johnny?"

"Go ahead."

"Missing a birthday."

May the story of Walt Jones inspire all of us to remain green and growing every day of our lives.

Bob Moawad

Are You Strong Enough To Handle Critics?

It is not the critic who counts, not the man who points out how the strong man stumbles or where the doer of deeds could have done them better. The credit belongs to the man who is actually in the arena, whose face is marred by dust and sweat and blood, who strives valiantly, who errs and comes short again and again because there is no effort without error and shortcomings, who knows the great devotion, who spends himself in a worthy cause, who at best knows in the end the high achievement of triumph and who at worst, if he fails while daring greatly, knows his place shall never be with those timid and cold souls who know neither victory nor defeat.

Theodore Roosevelt

Risking

Two seeds lay side by side in the fertile spring soil.

The first seed said, "I want to grow! I want to send my roots deep into the soil beneath me, and thrust my sprouts through the earth's crust above me... I want to unfurl my tender buds like banners to announce the arrival of spring... I want to feel the warmth of the sun on my face and the blessing of the morning dew on my petals!"

And so she grew.

The second seed said, "I am afraid. If I send my roots into the ground below, I don't know what I will encounter in the dark. If I push my way through the hard soil above me I may damage my delicate sprouts... what if I let my buds open and a snail tries to eat them? And if I were to open my blossoms, a small child may pull me from the ground. No, it is much better for me to wait until it is safe."

And so she waited.

A yard hen scratching around in the early spring ground for

food found the waiting seed and promptly ate it.

MORAL OF THE STORY

Those of us who refuse to risk and grow
get swallowed up by life.

Patty Hansen

Try Something Different

When we first read the following story, we had just begun teaching a course called "The Million Dollar Forum," a course designed to teach people to accelerate their income up to levels of a million dollars a year or more. Early on we discovered people get locked into a rut of trying harder without trying smarter. Trying harder doesn't always work. Sometimes we need to do something radically different to achieve greater levels of success. We need to break out of our paradigm prisons, our habit patterns and our comfort zones.

• • •

I'm sitting in a quiet room at the Milcroft Inn, a peaceful little place hidden back among the pine trees about an hour out of Toronto. It's just past noon, late July, and I'm listening to the desperate sounds of a life-or-death struggle going on a few feet away.

There's a small fly burning out the last of its short life's energies in a futile attempt to fly through the glass of the windowpane. The whining wings tell the poignant story of the fly's strategy: *Try harder*.

But it's not working.

The frenzied effort offers no hope for survival. Ironically, the struggle is part of the trap. It is impossible for the fly to try hard enough to succeed at breaking through the glass.

Nevertheless, this little insect has staked its life on reaching its goal through raw effort and determination.

This fly is doomed. It will die there on the windowsill.

Across the room, ten steps away, the door is open. Ten seconds of flying time and this small creature could reach the outside world it seeks. With only a fraction of the effort now being wasted, it could be free of this self-imposed trap. The breakthrough possibility is there. It would be so easy.

Why doesn't the fly try another approach, something dramatically different? How did it get so locked in on the idea that this particular route and determined effort offer the most promise for success? What logic is there in continuing until death to seek a breakthrough with more of the same?

No doubt this approach makes sense to the fly. Regrettably, it's an idea that will kill.

Trying harder isn't necessarily the solution to achieving more. It may not offer any real promise for getting what you want out of life. Sometimes, in fact, it's a big part of the problem.

If you stake your hopes for a breakthrough on trying harder than ever, you may kill your chances for success.

Price Pritchett

Obstacles

We who lived in the concentration camps can remember the men who walked through the huts comforting others, giving away their last piece of bread. They may have been few in number, but they offer sufficient proof that everything can be taken from a man but one thing: The last of his freedoms — to choose one's attitude in any given set of circumstances, to choose one's own way.

Viktor E. Frankl
Man's Search for Meaning

Consider This

Consider this:

- After Fred Astaire's first screen test, the memo from the testing director of MGM, dated 1933, said, "Can't act! Slightly bald! Can dance a little!" Astaire kept that memo over the fireplace in his Beverly Hills home.
- An expert said of Vince Lombardi: "He possesses minimal football knowledge. Lacks motivation."
- Socrates was called, "An immoral corrupter of youth."
- When Peter J. Daniel was in the fourth grade, his teacher, Mrs. Phillips, constantly said,' Peter J. Daniel, you're no good, you're a bad apple and you're never going to amount to anything." Peter was totally illiterate until he was 26. A friend stayed up with him all night and read him a copy of *Think and Grow Rich*. Now he owns the street corners he used to fight on and just published his latest book: *Mrs. Phillips, You Were Wrong*!
- Louisa May Alcott, the author of *Little Women*, was encouraged to find work as a servant or seamstress by her family.
- Beethoven handled the violin awkwardly and preferred playing his own compositions instead of improving his technique. His teacher called him hopeless as a composer.

- The parents of the famous opera singer Enrico Caruso wanted him to be an engineer. His teacher said he had no voice at all and could not sing.
- Charles Darwin, father of the Theory of Evolution, gave up a medical career and was told by his father, "You care for nothing but shooting, dogs and rat catching." In his autobiography, Darwin wrote, "I was considered by all my masters and by my father, a very ordinary boy, rather below the common standard in intellect."
- Walt Disney was fired by a newspaper editor for lack of ideas. Wald Disney also went bankrupt several times before he built Disneyland.
- Thomas Edison's teachers said he was too stupid to learn anything.
- Albert Einstein did not speak until he was four years old and didn't read until he was seven. His teacher described him as "mentally slow, unsociable and adrift forever in his foolish dreams." He was expelled and was refused admittance to the Zurich Polytechnic School.
- Louis Pasteur was only a mediocre pupil in undergraduate studies and ranked 15th out of 22 in chemistry.
- Isaac Newton did very poorly in grade school.
- The sculptor Rodin's father said, "I have an idiot for a son." Described as the worst pupil in the school, Rodin failed three times to secure admittance to the school of art. His uncle called him uneducable.
- Leo Tolstoy, author of *War and Peace*, flunked out of college. He was described as "both unable and unwilling to learn."
- Play wright Tennessee Williams was enraged when his play *Me, Vasha* was not chosen in a class competition at Washington University where he was enrolled in English

XVI. The teacher recalled that Williams denounced the judges's choices and their intelligence.

- F. W. Woolworth's employers at the dry goods store said he had not enough sense to wait upon customers.
- Henry Ford failed and went broke five times before he finally succeeded.
- Babe Ruth, considered by sports historians to be the greatest athlete of all time and famous for setting the home run record, also holds the record for strikeouts.
- Winston Churchill failed sixth grade. He did not become Prime Minister of England until he was 62, and then only after a lifetime of defeats and setbacks. His greatest contributions came when he was a "senior citizen."
- Eighteen publishers turned down Richard Bach's 10, 000-word story about a "soaring" seagull, *Jonathan Livingston Seagull*, before Macmillan finally published it in 1970. By 1975 it had sold more than 7 million copies in the U. S. alone.
- Richard Hooker worked for seven years on his humorous war novel, *M*A*S*H*, only to have it rejected by 21 publishers before Morrow decided to publish it. It became a runaway bestseller, spawning a blockbuster movie and a highly successful television series.

Jack Canfield and Mark V. Hansen

John Corcoran — The Man Who Couldn't Read

For as long as John Corcoran could remember, words had mocked him. The letters in sentences traded places, vowel sounds lost themselves in the tunnels of his ears. In school he'd sit at his desk, stupid and silent as a stone, knowing he would be different from everyone else forever. If only someone had sat next to that little boy, put an arm around his shoulder and said, "I'll help you, Don't be scared."

But no one had heard of dyslexia then. And John couldn't tell them that the left side of his brain, the lobe humans use to arrange symbols logically in a sequence, had always misfired.

Instead, in second grade they put him in the "dumb" row. In third grade a nun handed a yardstick to the other children when John refused to read or write and let each student have a crack at his legs. In fourth grade his teacher called on him to read and let one minute of quiet pile upon another until the child thought he would suffocate. Then he was passed on to the next grade and the next. John Corcoran never failed a year in his life.

In his senior year, John was voted homecoming king, went steady with the valedictorian and starred on the basketball team. His mom kissed him when he graduated — and kept talking about college. College? It would be insane to consider. But he finally decided on the University of Texas at El Paso where he could try out for the basketball team. He took a deep breath, closed his eyes... and recrossed enemy lines.

On campus John asked each new friend: Which teachers gave essay tests? Which gave multiple choice? The minute he stepped out of a class, he tore the pages of scribble from his notebook, in case anyone asked to see his notes. He stared at thick textbooks in the evening so his roommate wouldn't doubt. And he lay in bed, exhausted but unable to sleep, unable to make his whirring mind let go. John promised he'd go to Mass 30 days straight at the crack of dawn, if only God would let him get his degree.

He got the diploma. He gave God his 30 days of Mass. Now what? Maybe he was addicted to the edge. Maybe the thing he felt most insecure about — his mind — was what he needed most to have admired. Maybe that's why, in 1961, John became a teacher.

John taught in California. Each day he had a student read the textbook to the class. He gave standardized tests that he could grade by placing a form with holes over each correct answer and he lay in bed for hours on weekend mornings, depressed.

Then he met Kathy, an A student and a nurse. Not a leaf, like John. A rock. "There's something I have to tell you, Kathy," he said one night in 1965 before their marriage, "I... I can't read."

"He's a teacher," she thought. He must mean he can't read well. Kathy didn't understand until years later when she saw John unable to read a children's book to their 18-month-old daughter. Kathy filled out his forms, read and wrote his letters. Why didn't he simply ask her to teach him to read and write? He couldn't believe that anyone could teach him.

At age 28 John borrowed $2, 500, bought a second house, fixed it up and rented it. He bought and rented another. And another. His business got bigger and bigger until he needed a secretary, a lawyer and a partner.

Then one day his accountant told him he was a millionaire. Perfect. Who'd notice that a millionaire always pulled on the doors that said PUSH or paused before entering public bathrooms, waiting to see which one the men walked out of?

In 1982 the bottom began to fall out. His properties started to sit empty and investors pulled out. Threats of foreclosures and lawsuits tumbled out of envelopes. Every waking moment, it seemed, he was pleading with bankers to extend his loans, coaxing builders to stay on the job, trying to make sense of the pyramid of paper. Soon he knew they'd have him on the witness stand and the man in black robes would say: "The truth, John Corcoran. Can't you even read?"

Finally in the fall of 1986, at age 48, John did two things he swore he never would. He put up his house as collateral to obtain one last construction loan. And he walked into the Carlsbad City Library and told the woman in charge of the tutoring program, "I can't read."

Then he cried.

He was placed with a 65-year-old grandmother named Eleanor Condit. Painstakingly — letter by letter, phonetically — she began teaching him. Within 14 months, his land-development company began to revive. And John Corcoran was learning to read.

The next step was confession: a speech before 200 stunned

businessmen in San Diego. To heal, he had to come clean. He was placed on the board of directors of the San Diego Council on Literacy and began traveling across the country to give speeches.

"Illiteracy is a form of slavery!" he would cry. "We can't waste time blaming anyone. We need to become obsessed with teaching people to read!"

He read every book or magazine he could get his hands on, every road sign he passed, out loud, as long as Kathy could bear it. It was glorious, like singing, And now he could sleep.

Then one day it occurred to him — one more thing he could finally do. Yes, that dusty box in his office, that sheaf of papers bound by ribbon. . . a quarter-century later, John Corcoran could read his wife's love letters.

Gary Smith

Don't Be Afraid To Fail

You've failed many times, although you may not remember.
You fell down the first time you tried to walk.
You almost drowned the first time you tried to swim, didn't you?
Did you hit the ball the first time you swung a bat?
Heavy hitters, the ones who hit the most home runs, also strike out a lot.
R. H. Macy failed seven times before his store in New York caught on.
English novelist John Creasey got 753 rejection slips before he published 564 books.
Babe Ruth struck out 1,330 times, but he also hit 714 home runs.
Don't worry about failure.
Worry about the chances you miss when you don't *even try.*

A message as published in the Wall Street Journal *by United Technologies Corporation, Hartford, Connecticut 06101*

Abraham Lincoln Didn't Quit

The sense of obligation to continue is present in all of us. A duty to strive is the duty of us all. I felt a call to that duty.

Abraham Lincoln

Probably the greatest example of persistence is Abraham Lincoln. If you want to learn about somebody who didn't quit, look no further.

Born into poverty, Lincoln was faced with defeat throughout his life. He lost eight elections, twice failed in business and suffered a nervous breakdown.

He could have quit many times — but he didn't and because he didn't quit, he became one of the greatest presidents in the history of our country.

Lincoln was a champion and he never gave up. Here is a sketch of Lincoln's road to the White House:

1816 His family was forced out of their home. He had to work to support them.

1818 His mother died.

1831 Failed in business.

1832 Ran for state legislature — *lost.*

1832 Also lost his job — wanted to go to law school but

couldn't get in.

1833 Borrowed some money from a friend to begin a business and by the end of the year he was bankrupt. He spent the next 17 years of his life paying off this debt.

1834 Ran for state legislature again — *won.*

1835 Was engaged to be married, sweetheart died and his heart was broken.

1836 Had a total nervous breakdown and was in bed for six months.

1838 Sought to become speaker of the state legislature — *defeated.*

1840 Sought to become elector — *defeated.*

1843 Ran for Congress — *lost.*

1846 Ran for Congress again — *this time he won* — went to Washington and did a good job.

1848 Ran for re-election to Congress — *lost.*

1849 Sought the job of land officer in his home state — *rejected.*

1854 Ran for Senate of the United States — *lost.*

1856 Sought the Vice-Presidential nomination at his party's national convention — got less than 100 votes.

1858 Ran for U. S. Senate again — *again he lost.*

1860 *Elected president of the United States.*

The path was worn and slippery. My foot slipped from under me, knocking the other out of the way, but I recovered and said to myself, "It's a slip and not a fall."

Abraham Lincoln
After losing a senate race
Source Unknown

Lesson From A Son

My son Daniel's passion for surfing began at the age of 13. Before and after school each day, he donned his wet suit, paddled out beyond the surf line and waited to be challenged by his three- to six-foot companions. Daniel's love of the ride was tested one fateful afternoon.

"Your son's been in an accident," the lifeguard reported over the phone to my husband Mike.

"How bad?"

"Bad. When he surfaced to the top of the water, the point of the board was headed toward his eye."

Mike rushed him to the emergency room and they were then sent to a plastic surgeon's office. He received 26 stitches from the corner of his eye to the bridge of his nose.

I was on an airplane flying home from a speaking engagement while Dan's eye was being stitched. Mike drove directly to the airport after they left the doctor's office. He greeted me at the gate and told me Dan was waiting in the car.

"Daniel?" I questioned. I remember thinking the waves must have been lousy that day.

"He's been in an accident, but he's going to be fine."

A traveling working mother's worst nightmare had come true. I ran to the car so fast the heel of my shoe broke off. I swung open the door, and my youngest son with the patched eye was leaning forward with both arms stretched out toward me crying, "Oh, Ma, I'm so glad you're home."

I sobbed in his arms telling him how awful I felt about not being there when the lifeguard called.

"It's okay, Mom," he comforted me. "You don't know how to surf anyway."

"What?" I asked, confused by his logic.

"I'll be fine. The doctor says I can go back in the water in eight days."

Was he out of his mind? I wanted to tell him he wasn't allowed to go near water again until he was 35, but instead I bit my tongue and prayed he would forget about surfing forevermore.

For the next seven days he kept pressing me to let him go back on the board. One day after I emphatically repeated "No" to him for the 100th time, he beat me at my own game.

"Mom, you taught us never to give up what we love."

Then he handed me a bribe — a framed poem by Langston Hughes that he bought "because it reminded me of you."

Mother To Son

Well, son, I'll tell you:
Life for me ain't been no crystal stair.
It's had tacks in it.
And splinters,
And boards torn up,
And places with no carpet on the floor —
Bare.
But all the time

I'se been a-climbin' on,
And reachin' landin's
And turnin's corners,
And sometimes goin' in the dark
Where there ain't been no light.
So, boy, don't you turn back,
Don't you set down on the steps
'Cause you finds it's kinder hard.
Don't you fall now —
For I'se still goin', honey,
I'se still climbin'
And life for me ain't been no crystal stair.

I gave in.

Back then Daniel was a just a boy with a passion for surfing. Now he's a man with a responsibility. He ranks among the top 25 pro surfers in the world.

I was tested in my own backyard on an important principle that I teach audiences in distant cities: "Passionate people embrace what they love and never give up."

Danielle Kennedy

Ziggy ©Ziggy and Friends. Distributed by Universal Press Syndicate. Reprinted with permission. All rights reserved.

Failure? No! Just Temporary Setbacks

To see things in the seed, that is genius.

Lao-tzu

If you could come to my office in California to visit with me today, you would notice across one side of the room a beautiful old-fashioned Spanish tile and mahogany soda fountain with nine leather-covered stools (the kind they used to have in the old drug stores). Unusual? Yes. But if those stools could speak, they would tell you a story about the day I almost lost hope and gave up.

It was a recession period after World War II and jobs were scarce. Cowboy Bob, my husband, had purchased a small dry cleaning business with borrowed money. We had two darling babies, a tract home, a car and all the usual time payments. Then the bottom fell out. There was no money for the house payments or anything else.

I felt that I had no special talent, no training, no college education. I didn't think much of myself. But I remembered someone in my past who thought I had a little ability — my Alhambra High School English teacher. She inspired me to take journalism and named me advertising manager and feature editor of the school paper. I thought, "Now if I could write a 'shoppers Column' for the small weekly newspaper in our rural town, maybe I could earn that house payment."

I had no car and no baby-sitter. So I pushed my two children before me in a rickety baby stroller with a big pillow tied in the back. The wheel kept coming off, but I hit it back on with the heel of my shoe and kept going. I was determined that my children would not lose their home as I often had done as a child.

But at the newspaper office, there were no jobs available. Recession. So I caught an idea. I asked if I might buy advertising space at wholesale and sell it at retail as a "Shoppers Column." They agreed, telling me later that they mentally gave me about a week of pushing that beat up heavily laden stroller down those country roads before I gave up. But they were wrong.

The newspaper column idea worked. I made enough money for the house payment and to buy an old used car that Cowboy Bob found for me. Then I hired a high school girl to baby-sit from three to five each afternoon. When the clock struck three, I grabbed my newspaper samples and flew out of the door to drive to my appointments.

But on one dark rainy afternoon every advertising prospect I had worked on turned me down when I went to pick up their copy.

"Why?" I asked. They said they had noticed that Ruben Ahlman, the President of the Chamber of Commerce and the owner of the Rexall Drug store did not advertise with me. His store was the most popular in town. They respected his judgment. "There must be something wrong with your advertising," they explained.

My heart sank. Those four ads would have made the

house payment. Then I thought, I will try to speak with Mr. Ahlman one more time. Everyone loves and respects him. Surely he will listen. Every time I had tried to approach him in the past, he had refused to see me. He was always "out" or unavailable. I knew that if he advertised with me, the other merchants in town would follow his lead.

This time, as I walked into the Rexall drug store, he was there at the prescription counter in the back. I smiled my best smile and held up my precious "Shoppers Column" carefully marked in my children's green Crayola. I said, "Everyone respects your opinion, Mr. Ahlman. Would you just look at my work for a moment so that I can tell the other merchants what you think?"

His mouth turned perpendicular in an upside down U. Without saying a word he emphatically shook his head in the chilling negative gesture, "NO!" My knotted heart fell to the floor with such a thud, I thought everyone must have heard it.

Suddenly all of my enthusiasm left me. I made it as far as the beautiful old soda fountain at the front of the drug store, feeling that I didn't have the strength to drive home. I didn't want to sit at the soda fountain without buying something, so I pulled out my last dime and ordered a cherry Coke. I wondered desperately what to do. Would my babies lose their home as I had so many times when I was growing up? Was my journalism teacher wrong? Maybe that talent she talked about was just a dud. My eyes filled with tears.

A soft voice beside me on the next soda fountain stool said, "What is the matter, dear?" I looked up into the sympathetic face of a lovely grey haired lady. I poured out my story to her, ending it with, "But Mr. Ahlman, who everyone respects so much, will not look at my work."

"Let me see that Shoppers Column," she said. She took my marked issue of the newspaper in her hands and carefully read it all the way through. Then she spun around on the stool, stood up, looked back at the prescription counter and in a commanding voice that could be heard down the block, said, "Ruben Ahlman, come *here*!" The lady was Mrs. Ahlman!

She told Ruben to buy the advertising from me. His mouth turned up the other way in a big grin. Then she asked me for the names of the four merchants who had turned me down. She went to the phone and called each one. She gave me a hug and told me they were waiting for me and to go back and pick up their ads.

Ruben and Vivian Ahlman became our dear friends, as well as steady advertising customers. I learned that Ruben was a darling man who bought from everyone. He had promised Vivian not to buy any more advertising. He was just trying to keep his word to her. If I had only asked others in town, I might have learned that I should have been talking to Mrs. Ahlman from the beginning. That conversation on the stools of the soda fountain was the turning point. My advertising business prospered and grew into four offices, with 285 employees serving 4,000 continuous contract advertising accounts.

Later when Mr. Ahlman modernized the old drug store and removed the soda fountain, my sweet husband Bob bought it and installed it in my office. If you were here in California, we would sit on the soda fountain stools together. I'd pour you a cherry Coke and remind you to never give up, to remember that help is always closer than we know.

Then I would tell you that if you can't communicate with a key person, search for more information. Try another path around. Look for someone who can communicate for you in a third person endorsement. And, finally, I would serve you these sparkling, refreshing words of Bill Marriott of the Marriott Hotels:

Failure? I never encountered it.
All I ever met were temporary setbacks.

Dottie Walters

For Me To Be More Creative, I Am Waiting For...

1. Inspiration
2. Permission
3. Reassurance
4. The coffee to be ready
5. My turn
6. Someone to smooth the way
7. The rest of the rules
8. Someone to change
9. Wider fairways
10. Revenge
11. The stakes to be lower
12. More time
13. A significant relationship to:
    (a) improve
    (b) terminate
    (c) happen
14. The right person
15. A disaster
16. Time to almost run out
17. An obvious scapegoat
18. The kids to leave home
19. A Dow-Jones of 1500
20. The Lion to lie down with the Lamb
21. Mutual consent
22. A better time
23. A more favorable horoscope
24. My youth to return
25. The two-minute warning
26. The legal profession to reform
27. Richard Nixon to be re-elected
28. Age to grant me the right of eccentricity
29. Tomorrow
30. Jacks or better
31. My annual checkup
32. A better circle of friends

33. The stakes to be higher
34. The semester to start
35. My way to be clear
36. The cat to stop clawing the sofa
37. An absence of risk
38. The barking dog next door to leave town
39. My uncle to come home from the service
40. Someone to discover me
41. More adequate safeguards
42. A lower capital gains rate
43. The statute of limitations to run out
44. My parents to die (Joke!)
45. A cure for herpes/AIDS
46. The things that I do not understand or approve of to go away
47. Wars to end
48. My love to rekindle
49. Someone to be watching
50. A clearly written set of instructions
51. Better birth control
52. The ERA to pass
53. An end to poverty, injustice, cruelty, deceit, incompetence, pestilence, crime and offensive suggestions
54. A competing patent to expire
55. Chicken Little to return
56. My subordinates to mature
57. My ego to improve
58. The pot to boil
59. My new credit card
60. The piano tuner
61. This meeting to be over
62. My receivables to clear
63. The unemployment checks to run out
64. Spring
65. My suit to come back from the cleaners
66. My self-esteem to be restored
67. A signal from Heaven
68. The alimony payments to stop
69. The gems of brilliance buried within my first bumbling efforts to be recognized, applauded and substantially rewarded so that I can work on the second draft in comfort
70. A reinterpretation of

Robert'sRules of Order
71. Various aches and pains to subside
72. Shorter lines at the bank
73. The wind to freshen
74. My children to be thoughtful, neat, obedient and self-supporting
75. Next season
76. Someone else to screw up
77. My current life to be declared a dress rehearsal with some script changes permitted before opening night
78. Logic to prevail
79. The next time around
80. You to stand out of my light
81. My ship to come in
82. A better deodorant
83. My dissertation to be finished
84. A sharp pencil
85. The check to clear
86. My wife, film or boomerang to come back
87. My doctor's approval, my father's permission, my minister's blessing or my lawyer's okay
88. Morning
89. California to fall into the ocean
90. A less turbulent time
91. The Iceman to Cometh
92. An opportunity to call collect
93. A better write-off
94. My smoking urges to subside
95. The rates to go down
96. The rates to go up
97. The rates to stabilize
98. My grandfather's estate to be settled
99. Weekend rates
100. A cue card
101. You to go first

David B. Campbell

Everybody Can Do Something

The basic difference between an ordinary man and a warrior is that a warrior takes everything as a challenge, while an ordinary man takes everything either as a blessing or a curse.

Don Juan

Roger Crawford had everything he needed to play tennis — except two hands and a leg.

When Roger's parents saw their son for the first time, they saw a baby with a thumb-like projection extended directly out of his right forearm and a thumb and one finger stuck out of his left forearm. He had no palms. The baby's arms and legs were shortened, and he had only three toes on his shrunken right foot and a withered left leg, which would later be amputated.

The doctor said Roger suffered from ectrodactylism, a rare birth defect affecting only one out of 90,000 children born in the United States. The doctor said Roger would probably never walk or care for himself.

Fortunately Roger's parents didn't believe the doctor.

"My parents always taught me that I was only as handicapped as I wanted to be," said Roger. "They never allowed me to feel sorry for myself or take advantage of people because of my handicap. Once I got into trouble because my school papers were continually late," explained Roger, who had to hold his pencil with both "hands" to write slowly. "I asked Dad to write a note to my teachers, asking for a two-day extension on my assignments. Instead Dad made me start writing my paper two days early!"

Roger's father always encouraged him to get involved in sports, teaching Roger to catch and throw a volleyball, and play backyard football after school. At age 12, Roger managed to win a spot on the school football team.

Before every game, Roger would visualize his dream of scoring a touchdown. Then one day he got his chance. The ball landed in his arms and off he ran as fast as he could on his artificial leg toward the goal line, his coach and teammates cheering wildly. But at the ten-yard line, a guy from the other team caught up with Roger, grabbing his left ankle. Roger tried to pull his artificial leg free, but instead it ended up being pulled off.

"I was still standing up," recalls Roger. "I didn't know what else to do so I started hopping towards the goal line. The referee ran over and threw his hands into the air. Touchdown! You know, even better than the six points was the look on the face of the other kid who was holding my artificial leg."

Roger's love of sports grew and so did his self confidence. But not every obstacle gave way to Roger's determination. Eating in the lunchroom with the other kids watching him fumble with his food proved very painful to Roger, as did his repeated failure in typing class. "I learned a very good lesson from typing class," said Roger. "You can't do *everything* — it's better to concentrate on what you can do."

One thing Roger could do was swing a tennis racket. Unfortunately, when he swung it hard, his weak grip usually launched it into space. By luck, Roger stumbled upon an odd-looking tennis racket in a sports shop and accidentally wedged his finger between its double-barred handle when he picked it up. The snug fit made it possible for Roger to swing, serve and volley like an ablebodied player. He practiced every day and was soon playing — and losing — matches.

But Roger persisted. He practiced and practiced and played and played. Surgery on the two fingers of his left hand enabled Roger to grip his special racket better, greatly improving his game. Although he had no role models to guide him, Roger became obsessed with tennis and in time he started to win.

Roger went on to play college tennis, finishing his tennis career with 22 wins and 11 losses. He later became the first physically handicapped tennis player to be certified as a teaching professional by the United States Professional Tennis Association. Roger now tours the country, speaking to groups about what it takes to be a winner, no matter who you are.

"The only difference between you and me is that you can see my handicap, but I can't see yours. We *all* have them. When people ask me how I've been able to overcome my physical handicaps, I tell them that I haven't overcome anything. I've simply learned what I can't do — such as play the piano or eat with chopsticks — but more importantly, I've learned what I *can* do. Then I do what I can with all my heart and soul."

Jack Canfield

Yes, You Can

Experience is not what happens to a man. It is what a man does with what happens to him.

Aldous Huxley

What if at age 46 you were burned beyond recognition in a terrible motorcycle accident, and then four years later were paralyzed from the waist down in an airplane crash? Then, can you imagine yourself becoming a millionaire, a respected public speaker, a happy newlywed and a successful business person? Can you see yourself going white water rafting? Sky diving? Running for political office?

W. Mitchell has done all these things and more *after* two horrible accidents left his face a quilt of multicolored skin grafts, his hands fingerless and his legs thin and motionless in a wheelchair.

The 16 surgeries Mitchell endured after the motorcycle accident burned more than 65 percent of his body, left him unable to pick up a fork, dial a telephone or go to the bathroom without help. But Mitchell, a former Marine, never believed he was defeated. "I am in charge of my own spaceship," he said. "It's my up, my down. I could choose to see this situation as a setback or a starting point." Six months later he was piloting a plane again.

Mitchell bought himself a Victorian home in Colorado, so me real estate, a plane and a bar. Later he teamed up with two friends and co-founded a wood-burning stove company that grew to be Vermont's second largest private employer.

Then four years after the motorcycle accident, the plane Mitchell was piloting crashed back onto the runway during takeoff, crushing Mitchell's 12 thoracic vertebrae and permanently paralyzing him from the waist down. "I wondered what the hell was happening to me. What did I do to deserve this?"

Undaunted, Mitchell worked day and night to regain as much independence as possible. He was elected Mayor of Crested Butte, Colorado, to save the town from mineral mining that would ruin its beauty and environment. Mitchell later ran for Congress, turning his odd appearance into an asset with slogans such as, "Not just another pretty face."

Despite his initially shocking looks and physical challenges, Mitchell began white water rafting, he fell in love and married, earned a master's degree in public administration and continued flying, environmental activism and public speaking.

Mitchell's unshakable Positive Mental Attitude has earned him appearances on the "Today Show" and "Good Morning America" as well as feature articles in *Parade*, *Time*, *The New York Times* and other publications.

"Before I was paralyzed, there were 10,000 things I could do," Mitchell says. "Now there are 9,000. I can either dwell on the 1,000 I lost or focus on the 9,000 I have left. I tell people that I have had two big bumps in my life. If I have chosen not to use them as an excuse to quit, then maybe some of the experiences you are having which are pulling you back can be put into a new perspective. You can step back, take a wider view and have a chance to say, "Maybe that isn't such a big deal after all."

Remember: "It's not what happens to you, it's what you do about it."

Jack Canfield and Mark V. Hansen

Run, Patti, Run

At a young and tender age, Patti Wilson was told by her doctor that she was an epileptic. Her father, Jim Wilson, is a morning jogger. One day she smiled through her teenage braces and said, "Daddy what I'd really love to do is run with you every day, but I'm afraid I'll have a seizure."

Her father told her, "If you do, I know how to handle it so let's start running!"

That's just what they did every day. It was a wonderful experience for them to share and there were no seizures at all while she was running. After a few weeks, she told her father, "Daddy, what I'd really love to do is break the world's long-distance running record for women."

Her father checked the *Guiness Book of World Records* and found that the farthest any woman had run was 80 miles. As a freshman in high school, Patti announced, "I'm going to run from Orange County up to San Francisco." (A distance of 400 miles.) "As a sophomore," she went on, "I'm going to run to Portland, Oregon." (Over 1,500 miles.) "As a junior I'll run to St. Louis. (About 2,000 miles.) "As a senior I'll run to the White House." (More than 3, 000 miles away.)

In view of her handicap, Patti was as ambitious as she was enthusiastic, but she said she looked at the handicap of being an epileptic as simply "an inconvenience." She focused not on what she had lost, but on what she had *left*.

That year she completed her run to San Francisco wearing a T-shirt that read, "I Love Epileptics." Her dad ran every mile at her side, and her mom, a nurse, followed in a motor home behind them in case anything went wrong.

In her sophomore year Patti's classmates got behind her. They built a giant poster that read, "Run, Patti, Run!" (This has since become her motto and the title of a book she has written.) On her second marathon, en route to Portland, she fractured a bone in her foot. A doctor told her she had to stop her run. He said, "I've got to put a cast on your ankle so that you don't sustain permanent damage."

"Doc, you don't understand," she said. "This isn't just a whim of mine, it's amagnificent obsession! I'm not just doing it for me, I'm doing it to break the chains on the brains that limit so many others. Isn't there a way I can keep running?" He gave her one option. He could wrap it in adhesive instead of putting it in a cast. He warned her that it would be incredibly painful, and he told her, "It will blister." She told the doctor to wrap it up.

She finished the run to Portland, completing her last mile with the governor of Oregon. You may have seen the headlines: "Super Runner, Patti Wilson Ends Marathon For Epilepsy On Her 17th Birthday."

After four months of almost continuous running from the West Coast to the East Coast, Patti arrived in Washington and shook the hand of the President of the United States. She told him, "I wanted people to know that epileptics are normal human beings with normal lives."

I told this story at one of my seminars not long ago, and afterward a big teary-eyed man came up to me, stuck out his big meaty hand and said, "Mark, my name is Jim Wilson. You were talking about my daughter, Patti." Because of her noble efforts, he told me, enough money had been raised to open up 19 multi-million-dollar epileptic centers around the country.

If Patti Wilson can do so much with so little, what can you do to outperform yourself in a state of total wellness?

Mark V. Hansen

er Of Determination

hoolhouse was heated by an old-fash-
stove. A little boy had the job of com-
ch day to start the fire and warm the
er and his classmates arrived.
rrived to find the schoolhouse engulfed
gged the unconscious little boy out of
more dead than alive. He had major
half of his body and was taken to the
tal.
dreadfully burned, semi-conscious little
e doctor talking to his mother. The
mother that her son would surely die —
best, really — for the terrible fire had
devastated the lower half of his body.

But the brave boy didn't want to die. He made up his mind that he would survive. Somehow, to the amazement of the physician, he did survive. When the mortal danger was past, he again heard the doctor and his mother speaking quietly. The mother was told that since the fire had destroyed so much flesh in the lower part of his body, it would almost be better if he had died, since he was doomed to be a lifetime cripple with no use at all of his lower limbs.

Once more the brave boy made up his mind. He would not

be a cripple. He would walk. But unfortunately from the waist down, he had no motor ability. His thin legs just dangled there, all but lifeless.

Ultimately he was released from the hospital. Every day his mother would massage his little legs, but there was no feeling, no control, nothing. Yet his determination that he would walk was as strong as ever.

When he wasn't in bed, he was confined to a wheelchair. One sunny day his mother wheeled him out into the yard to get some fresh air. This day, instead of sitting there, he threw himself from the chair. He pulled himself across the grass, dragging his legs behind him.

He worked his way to the white picket fence bordering their lot. With great effort, he raised himself up on the fence. Then, stake by stake, he began dragging himself along the fence, resolved that he would walk. He started to do this every day until he wore a smooth path all around the yard beside the fence. There was nothing he wanted more than to develop life in those legs.

Ultimately through his daily massages, his iron persistence and his resolute determination, he did develop the ability to stand up, then to walk haltingly, then to walk by himself — and then — to run.

He began to walk to school, then to run to school, to run for the sheer joy of running. Later in college he made the track team.

Still later in Madison Square Garden this young man who was not expected to survive, who would surely never walk, who could never hope to run — this determined young man, Dr. Glenn Cunningham, ran the world's fastest mile!

Burt Dubin

The Power Of Optimism

The years of the Vietnam War were a confused troubled time for American foreign policy, making the suffering of the participants all the more tragic. But out of it has come the marvelous story about Captain Gerald L. Coffee.

His plane was shot down over the China Sea on February 3, 1966, and he spent the next seven years in a succession of prison camps. The POWs who survived, he says, did so by a regimen of physical exercise, prayer and stubborn communication with one another. After days of torture on the Vietnamese version of the rack, he signed the confession they demanded. Then he was thrown back into his cell to writhe in pain. Even worse was his guilt over having cracked. He did not know if there were other American prisoners in the cell block, but then he heard a voice: "Man in cell number 6 with the broken arm, can you hear me?"

It was Col. Robinson Risner. "It's safe to talk. Welcome to Heartbreak Hotel," he said.

"Colonel, any word about my navigator, Bob Hansen?" Coffee asked.

"No. Listen, Jerry, you must learn to communicate by tapping on the walls. It's the only dependable link we have to each other."

Risner had said "We"! That meant there were others.

"Thank god, now I'm back with the others," Coffee thought.

"Have they tortured you, Jerry?" Risner asked.

"Yes, And I feel terrible that they got anything out of me."

"Listen," Risner said, "once they decide to break a man, they do it. The important thing is how you come back. Just follow the Code. Resist to the utmost of your ability. If they break you, just don't stay broken. Lick your wounds and bounce back. Talk to someone if you can. Don't get down on yourself. We need to take care of one another."

For days at a time Coffee would be punished for some minor infraction by being stretched on the ropes. His buddy in the next cell would tap on the wall, telling him to "hang tough," that he was praying for him. "Then, when he was being punished," Coffee says, "I would be on the wall doing the same for him."

At last Coffee received a letter from his wife:

Dear Jerry,
It has been a beautiful spring but of course we miss you. The kids are doing great. Kim skis all the way around the lake now. The boys swim and dive off the dock, and little Jerry splashes around with a plastic bubble on his back.

Coffee stopped reading because his eyes were filling with tears as he clutched his wife's letter to his chest. "Little Jerry? Who's Jerry?" Then he realized. Their baby, born after his imprisonment, had been a son and she had named him Jerry. There was no way she could know that all her previous letters had been undelivered, so she talked about their new son matter of-factly. Coffee says:

"Holding her letter, I was full of emotions: relief at finally knowing that the family was well, sorrow for missing out on Jerry's entire first year, gratitude for the blessing of simply being alive." The letter concluded:

> *All of us, plus so many others, are praying for your safety and return soon. Take good care of yourself, honey.*
> *I love you.*
>
> *Bea*

Coffee tells about the long, long hours during which the prisoners played movies in their minds, of going from room to room in their houses back home, the camera taking in every detail. Over and over they played scenes of what it was going to be like to be back. Coffee says it was his friends and his faith that helped him through. Every Sunday the senior officer in each cell block would pass a signal — church call. Every man stood up in his cell, if he was able, and then with a semblance of togetherness, they would recite the Twenty-Third Psalm: "Thou prepares" a table before me in the presence of mine enemies, thou anointest my head with oil; my cup runneth over."

Coffee says, "I realized that despite being incarcerated in this terrible place, it was my cup that runneth over because someday, however, whenever, I would return to a beautiful and free country."

Finally, the peace treaty was signed, and on February 3, 1973, the seventh anniversary of his capture, Coffee was called before two young Vietnamese officers.

"Today it is our duty to return your belongings," one said.

"What belongings?" he asked.

"This."

He swallowed hard and reached for the gold wedding band the soldier held between his thumb and forefinger. Yes, it was his. He slipped it onto his finger. A little loose, but definitely his ring. He had never expected to see it again.

[My] kids were 11 or 12 years old when my ring had been taken away. Suddenly I felt old and weary. During the prime years of my life, I had sat in a medieval dungeon, had my arm screwed up, had contracted worms and God knows what else. I wondered if my children, now older and changed so much, would accept me back into the family and what our reunion would be like. And I thought of Bea. Would I be okay for her? Did she still love me? Could she possibly know how much she had meant to me all these years?

The bus trip to the Hanoi airport was a blur, but one thing stood out with clarity for Coffee: The bright beautiful, red, white, and blue flag painted on the tail of the enormous Air Force C-141 transport that gleamed in the sun, awaiting the first load of freed prisoners.

Next to the aircraft were several dozen American military people who smiled at them through the fence and gave them the thumbs-up signal. As they lined up by twos, the Vietnamese officer reeled off their names, rank and service.

"Commander Gerald L. Coffee, United States Navy." (He had been promoted two ranks in his absence.)

As Coffee stepped forward, his attention was riveted on an American colonel wearing crisp Air Force blues, wings and ribbons. It was the first American military uniform he had seen in many years. The colonel returned Coffee's brisk salute.

"Commander Gerald L. Coffee reporting for duty, sir."

"Welcome back, Jerry." Then colonel reached forward with both hands and shook Coffee's hand. When the plane was loaded, the pilot taxied directly onto the runway without holding short, then locked the brakes and jammed his throttles forward. The huge beast rocked and vibrated as the pilot made his final checks of the engine's performance. The roar was horrendous as the brakes were released and they lurched forward on the runway. When they were airborne, the pilot's voice came onto the speaker and filled the cabin. It was a strong, sure voice."

"Congratulations, gentlemen. We've just left North Vietnam." Only then did they erupt into cheers.

The first leg of their trip home took them to Clark Air Force Base in the Philippines. The crowd held up banners: "Welcome Home! We love you. God bless." From behind the security lines they applauded wildly as the name of each debarking POW was announced. There were television cameras, but the men had no idea that at that very moment in the small hours of the morning, millions of Americans back home were riveted to their television sets, cheering and weeping.

Special telephones had been set up to accommodate their initial calls home. Coffee's stomach churned as he waited the interminable few seconds for Bea to pick up the phone in Sanford, Florida, where she and the children were waiting.

"Hello, babe. It's me. Can you believe it?"

"Hi, honey. Yes. We watched you on TV when you came off the airplane. I think everybody in America saw you. You look great!"

"I dunno. I'm kinda scrawny. But I'm okay. I'm just anxious to get home."

After his long-awaited reunion with his wife and children,

he and his family attended mass the following Sunday. Afterwards, in response to the parish priest's welcome, here is what Coffee said. It summarizes as well as anything I know of the optimist's code:

"Faith was really the key to my survival all those years. Faith in myself to simply pursue my duty to the best of my ability and ultimately return home with honor. Faith in my fellow man, starting with all of you here, knowing you would be looking out for my family, and faith in my comrades in those various cells and cell blocks in prison, men upon whom I depended and who in turn depended upon me, sometimes desperately. Faith in my country, its institutions and our national purpose and cause... And, of course, faith in God — truly, as all of you know, the foundation for it all... Our lives are a continuing journey — and we must learn and grow at every bend as we make our way, sometimes stumbling, but always moving, toward the finest within us."

David McNally
From The Power of Potimism
by Alan Loy McGinnis

Faith

We're a rugged breed, us quads. If we weren't, we wouldn't be around today. Yes, we're a rugged breed. In many ways, we've been blessed with a savvy and spirit that isn't given to everybody.

And let me say that this refusal of total or full acceptance of one's disability all hooks up with one thing — faith, an almost divine faith.

Down in the reception room of the Institute of Physical Medicine and Rehabilitation, over on the East River at 400 East 34th Street in New York City, there's a bronze plaque that's riveted to the wall. Duringthe months of coming back to the Institute for treatment — two or three times a week — I rolled through that reception room many times, coming and going. But I never quite made the time to pull over to one side and read the words on that plaque that were written, it's said, by an unknown Confederate soldier. Then one afternoon, I did. I read it and then I read it again. When I finished it for the second time, I was near to bursting — not in despair, but with an inner glow that had me straining to grip the arms of my wheelchair. I'd like to share it with you.

A Creed For Those Who Have Suffered

I asked God for strength, that I might achieve.

I was made weak, that I might learn humbly to obey...

I asked for health, that I might do great things.
I was given infirmity, that I might do better things...

I asked for riches, that I might be happy.
I was given poverty, that I might be wise...

I asked for power, that I might have the praise of men.
I was given weakness, that I might feel the need of God...

I asked for all things, that I might enjoy life.
I was given life, that I might enjoy all things...

I got nothing I asked for — but everything I had hoped for.
Almost despite myself, my unspoken prayers were answered.

I am, among men, most richly blessed!

Roy Campanella

She Saved 219 Lives

Mrs. Betty Tisdale is a world-class heroine. When the war in Vietnam heated up back in April of 1975, she knew she had to save the 400 orphans who were about to be put on the streets. She had already adopted five orphaned Vietnamese girls with her former pediatrician husband, Col. Patrick Tisdale, who was a widower and already had five children.

As a U. S. Naval doctor in Vietnam in 1954, Tom Dooley had helped refugees flee from the communist north. Betty says, "I really feel Tom Dooley was a saint. His influence changed my life forever." Because of Dooley's book, she took her life savings and traveled to Vietnam 14 times on her vacations to visit and work in the hospitals and orphanages he had founded. While in Saigon, she fell in love with the orphans at An Lac (Happy Place), run by Madame Vu Thi Ngai, who was later evacuated by Betty the day Vietnam fell, and returned with her to Georgia to live with Betty and her ten children.

When Betty, a do-it-now and invent-solutions-as-problems-arise kind of person, realized the 400 children's plight, she went into warp-speed action. She called Madame Ngai and said, "Yes! I'll come and get the children and get them all adopted." She didn't know how she would do it. She just knew that she'd do it. Later, in a movie of the evacuation, "The Children of An Lac," Shirley Jones portrayed Betty.

In moments she began to move mountains. She raised the necessary money in many different ways, even including accepting green stamps. Shc simply decided to do it and she did it. She said, "I visualized all those babies growing up in good Christian homes in America, not under communism." That kept her motivated.

She left for Vietnam from Fort Benning, Georgia, on Sunday, arrived on Tuesday in Saigon, and miraculously and sleeplessly conquered every obstacle to airlift 400 children out of Saigon by Saturday morning. However, upon her arrival, the head of Vietnam's social welfare, Dr. Dan, suddenly announced he would only approve children under ten years old and all the children must have birth certificates. She quickly discovered war orphans are fortunate to simply be alive. They don't have birth certificates.

Betty went to the hospital pediatric department, obtained 225 birth certificates, and quickly created birth dates, times and places for the 219 eligible babies, toddlers and youngsters. She says, "I have no idea when, where and to whom they were born. My fingers just created birth certificates." Birth certificates were the only hope they had to depart the place safely and have a viable future with freedom. It was now or never.

Now she needed a place to house the orphans once they were evacuated... The military at Ft. Benning resisted, but Betty brilliantly and tenaciously persisted. Try as she might, she could not get the Commanding General on the phone, so she called the office of the Secretary of the Army, Bo Callaway. His duty, too, was not answering Betty's calls, no matter how urgent and of life-saving importance they were.

However, Betty was not to be beaten. She had come too far and done too much to be stopped now. So since he was from Georgia, she called his mother and pleaded her case. Betty enrolled her with her heart and asked her to intercede. Virtually overnight, the Secretary of the Army, her son, responded and arranged that a school at Ft. Benning be used as the interim home for the orphans of An Lac.

But the challenge of how to get the children out was still to be accomplished. When Betty arrived in Saigon, she went to Ambassador Graham Martin immediately and pleaded for some sort of transportation for the children. She had tried to charter a Pan Am plane, but Lloyds of London had raised the insurance so high that it was impossible to negotiate at this time. The Ambassador agreed to help if all the papers were cleared through the Vietnamese government. Dr. Dan signed the last manifest, literally, as the children were boarding the two airforce planes.

The orphans were malnourished and sickly. Most had never been away from the orphanage. They were scared. She had recruited soldiers and the ABC crew to help strap them in, transport them and feed them. You can't believe how deeply and permanently those volunteers' hearts were touched that beautiful Saturday as 219 children were transported to freedom. Every volunteer cried with joy and appreciation that they had tangibly contributed to another's freedom.

Chartering airlines home from the Philippines was a huge hassle. There was a $21,000 expense for a United Airlines plane. Dr. Tisdale guaranteed payment because of his love for the orphans. Had Betty had more time, she could have probably got it for free! But time was a factor so she moved quickly.

Every child was adopted within one month of arriving in the United States. The Tressler Lutheran Agency in York, Pennsylvania, which specializes in getting handicapped children adopted, found a home for each orphan.

Betty has proven over and over again that you can do anything at all if you are simply willing to ask, to not settle for a "no," to do whatever it takes and to persevere.

As Dr. Tom Dooley once said, "It takes ordinary people to do extraordinary things."

Jack Canfield and Mark V. Hansen

Are You Going To Help Me?

In 1989 an 8. 2 earthquake almost flattened Armenia, killing over 30, 000 people in less than four minutes.

In the midst of utter devastation and chaos, a father left his wife securely at home and rushed to the school where his son was supposed to be, only to discover that the building was as flat as a pancake.

After the traumatic initial shock, he remembered the promise he had made to his son: "No matter what, I'll always be there for you!" And tears began to fill his eyes. As he looked at the pile of debris that once was the school, it looked hopeless, but he kept remembering his commitment to his son.

He began to concentrate on where he walked his son to class at school each morning. Remembering his son's classroom would be in the back right corner of the building, he rushed there and started digging through the rubble.

As he was digging, other forlorn parents arrived, clutching their hearts, saying: "My son!" "My daughter!" Other well meaning parents tried to pull him off of what was left of the school saying:

"It's too late!" "They're dead!"

"You can't help!" "Go home!"

"Come on, face reality, there's nothing you can do!"

"You're just going to make things worse!"

To each parent he responded with one line: "Are you going to help me now?" And then he proceeded to dig for his son, stone by stone.

The fire chief showed up and tried to pull him off of the school's debris saying, "Fires are breaking out, explosions are happening everywhere. You're in danger. We'll take care of it. Go home." To which this loving, caring Armenian father asked, "Are you going to help me now?"

The police came and said, "You're angry, distraught and it's over. You're endangering others. Go home. We'll handle it!" To which he replied, "Are you going to help me now?" No one helped.

Courageously he proceeded alone because he needed to know for himself: "Is my boy alive or is he dead?"

He dug for eight hours... 12 hours... 24 hours... 36 hours... then, in the 38th hour, he pulled back a boulder and heard his son's voice. He screamed his son's name, "*ARMAND*!" He heard back, "Dad!?! It's me, Dad! I told the other kids not to worry. I told 'em that if you were alive, you'd save me and when you saved me, they'd be saved. You promised, 'No matter what, I'll always be there for you!' You did it, Dad!"

"What's going on in there? How it it?" The father asked.

"There are 14 of us left out of 33, Dad. We're scared, hungry, thirsty and thankful you're here. When the building collapsed, it mad a wedge, like a triangle, and it saved us."

"Come on out, boy!"

"No, Dad! Let the other kids out first, 'cause I know you 'll get me! No matter what, I know you'll be there for me!"

Mark V. Hansen

Just One More Time

There's a 19th-century English novel set in a small Welsh town in which every year for the past 500 years the people all gather in church on Christmas Eve and pray. Shortly before midnight, they light candle lanterns and singing carols and hymns, they walk down a country path several miles to an old abandoned stone shack. There they set up a creche scene, complete with manger. And in simple piety, they kneel and pray. Their hymns warm the chilly December air. Everyone in town capable of walking is there.

There is a myth in that town, a belief that if all citizens are present on Christmas Eve, and if all are praying with perfect faith, then and only then, at the stroke of midnight, the Second Coming will be at hand. And for 500 years they've come to that stone ruin and prayed. Yet the Second Coming has eluded them.

One of the main characters in this novel is asked, "Do you believe that He will come again on Christmas Eve in our town?"

"No," He answers, shaking his head sadly, "no, I don't."

"Then why do you go each year?" he asked.

"Ah," he says smiling, "what if I were the only one who wasn't there when it happened?"

Well, that's very little faith he has, isn't it? But it is some faith. As it says in the New Testament, we need only have faith as small as a grain of mustard seed to get into the Kingdom of Heaven. And sometimes, when we work with disturbed children, at-risk youth, troubled teens, alcoholic or abusive or depressed and suicidal partners, friends or clients... it is at those moments that we need that small bit of faith that kept that man coming back to the stone ruin on Christmas Eve. Just one more time. Just this next time, perhaps I'll make the breakthrough then.

We sometimes are called upon to work with people for whom others have abandoned all hope. Perhaps we have even come to the conclusion that there's no possibility of change or growth. It's at that time that, if we can find the tiniest scrap of hope, we may turn the corner, achieve a measurable gain, save someone worth saving. Please go back, my friend, just this one more time.

Hanoch McCarty

There Is Greatness All Around You —Use It

There are many people who could be Olympic champions, All-Americans who have never tried. I'd estimate five million people could have beaten me in the pole vault the years I won it, at *least* five million. Men who were stronger, bigger and faster than I was could have done it, but they never picked up a pole, never made the feeble effort to pick their legs off the ground to try to get over the bar.

Greatness is all around us. It's easy to be great because great people will help you. What is fantastic about all the conventions I go to is that the greatest in the business will come and share their ideas, their methods and their techniques with everyone else. I have seen the greatest salesmen open up and show young salesmen exactly how they did it. They don't hold back. I have also found it true in the world of sports.

I'll never forget the time I was trying to break Dutch WarmerDam's record. I was about a foot below his record, so I called him on the phone. I said, "Dutch, can you help me? I seem to have leveled off. I can't get any higher."

He said, "Sure, Bob, come on up to visit me and I'll give you all I got." I spent three days with the master, the greatest pole vaulter in the world. For three days, Dutch gave me everything that he'd seen. There were things that I was doing wrong and he corrected them. To make a long story short, I went up eight inches. That great guy gave me the best that he had. I've found that sports champions and heroes willingly do this just to help you become great, too.

John Wooden, the great UCLA basketball coach, has a philosophy that every day he is supposed to help someone who can never reciprocate. That's his obligation.

When in college working on his masters thesis on scouting and defensive football, George Allen wrote up a 30-page survey and sent it out to the great coaches in the country. Eighty-five percent answered it completely.

Great people will share, which is what made George Allen one of the greatest football coaches in the world. Great people will tell you their secrets. Look for them, call them on the phone or buy their books. Go where they are, get around them, talk to them. It is easy to be great when you get around great people.

Bob Richards
Olympic Athlete

7

ECLECTIC WISDOM

This life is a test.
It is only a test.
Had it been
an actual life
You would have received
Further instructions on
Where to go and what to do!

Found on a bulletin board

You've Got Yourself A Deal!

When Marita was 13, it was the era of tie-dyed T-shirts and frayed jeans. Even though I had grown up in the Depression and had no money for clothes, I had never dressed this poorly. One day I saw her out in the driveway rubbing the hems of her new jeans with dirt and rocks. I was aghast at her ruining these pants I had just paid for and ran out to tell her so. She continued to grind on as I recounted my soap opera of childhood deprivation. As I concluded without having moved her to tears of repentance, I asked why she was wrecking her new jeans. She replied without looking up, "You can't wear new ones."

"Why not?"

"You just can't, so I'm messing them up to make them look old." Such total loss of logic! How could it be the style to ruin new clothes?

Each morning as she would leave for school I would stare at her and sigh, "My daughter looking like that." There she'd stand in her father's old T-shirt, tie-dyed with big blue spots and streaks. Fit for a duster, I thought. And those jeans — so low-slung I feared if she took a deep breath, they'd drop off her rear. But where would they go? They were so tight and stiff they couldn't move. The frayed bottoms, helped by the rocks, had strings that dragged behind her as she walked.

One day after she had left for school, it was as if the Lord got my attention and said, "Do you realize what your last words are to Marita each morning? 'My daughter looking like that.' When she gets to school and her friends talk about their old-fashioned mothers who complain all the time, she'll have your constant comments to contribute. Have you ever looked at the other girls in junior high? Why not give them a glance?"

I drove over to pick her up that day and observed that many of the other girls looked even worse. On the way home I mentioned how I had over-reacted to her ruining her jeans. I offered a compromise: "From now on you can wear anything you want to school and with your friends, and I won't bug you about it."

"That'll be a relief."

"But when I take you out with me to church or shopping or to my friends, I'd like you to dress in something you know I like without my having to say a word."

She thought about it.

Then I added, "That means you get 95 percent your way and I get 5 percent for me. What do you think?"

She got a twinkle in her eye as she put out her hand and shook mine. "Mother, you've got yourself a deal!"

From then on I gave her a happy farewell in the morning and didn't bug her about her clothes. When I took her out with me, she dressed properly without fussing. We had ourselves a deal!

Florence Littauer

Take A Moment To Really See

We have all heard the expression: "Remember to stop and smell the roses." But, how often do we really take time out of our hectic fast-paced lives to notice the world around us? Too often we get caught up in our busy schedules, thoughts of our next appointment, the traffic or life in general, to even realize there are other people nearby.

I am as guilty as anyone of tuning out the world in this manner, especially when I am driving on California's over-crowded streets. A short time ago, however, I witnessed an event that showed me how being wrapped up in my own little world has kept me from being fully aware of the bigger world picture around me.

I was driving to a business appointment and, as usual, I was planning in my mind what I was going to say. I came to a very busy intersection where the stoplight had just turned red. "All right," I thought to myself, "I can beat the next light if I race ahead of the pack."

My mind and car were in auto pilot, ready to go when suddenly my trance was broken by an unforgettable sight. A young couple, both blind, were walking arm-in-arm across this busy intersection with cars whizzing by in every direction. The man was holding the hand of a little boy, while the woman was clutching a baby sling to her chest, obviously carrying a child. Each of them had a white cane extended, searching for clues to navigate them across the intersection.

Initially I was moved. They were overcoming what I felt was one of the most feared handicaps — blindness. "Wouldn't it be terrible to be blind?" I thought. My thought was quickly interrupted by horror when I saw that the couple was not walking in the crosswalk, but was instead veering diagonally, directly toward the middle of the intersection. Without realizing the danger they were in, they were walking right smack into the path of oncoming cars. I was frightened for them because I didn't know if the other drivers understood what was happening.

As I watched from the front line of traffic (I had the best seat in the house), I saw a miracle unfold before my eyes. *Every* car in *every* direction came to a simultaneous stop. I never heard the screech of brakes or even the peep of a car horn. Nobody even yelled, "Get out of the way!" Everything froze. In that moment, time seemed to stand still for this family.

Amazed, I looked at the cars around me to verify that we were all seeing the same thing. I noticed that everyone's attention was also fixed on the couple. Suddenly the driver to my right reacted. Craning his head out of his car, he yelled, "To your right. To your right!" Other people followed in unison, shouting, "To your right!"

Never skipping a beat, the couple adjusted their course as they followed the coaching. Trusting their white canes and the calls from some concerned citizens, they made it to the other side of the road. As they arrived at the curb, one thing struck me — they were still arm-in-arm.

I was taken aback by the emotionless expressions on their faces and judged that they had no idea what was really going on around them. Yet I immediately sensed the sighs of relief exhaled by everyone stopped at that intersection.

As I glanced into the cars around me, the driver on my right was mouthing the words "Whew, did you see that?!" The driver to the left of me was saying, "I can't believe it!" I think all of us were deeply moved by what we had just witnessed. Here were human beings stepping outside themselves for a moment to help four people in need.

I have reflected back on this situation many times since it happened and have learned several powerful lessons from it. The first is: "Slow down and smell the roses." (Something I had rarely done up until then.) Take time to look around and really see what is going on in front of you right now. Do this and you will realize that this moment is all there is, more importantly, this moment is all that you have to make a difference in life.

The second lesson I learned is that the goals we set for ourselves can be attained through faith in ourselves and trust in others, despite seemingly insurmountable obstacles.

The blind couple's goal was simply to get to the other side of the road intact. Their obstacle was eight lines of cars aimed straight at them. Yet, without panic or doubt, they walked forward until they reached their goal.

We too can move forward in attaining our goals, putting blinders on to the obstacles that would stand in our way. We just need to trust our intuition and accept the guidance of others who may have greater insight.

Finally, I learned to really appreciate my gift of sight, something I had taken for granted all too often.

Can you imagine how different life would be without your eyes? Try to imagine for a moment, walking into a busy intersection without being able to see. How often we forget the simple yet incredible gifts we have in our life.

As I drove away from that busy intersection, I did so with more awareness of life and compassion for others than I had arrived there with. Since then I have made the decision to really see life as I go about my daily activities and use my God-given talents to help others less fortunate.

Do yourself a favor as you walk through life: Slow down and take the time to really *see*. Take a moment to see what is going on around you right now, right where you are. You may be missing something wonderful.

Jeffrey Michael Thomas

If I Had My Life To Live Over

Interviews with the elderly and the terminally ill do not report that people have regret for the things they have done but rather people talk about the things they regret not having done.

I'd dare to make more mistakes next time.
I'd relax. I would limber up.
I would be sillier than I have been this trip.
I would take fewer things seriously.
I would take more chances.
I would take more trips.
I would climb more mountains and swim more rivers. I would eat more ice cream and less beans.
I would perhaps have more actual troubles but I'd have fewer imaginary ones.
You see, I'm one of those people who live sensibly and sanely hour after hour, day after day.
Oh, I've had my moments and if I had it to do over again, I'd have more of them. In fact, I'd try to have nothing else. Just moments.
One after another, instead of living so many years ahead of each day.
I've been one of those people who never go anywhere with-

out a thermometer, a hot water bottle, a raincoat and a parachute.
If I had it to do again, I would travel lighter next time.

If I had my life to live over, I would start barefoot earlier in the spring and stay that way later in the fall.
I would go to more dances.
I would ride more merry-go-rounds.
I would pick more daisies.

Nadine Stair
(*age* 85)

Two Monks

Two monks on a pilgrimage came to the ford of a river. There they saw a girl dressed in all her finery, obviously not knowing what to do since the river was high and she did not want to spoil her clothes. Without more ado, one of the monks took her on his back, carried her across and put her down on dry ground on the other side.

Then the monks continued on their way. But the other monk after an hour started complaining, "Surely it is not right to touch a woman; it is against the commandments to have close contact with women. How could you go against the rules of monks?"

The monk who had carried the girl walked along silently, but finally he remarked, "I set her down by the river an hour ago, why are you still carrying her?"

Irmgard Schloegl
The Wisdom of Zen Masters

Sachi

Soon after her brother was born, little Sachi began to ask her parents to leave her alone with the new baby. They worried that like most four-year-olds, she might feel jealous and want to hit or shake him, so they said no. But she showed no signs of jealousy. She treated the baby with kindness and her pleas to be left alone with him became more urgent. They decided to allow it.

Elated, she went into the baby's room and shut the door, but it opened a crack — enough for her curious parents to peek in and listen. They saw little Sachi walk quietly up to her baby brother, put her face close to his and say quietly, "Baby, tell me what God feels like. I'm starting to forget."

Dan Millman

The Dolphin's Gift

I was in about 40 feet of water, alone. I knew I should not have gone alone, but I was very competent and just took a chance. There was not much current, and the water was so warm, clear and enticing. When I got a cramp, I realized at once how foolish I was. I was not too alarmed, but *was* completely doubled up with stomach cramps. I tried to remove my weight belt, but I was so doubled up I could not get to the catch. I was sinking and began to feel more frightened, unable to move. I could see my watch and knew there was only a little more time on the tank before I would be out of air. I tried to massage my abdomen. I wasn't wearing a wet suit, but couldn't straighten out and couldn't get to the cramped muscles with my hands.

I thought, "I can't go like this! I have things to do!" I just couldn't die anonymously this way with no one to even know what happened to me. I called out in my mind, "Somebody, something, help me!"

I was not prepared for what happened. Suddenly I felt a prodding from behind me under the armpit. I thought, "Oh no, sharks!" I felt real terror and despair. But my arm was being lifted forcibly. Around into my field of vision came an eye — the most marvelous eye I could ever imagine. I swear it was smiling. It was the eye of a big dolphin. Looking into that eye, I knew I was safe.

It moved farther forward, nudging under and hooking its dorsal fin below my armpit with my arm over its back. I relaxed, hugging it, flooded with relief. I felt that the animal was conveying security to me, that it was healing me as well as lifting me toward the surface. My stomach cramps went away as we ascended and I relaxed with security, but I felt very strongly that it healed me too.

At the surface it drew me all the way into shore. It took me into water so shallow that I began to be concerned that it might be beached, and I pushed it back a little deeper, where it waited, watching me, I guess to see if I was all right.

It felt like another lifetime. When I took off the weight belt and oxygen tank, I just took everything off and went naked back into the ocean to the dolphin. I felt so light and free and alive, and just wanted to play in the sun and the water in all that freedom. The dolphin took me back out and played around in the water with me. I noticed that there were a lot of dolphins there, farther out.

After a while it brought me back to shore. I was very tired then, almost collapsing and he made sure I was safe in the shallowest water. Then he turned sideways with one eye looking into mine. We stayed that way for what seemed like a very long time, timeless I guess, in a trance almost, with personal thoughts from the past going through my mind. Then he made just one sound and went out to join the others. And all of them left.

Elizabeth Gawain

The Touch Of The Master's Hand

'Twas battered and scarred, and the auctioneer
Thought it scarcely worth his while
To waste much time on the old violin,
But held it up with a smile.
"What am I bidden, good folks," he cried,
"Who'll start the bidding for me?"
"A dollar, a dollar," then, two! Only two?
"Two dollars, and who'll make it three?
"Three dollars, once; three dollars, twice;
Goin for three..." But no,
From the room, far back, a gray-haired man
Came forward and picked up the bow;
Then, wiping the dust from the old violin,
And tightening the loose strings,
He played a melody pure and sweet
As a caroling angel sings.

The music ceased, and the auctioneer,
With a voice that was quiet and low,
Said: "What am I bid for the old violin?"
And he held it up with the bow.
"A thousand dollars, and who'll make it two?
Two thousand! And who'll make it three?

Three thousand, once; three thousand, twice;
And going and gone," said he.
The people cheered, but some of them cried,
"We do not quite understand
What changed its worth?"
Swift came the reply:
"The touch of a master's hand."

And many a man with life out of tune,
And battered and scarred with sin,
Is auctioned cheap to the thoughtless crowd,
Much like the old violin.
A "mess of potage," a glass of wine;
A game — and he travels on.
He is "going" once, and "going" twice,
He's "going" and almost "gone."
But the Master comes and the foolish crowd
Never can quite understand
The worth of a soul and the change that's wrought
By the touch of the Master's hand.

Myra B. Welch

Who Is Jack Canfield?

Jack Canfield is one of America's leading experts in the development of human potential and personal effectiveness. He is both a dynamic, entertaining speaker and a highly sought-after trainer. Jack has a wonderful ability to inform and inspire audiences toward increased levels of self-esteem and peak performance.

He is the author and narrator of several bestselling audio- and videocassette programs, including *Self-Esteem And Peak Performance*, *How To Build High Self-Esteem*, *Self-Esteem In The Classroom and Chicken Soup For The Soul — Live*. He is regularly seen on television shows such as *Good Morning America*, 20/20 and *NBC Nightly News*. Jack has coauthored numerous books, including the Chicken Soup For The Soul *series*, *Dare To Win* and *Factor* (all with Mark Victor Hansen), 100 *Ways To Build Self-Concept In The Classroom* (with Harold C. Wells) and *Heart At Work* (with Jacqueline Miller).

Jack is a regularly featured speaker for professional associations, school districts, government agencies, churches, hospitals, sales organizations and corporations. His clients have included the American Dental Association, the American Management Association, AT&T, Johnson & Johnson, the Million Dollar Roundtable, NCR, New England Telephone, Re/Max, Scott Paper, TRW and Virgin Records. Jack is also on the faculty of Income Builders International, a school for entrepreneurs.

Jack conducts an annual eight-day Training of Trainers program in the areas of self-esteem and peak performance. It attracts educators, counselors, parenting trainers, corporate trainers, professional speakers, ministers and others interested in developing their speaking and seminar leading skills.

For further information about Jack's books, tapes and training programs, or to schedule him for a presentation, please contact:

The Canfield Training Group
P. O. Box 30880 • Santa Barbara, CA 93130
phone: 805-563-2935 • fax: 805-563-2945
Web site: *www. chickensoup. com*

Who Is Mark Victor Hansen?

Mark Victor Hansen is a professional speaker who, in the last 20 years, has made over 4, 000 presentations to more than 2 million people in 32 countries. His presentations cover sales excellence and strategies; personal empowerment and development; and how to triple your income and double your time off.

Mark has spent a lifetime dedicated to his mission of making a profound and positive difference in people's lives. Throughout his career, he has inspired hundreds of thousands of people's lives. Throughout his career, he has inspired hundreds of thousands of people to create a more powerful and purposeful future for themselves while stimulating the sale of billions of dollars worth of goods and services.

Mark is a prolific writer and has authored *Future Diary*, *How To Achieve Total Prosperity* and *The Miracle Of Tithing*. He is coauthor of the *Chicken Soup For The Soul* series, *Dare To Win* and *The Aladdin Factor* (all with Jack Canfield) and *The Master Motivator* (with Joe Batten).

Mark has also produced a complete library of personal empowerment audio and videocassette programs that have enabled his listeners to recognize and use their innate abilites in their business and personal lives. His message has made him a popular television and radio personality, with appearances on ABC, NBC, CBS, HBO, PBS and CNN. He has also appeared on the cover of numerous magazines, including *Success*, *Entrepreneur* and *Changes*.

Mark is a big man with a heart and spirit to match — an inspiration to all who seek to better themselves.

You can contact Mark at:

P. O. Box 7665
Newport Beach, CA 92658
phone: 949-759-9304 or 800-433-2314
fax: 949-722-6912
Web site: *www. chichensoup. com*

What People Are Saying About...

"After interviewing hundreds of rich and famous people, it is clear to me that money and fame don't automatically make people happy. It has to come from within. I'd rather have a million smiles in my heart than a million dollars in my pocket. *Chicken Soup for the Soul* will help you put a million smiles in your heart."

Robin Leach
TV personality and autor

"Telling stories is one of the most powerful ways to teach values and open doors to new possibilities. In this rich and varied collection, everyone will find at least a few stories that strike a special resonance — stories one will treasure and want to share."

Nathaniel Branden
Author, *The Power Of Self-Esteem*

"This is a warm, wonderful, uplifting and inspiring book full of ideas and insights that anyone can use to improve any part of his or her life. It should be read, reflected upon and reread over and over."

Brian Tracy
Autory, *The Psychology of Achievement*

"This book is wisdom and solace for the ages. It is as contemporary as a space walk and as timeless as a pyramid. The world needs storytellers to help us make sense out of the confusion and chaos of these complex times. Jack and Mark are consummate tellers and collectors of real-life stories. What a gift: to teachers, to speechmakers, to anyone on his or her own journey of growth and healing. It's all here, and written with wit, compassion and integrity."

Sidney B. Simon
Professor Emeritus, University of Massachusetts,
and coauthor of *Values Clarification*, *Forgiveness*
and 14 other books

"I enjoyed every page. The stories are heart-rending and extremely motivational, the poetry is beautiful and the quotes are highly profound and meaningful. Jack and Mark have truly compiled a tremendous amount of wisdom. Its contents provide great insight into all dimensions of life.

"This book would make a wonderful gift for others to share with their loved ones, and you can rest assured that I will be purchasing additional copies for my family and friends."

Richard Loughlin
President, Century 21 Real Estate Corp.

"What a great book! Jack Canfield and Mark Victor Hansen have written a book that has the same effect as my grand. mother's chicken soup did... It's warm and it's soothing. I plan on using it whenever I need a little love."

Dawn Steel
Former President, Columbia Pictures

"*Chicken Soup For the Soul* is a powerful reminder that the main ingredient in life is *Love*. It should be required reading for all."

Wally Amos
Famous Amos Cookies

"What a wonderful gift you have given us with this collection of inspirational stories! And what a wonderful gift it will be for my friends! I'm convinced that *Chicken Soup For The Soul* should be on everyone's bedside table to read for 30 minutes at the end of the day to retain one's faith in human nature and the basic goodness in all people.

"The stories you have selected warm one's heart and balance the news that we hear through the media each day. Your book restores the soul and gives one a positive sense of what life is really all about. Great job! I'm sure it will be a tremendous success."

Bob Reasoner
President, International Council for Self-Esteem
Author, *Building Self-Esteem*

英文版《心灵鸡汤》系列丛书

《关于工作》工作的人是快乐的，但也是多感的。18.00元

《致天下有情人》沐浴着爱情雨露的人让世界更精彩。19.00元

《女人心语》事业、家庭、爱情中的美国当代女性心语。19.00元

《象牙塔里的日子》美国大学生情感生活的真实再现。19.00元

"Jo Ann Beard's work impresses me no end. Funny without being sitcomish, self-aware without being self-absorbed, scrupulous without being fussy, emotional without being sentimental, pointed without being cruel—I could go on and on with these distinctions, all in Beard's favor, but instead I'll just say that Jo Ann Beard is a fantastic writer, an Athena born fully formed out of her own painstaking head."

—JEFFREY EUGENIDES, author of *The Virgin Suicides*

"It's hard to talk about Jo Ann Beard without sounding like an adjective machine: her writing is elaborately wonderful. Now, when I get cornered at parties and asked, 'So, just what is Creative Nonfiction?' I can hold up this book and say, 'This. This is it.'"

—LUCY GREALY, author of *Autobiography of a Face*

ISBN 0-965-57948-4

90000>

9 780965 579483

Printed in the U.S.A.

The Boys of My Youth

The Boys of My Youth

JO ANN BEARD

LITTLE, BROWN AND COMPANY

Boston New York Toronto London

First Edition

The events described in these stories are real. Some characters are composites and some have been given fictitious names and identifying characteristics in order to protect their anonymity.

"Coyotes" first appeared in *Story;* "Out There" and "Waiting" appeared in *Iowa Woman;* "Bonanza" appeared in *The Iowa Review;* "Cousins" appeared in *Prairie Schooner;* and "The Fourth State of Matter" appeared in *The New Yorker.*

The author is grateful for permission to include the following previously copyrighted material: Excerpts from "Over My Head" by Christine McVie. Copyright © 1977 by Fleetwood Mac Music (BMI). Reprinted by permission of NEM Entertainment. Excerpts from "Good Hearted Woman" by Willie Nelson and Waylon Jennings. Copyright © 1971 by Full Nelson Music, Inc., and Songs of Polygram International, Inc. All rights on behalf of Full Nelson Music, Inc., administered by Windswept Pacific Entertainment Co. d/b/a Longitude Music Co. Reprinted by permission of Full Nelson Music, Inc., and songs of Polygram International, Inc.

LIBRARY OF CONGRESS CATALOGING-IN-PUBLICATION DATA
Beard, Jo Ann.
The boys of my youth / Jo Ann Beard. — 1st ed.
p. cm.
ISBN 0-316-08554-5
1. Beard, Jo Ann. 2. United States — Biography. I. Title.
CT275.B5394A3 1998
973 — dc21
[B] 97-29710

10 9 8 7 6 5 4 3

MV-NY

Book design by Julia Sedykh

Published simultaneously in Canada by Little, Brown & Company (Canada) Limited
Printed in the United States of America

for BRAD *and* LINDA

Contents

Acknowledgments

I would like to express my gratitude to the Corporation of Yaddo and the MacDowell Colony, for their generous gift of time, and the Constance Saltonstall Foundation in Ithaca, for much-needed financial support. My sincere appreciation to Lizzie Grossman for her sustained belief in my writing, her sanity, and her charming unwillingness to accept rejection when it came our way.

For their friendship, support, and encouragement, I offer profound thanks to Marilyn Abildskov, Mary Allen, Julene Bair, Charlie Buck, Barbara Camillo, Martha Christiansen, Marian Clark, Tory Dent, Sara DiDonato, Ellen Fagg, Gaile Gallatin, Wesley Gibson, Kathy Harris, Tony Hoagland, Will Jennings, Kathy Kiley, Carl Klaus, Edward Lawler, Jane and Michael O'Melia, Maxine Rodburg, Corbin Sexton, Bob Shacochis, Kathy Siebenmann, Jo Southard, David Stern, Patricia Stevens, Shirley Tarbell, and that beloved girl of my youth, Elizabeth White.

Preface

H*ere's one of my pre-verbal* memories: I'm very little and I'm behind bars, like a baby monkey in a cage. My parents have just put me to bed in a room with bright yellow walls. This is fine with me because in my crib there are various companions — the satin edge of my blue blanket, the chewable plastic circle that hangs down almost to mouth level on a piece of green cord, and a boy doll named Hal with blue eyes and lickable hands and feet made of vinyl. At this point in my life, I love Hal and the satin borders of blankets better than I love any of the humans I know. My mother puts Hal up next to my head as soon as I lie down, which is exactly where I don't want him. I smack him in the face.

"You don't want to hurt *Hal,*" my mother says sadly. "I thought Hal was your *friend.*"

Hal and I have an agreement that he isn't supposed to come up by my pillow; if I want him I'll go down to his end of the

crib. My mother snaps off the light and as she does so the night-light is illuminated, a new thing that I've never seen before. The door closes.

I can see the night-light through the bars of my crib. It is a garish depiction of Mary and Joseph and Jesus, although I don't know that then. Jesus is about my age but he looks mean, and the mom and dad are wearing long coats and no shoes. All three of them are staring at me funny. I start crying without taking my eyes off them.

The door opens and when the light goes on the night-light goes off. I stop crying and sit down by Hal while my mother looks at me. She puts the blanket back over me and leaves. Light off, night-light back on. More crying. This time my father comes in and picks me up, walks me around in a circle, puts me back in the crib with Hal, and leaves. When the light goes off and Jesus comes back on I cry again. This time both of them come in to look at me. My mother is smoking a cigarette.

"Don't ask me," she tells my father.

About three more times and they give up. I am left to wail loudly, which I do for a while, until I happen to turn on my side, looking for the bottle of water they had tried to bribe me with. As soon as I turn over the night-light miraculously disappears. The water is warm, just how I like it, and Hal's face is resting against the soles of my feet. I let go of the bottle and wrap the satin border of the blue blanket around my thumb, put the thumb in my mouth, and close my eyes for the night.

I tried to check out that particular memory with my mother when I grew up. I asked her if she remembered a night when I cried and cried, and couldn't be consoled, and they kept coming in and going back out and nothing they did could help me.

"I don't remember any that *weren't* like that," she said, smoking the same cigarette she'd been smoking for thirty years.

So. Here's a recent memory, from two nights ago. I was riding through upstate New York on a dark blue highway, no particular destination. It was cloudy, the air was springy and cool, the dashboard looked like the control panel of a spaceship. Piano music on the tape deck, a charming guy in the driver's seat. I thought to myself, not for the first time in this life, *Everything is perfect; all those things that I always think are so bad really aren't bad at all.* Then I noticed that out my window the clouds had parted, the clear night sky was suddenly visible, and the moon — a garish yellow disk against a dark wall — seemed to be looking at me funny.

The Boys of My Youth

In the Current

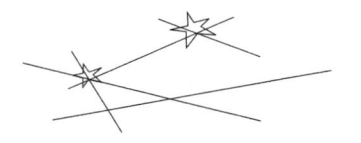

The family vacation. Heat, flies, sand, and dirt. My mother sweeps and complains, my father forever baits hooks and untangles lines. My younger brother has brought along his imaginary friend, Charcoal, and my older sister has brought along a real-life majorette by the name of Nan. My brother continually practices all-star wrestling moves on poor Charcoal. "I got him in a figure-four leg lock!" he will call from the ground, propped up on one elbow, his legs twisted together. My sister and Nan wear leg makeup, white lipstick, and say things about me in French. A river runs in front of our cabin, the color of bourbon, foamy at the banks, full of water moccasins and doomed fish. I am ten. The only thing to do is sit on the dock and read, drink watered-down Pepsi, and squint. No swimming allowed.

One afternoon three teenagers get caught in the current

while I watch. They come sweeping downstream, hollering and gurgling while I stand on the bank, forbidden to step into the water, and stare at them. They are waving their arms.

I am embarrassed because teenagers are yelling at me. Within five seconds men are throwing off their shoes and diving from the dock; my own dad gets hold of one girl and swims her back in. Black hair plastered to her neck, she throws up on the mud about eight times before they carry her back to wherever she came from. One teenager is unconscious when they drag him out and a guy pushes on his chest until a low fountain of water springs up out of his mouth and nose. That kid eventually walks away on his own, but he's crying. The third teenager lands a ways down the bank and comes walking by fifteen minutes later, a grown-up on either side of him and a towel around his waist. His skin looks like Silly Putty.

"Oh man," he says when he sees me. "I saw her go by about ninety miles an hour!" He stops and points at me. I just stand there, embarrassed to be noticed by a teenager. I hope my shorts aren't bagging out again. I put one hand in my pocket and slouch sideways a little. "Man, I thought she was gonna be the last thing I ever seen!" he says, shaking his head.

The girl teenager had had on a swimming suit top with a built-in bra. I cross my arms nonchalantly across my chest and smile at the teenage boy. He keeps walking and talking, the grown-ups supporting him and giving each other looks over the top of his head. His legs are shaking like crazy. "I thought, Man oh man, that skinny little chick is gonna be the last thing *ever*," he exclaims.

I look down. My shorts are bagging out.

Bonanza

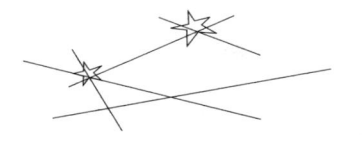

M*y grandmother married a* guy named Ralph, about a year and a half after Pokey, my real grandfather, died of a stroke in the upstairs bedroom of Uncle Rex's house. At Grandma and Ralph's wedding ceremony a man sang opera-style, which took the children by surprise and caused an uproar among the grandchildren, who were barely able to sit still as it was. Afterward, there was white cake with white frosting in the church basement, and bowls of peanuts. My mother and my aunts were quite upset about Grandma marrying Ralph barely a year after their dad had died. They sat in clumps in the church basement, a few here, a few there, and ate their cake while giving each other meaningful looks, shaking their heads ominously. My grandmother, a kind woman, was way above reproach. So, it was all Ralph's fault.

He took her to Florida on a honeymoon, a place where no

one in the family had ever been. There was an ocean there. They walked the beach morning and night, and Grandma brought home shells. She divided them up evenly, put them in cigar boxes, and gave them to each of her thirty-five grandchildren. The cigar boxes were painted flat white and glued to the top were pictures cut from greeting cards: a lamb, a big-eyed kitty, a bunch of flowers. On that trip to Florida, I always imagine my grandmother walking in the foamy tide, picking up dead starfish, while Ralph sat silently in a beach chair, not smiling at anyone.

When we'd drive down to Knoxville for a visit, everyone would be hale and hearty, the food eaten, the iced tea drunk, the new rag rugs admired, and then we'd pile back into the car for the hour ride home. Ralph was always grouchy and harsh, with big fingers that he pointed at everyone while he talked. As soon as we pulled out of the driveway, my mother would look at my father and say, "That old sonuvabitch, I'd like to *kill* him."

I went to visit Grandma and Ralph for a week right after having learned how to whistle. I whistled at all times, with dedication and complete concentration. When I was asked a question I whistled the answer, I whistled along with people as they talked, I whistled while I worked, I whistled while I played. Eventually they made a rule that whistling was forbidden in their house. I felt bereft and didn't know what to do with my lips if I couldn't whistle. I would blow gently, without making a sound, while helping my grandmother get dinner. She must have felt sorry for me because she said once, kindly, "Honey, you *can* whistle when you're outside." But that was no comfort to me. Part of the joy of whistling was knowing that it was always available, you carried the equipment right on your own face. If I couldn't whistle *at all times*, then I didn't care to whistle outdoors. I couldn't wait to get home, where no one could make me do anything.

Grandma and Ralph both worked, so when I went to visit I had hours and hours each day to occupy myself. Grandma took care of senior citizens, some of them younger than she was, shut-ins and disabled folk who needed company and assistance with some of the necessities — cooking, talking. She was a volunteer. Ralph was a butcher and a sheepshearer. He drove a panel truck out to people's farms and killed their cattle for them. Eyes like pebbles, tanned face pulled into a knotty smile, bald head glinting in the sun, a foot-long knife blade aimed at unsuspecting furred throats. Afterward he would use a garden hose to spray out the back of his truck. White walls and floor, pools and spatters of brilliant red. I glimpsed it once, without knowing what I was looking at. I remember thinking, "That looks like *blood*." It never occurred to me it *was* blood. The sheep, after being sheared, stood stunned, in masses, their sides heaving, long cuts and gashes on their pink, exposed skin. The wool stank like crazy and lay in mounds everywhere, gray and filthy. I was taken along on his sprees, sent off to play with complete strangers, farm children, while he went to work with his long knife, his buzzing clippers. I was known for being sensitive to the plight of farm animals and bunnies killed on the road, but I steadfastly refused to acknowledge what was taking place on those visits. I never figured out what was going on around me, even when it was written on the walls in red.

I went along with Grandma sometimes, too. I saw a lady who slept in a crib, curled like a four-year-old, so tiny. She stared out from the bars at me with blank blue eyes. My grandma helped her husband turn her over. Their living room smelled like pee and something else. We had a covered dish for the husband in our trunk and I carried it in. The old woman had white hair that stuck up in patches on her head. I couldn't get over that she slept in a crib, and I couldn't stop looking at her. My grandma called out to her before we left. "Eva!" she called,

"we brung Walter your noodle ring! But it don't taste nothing like what you made; I didn't have pumpernickel so I used white!" The words of grown-ups rarely made real sense to me. But Eva understood, and smiled faintly at us, her blue eyes staring through the bars.

"Oh, I got her smilin'," my grandma crowed. Walter walked us out to the car and stood while we drove away, a wide man in overalls and a pressed shirt. He waved to us by touching his temple gently with two fingers, and then pointing them at us. I waved back at him that way.

But mostly I stayed behind, at their house, and wandered through the rooms, picking things up and putting them back down. There were unimaginable treasures there, old things that you didn't know the purpose of, beautiful spindly-legged furniture, and things with exotic, lost names. Chifforobes and highboys, antimacassars and lowboys. Every surface of every wall was covered, and nearly every inch of floor space was, too. Only in the middle of each room was a cleared space for living, a more or less empty zone. Jars of buttons, every kind imaginable, homemade ones, bone ones, small pink and white ones ("Them're for a baby's dress," she told me), enormous black ones. They were endlessly fascinating to me, all their colors and textures, the satisfying *churrr* as they poured out of the jar and onto a table. I didn't quite know what to do with them then; they seemed to call out for some special kind of play, something that would lend itself to a pile of buttons. But I could never think of what to do with them next, so I would put them back in the jar, put the jar back on the table or shelf or closet that it had come out of, and wander on to the next thing. A small drawer in a small dresser, long thin tools with carved handles, a whole bunch of them rubber-banded together. "Them're buttonhooks," she told me, "from when you had buttons on your shoes." I didn't know what she was talking about, and set them back in their small drawer, closed it. On almost

every surface there was an antique vase with a bouquet of flowers in it, set in the middle of a starched doily. Beautiful, exotic blooms, all plastic, all covered with a heavy layer of dust. "They throw 'em away, just like they didn't cost money," my grandma would explain.

I spent long days of blistering, stupefying boredom in that house, opening the refrigerator and staring into it forty times in an afternoon. Butter, milk, bowls with clumped food visible through their Saran Wrapped tops. There was stuff to eat to make you go to the bathroom, stuff to drink to make you go to the bathroom, and then several things to make you *stop* going to the bathroom. Nothing sweet whatsoever. She'd make a batch of cookies before I came and put them in the fat-chef cookie jar. I would eat all the cookies on the first morning, and then hunt relentlessly the rest of the week for something sweet. I would remember the cookies — greasy peanut butter ones with peanuts stuck in them, or chocolate chip ones with oatmeal — with a kind of hysterical longing. I couldn't believe I had eaten every one of them the first morning. What could I have been thinking?

I ate sugar cubes from the sugar bowl, one every hour or so. They were actually *too* sugary and each time I ate one I swore I wouldn't do it again. But another hour later would find me creeping sock-footed out to the kitchen, lifting the plastic lid of the sugar bowl, and selecting another.

Sometimes I would jump energetically on the beds, two twin ones that were in the room where I slept. I'd kung fu all the embroidered throw pillows onto the floor, and then jump and jump and jump, saying a Chinese jump-rope chant: "Chicka-chicka China, sitting on a fence, tried to make a dollar outta fifty-nine cents," until I was so out of breath I had to collapse on my back and wait for the rotating fan to turn in my direction.

Oh, the rotating fan.

The lovely rotating fan, something that moved of its own accord in the dead house during the long afternoons. I would set the rotating fan on a footstool in the long, narrow bedroom. My job was to feed Kleenexes into it and then pick up the shredded pieces. By the end of one of those stultifying afternoons, I'd have an empty Kleenex box and a whole wastebasket full of soft pink confetti. Nobody ever questioned where the Kleenexes went when I was visiting, but once my grandma gave me another white painted cigar box that was full of handkerchiefs, neatly pressed and folded. Every kind imaginable: flowered, embroidered, ones with Scottie terriers, ones with lace edges, the whole bit.

They ate terrible food, things mixed together that weren't supposed to be. Mashed potatoes with corn, pieces of white bread with gravy poured on top, peas and carrots in the same bowl. Ralph would have a dish towel tucked into his collar and hold a fork and spoon in his enormous paws. He'd get something on the spoon, a great gob of potatoes, say, and then open his mouth as wide as it would go, like a bird in a nest getting fed a chewed worm. He had deep creases on either side of his mouth, and as he chewed, gravy would run down the gullies in rivulets, land on the dish towel, and stay there. It was an amazing and horrifying thing to watch. I had a sensitive stomach and sometimes, sitting across from him — eyes carefully averted, fastened on the Aunt Jemima potholder hanging on a hook or on a pan lid with a screw and a block of wood jimmied up for a handle — just hearing him eat could make me gag. I was in the habit of rising from the table and walking around the kitchen every few minutes, breathing through my nose, deeply, to keep from gagging. Then I'd sit back down, pick up two peas with my spoon, and put them in my mouth. This is what my grandma said to me once: "Eat your chicken, why don't you? And don't take the skin off, that's what's good."

They were trying to make me eat something with *skin* on it. At my own house, everyone knew enough not to say *skin* in relation to food.

My grandma, when she was cooking dinner, would send me down to the fruit cellar for jars of home-canned stuff. Then when I'd bring them up she'd open the jars and smell the contents thoughtfully; sometimes she'd have me take the jar outside to where Ralph was and have him smell it. He always said the same things: "There ain't nothing wrong with *that*, tell her" or he'd bawl toward the house as I was walking back in, "Maw, that'll be okay if you cook it longer!"

Once she served me red raspberries that she'd put up; poured them in a plastic bowl and put cream on them. As I started to dig in I noticed that there were some black things floating around. "Grandma, there's bugs in this," I said. She came over and looked into my bowl, head tipped back to see out of the bottoms of her glasses. "Them're dead," she told me. "Just push 'em to the side; the berries is okay." And I did, and the berries *were* okay.

At night we watched one show on TV and then had to go to bed, when it was still a little bit light out. They'd go in their room and my grandma would come out with her nightgown on and her teeth out to tuck me in. I'd be lying stiff as a plank under the bedspread and here she'd come, without her regular clothes on, with her arms and feet exposed, her mouth folded in on itself. "G'night, honey-Jo," she would lisp, pat me on the shoulder, and turn out the light. And there I'd be, while they snored up one side and down the other in the room across the hall. I'd tiptoe all over the bedroom, gazing for a while out the window, watching the sky turn black, the stars come out. I'd quietly open all the drawers of all the dressers in the room, take out things, examine them, put them back. I didn't dare jump on the bed, although sometimes I said "Chicka-chicka China"

to myself out of boredom. I tried counting sheep like on the cartoons, but I couldn't concentrate, couldn't for the life of me imagine what sheep looked like. I knew but I didn't know, just as I couldn't conjure up the faces of my long-lost parents and siblings. I was wide-awake, staring out at the vast Milky Way while the grown-ups snored on and on and the moon rose and sank.

The strange thing was, I always asked to go there. I don't remember them ever inviting me, or my parents suggesting it. It was me. From far away the idea of their house was magical to me, all those nooks, all those crannies, all those things to play with — the button jars, the lowboy with a little drawer full of marbles, the flower arrangements, the rotating fan. So, every July I got dropped off on a Sunday and picked up the following Sunday. By Tuesday I'd be counting the hours, sitting on the backyard glider, staring at the black lawn jockey and the flagstone path that took you to the garden, the broken bird bath with a pool of rusty, skanky water in it. Their yard had as much stuff in it as their house did, only the yard stuff was filthy, full of dirt and rainwater.

The last time I went there my parents drove off on a Sunday afternoon as I stood on the gravel sidewalk and waved, already regretting my visit. My grandma fed us, dinner was the usual ordeal of gravy rivulets and tainted food, and then they turned *Bonanza* on. I lay on the living room floor, in the cleared-out space in the center; on either end of the couch were Grandma and Ralph. She was knitting an afghan and he was sharpening a stack of scissors.

We were watching my favorite show. The dad, Ben, had a buckskin, Hoss had a black horse, and Little Joe had a pinto pony. They had Hop Sing for a servant, in place of a mom. Back home my little brother would be humming to himself through the whole show, "Umbuddy-umbuddy-umbuddy-ummm Bo-

nanza," and everyone would be telling him to shut up. My mom would be smoking her cigarettes and drinking beer out of a bottle, my dad would have his socks off and be stretching his bare toes, drinking his beer out of a glass. My sister would be trying to do homework at the dining room table.

Here I was with Grandma and Ralph, staying up one hour later than I would the rest of the century-long week. Little Joe falls in love with a schoolteacher who comes past the Ponderosa in a buggy. He kisses her a long one, it stretches out forever in the silence of the living room. There isn't a sound from behind me, on the couch. No one is moving while the kiss is going on. It's horrible. I look around the room, at the pictures that cover every inch of wall space, my aunts and uncles and their families, framed sayings from the olden days, plaques with jokes about outhouses, a pair of flying ceramic ducks with orange beaks and feet, and on and on. Too much to look at. The pecking-hen salt and pepper shakers, the donkey with a dead plant coming out of his back, the stacks of old magazines under tables and on the seats of chairs. Underneath me are three scatter rugs, converging their corners in a lump under my back. Rag rugs, one of them made from bread wrappers. Hoss Cartwright saves the schoolteacher when her horse shies and now she's in love with him. Little Joe tries to punch Hoss out. Behind me my grandmother's knitting needles click together in a sad and empty way, Ralph's breathing is audible over the scratch of scissor blades on stone. In the dim circle of light that I lay in, my head cushioned on an Arkansas Razorback pillow, I feel completely separate from them because of the simple fact that in seven days I will be rescued, removed from this terrible lonely place and put back in the noisy house I came from.

It occurs to me that Grandma and Ralph have nothing, they don't even enjoy *Bonanza* all that much, they just turned it on because my mom told them to let me watch it. There can't be

anything for them to enjoy, with their long empty days, full of curled-up old ladies and dirty sheep. They don't even drink pop.

I am crying on the floor, the tears go sideways and land coldly in my ears or on the velveteen pillow. I can't bear, suddenly, the way the television sends out its sad blue light, making the edges of the room seem darker. A coffee can covered with contact paper holds red, white, and blue Fourth of July flowers, taken from a dead person. I wish suddenly that my grandma was dead, so she wouldn't have to knit that afghan anymore. The rest of the year, while I'm gone back home and am playing with my friends, this is where my grandma is, her needles going, her teeth in the bathroom in a plastic bowl. My ears are swimming pools, and I feel trapped suddenly inside the small circle of light in the center of the room. I'm tiny Eva, watching Little Joe Cartwright through the bars of my crib, I'm a monkey, strapped into a space capsule and flung far out into the galaxy, weightless, hurtling along upside down through the Milky Way. Alone, alone, and alone. Against my will, I sob out loud. I turn over and weep into the Arkansas pillow, wrecking the velveteen. Suddenly my grandma's hand is on my hair, the knitting needles have been set down.

There is telephone talk, and muffled comments from Grandma to Ralph, from Ralph to the person on the other end of the phone. My nose is pressed against the pillow and I'm still crying, or trying to. I suddenly want to hear what's going on but I don't have the nerve to sit up. My clothes are gathered, the television is shut off, I am walked outside and put in the back seat of their great big yellow car. In the back window, there's a dog with a bobbing head that I usually like to mess around with when I'm riding in the car. I don't even bother to look at it; I just stare out the back window at the night sky.

After about a half hour of driving we pull over and sit at the

side of the road. I'm no longer weightless, but unbearably heavy, and tired. My dad pulls up with a crunch of gravel, words are exchanged through open windows, quiet chuckles, I am placed in the front seat between my parents. We pull away, and as we head toward home, the galaxy recedes, the stars move back into position, and the sky stretches out overhead, black and familiar.

They've decided not to hassle me about this. "What happened, honey?" my mom asks once, gently.

"*Bonanza* made me sad," I reply.

Cousins

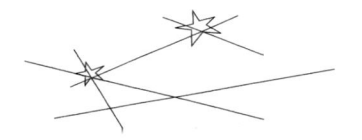

H*ere is a scene. Two sisters are* fishing together in a flat-bottomed boat on an olive green lake. They sit slumped like men, facing in opposite directions, drinking coffee out of a metal-sided thermos, smoking intently. Without their lipstick they look strangely weary, and passive, like pale replicas of their real selves. They both have a touch of morning sickness but neither is admitting it. Instead, they watch their bobbers and argue about worms versus minnows.

My cousin and I are floating in separate, saline oceans. I'm the size of a cocktail shrimp and she's the size of a man's thumb. My mother is the one on the left, wearing baggy gabardine trousers and a man's shirt. My cousin's mother is wearing blue jeans, cuffed at the bottom, and a cotton blouse printed with wild cowboys roping steers. Their voices carry, as usual, but at this point we can't hear them.

It is five A.M. A duck stands up, shakes out its feathers, and peers above the still grass at the edge of the water. The skin of the lake twitches suddenly and a fish springs loose into the air, drops back down with a flat splash. Ripples move across the surface like radio waves. The sun hoists itself up and gets busy, laying a sparkling rug across the water, burning the beads of dew off the reeds, baking the tops of our mothers' heads. One puts on sunglasses and the other a plaid fishing cap with a wide brim.

In the cold dark underwater, a long fish with a tattered tail discovers something interesting. He circles once and then has his breakfast before becoming theirs. As he breaks from the water to the air he twists hard, sending out a cold spray, sparks of green light. My aunt reels him in, triumphant, and grins at her sister, big teeth in a friendly mouth.

"Why you dirty rotten so-and-so," my mother says admiringly.

It is nine o'clock on Saturday night, the sky is black and glittering with pinholes, old trees are bent down over the highway. In the dark field behind, the corn gathers its strength, grows an inch in the silence, then stops to rest. Next to the highway, screened in vegetation, a deer with muscular ears and glamorous eyes stands waiting to spring out from the wings into the next moving spotlight. The asphalt sighs in anticipation.

The car is a late-model Firebird, black on black with a T-roof and a tape deck that pelts out anguish, Fleetwood Mac. My cousin looks just like me except she has coarse hair and the jawline of an angel. She's driving and I'm shotgun, talking to her profile. The story I'm recounting to her is full of what I said back to people when they said things to me. She can sing and

listen at the same time, so she does that, nodding and grimacing when necessary.

She interrupts me once. "What's my hair doing?"

"Laying down. I'll tell you if it tries anything." Her hair is short but so dense it has a tendency to stay wherever the wind pushes it. When she wakes up in the morning her head is like a landscape, with cliffs and valleys, spectacular pinnacles.

"Okay, go ahead," she says. I finish my story before my favorite song comes on so I can devote myself to it.

We sing along to a tune about a woman who rings like a bell through the night. Neither of us knows what that means, but we're in favor of it. We want to ring like bells, we want our hair to act right, we want to go out with guys who wear boots with turned-up toes and worn-down heels. We're out in the country, on my cousin's turf. My car is stalled in the city somewhere on four low tires, a blue-and-rust Volkswagen with the door coat-hangered shut. Her car is this streamlined, dark-eyed Firebird with its back end hiked up like a skirt. We are hurtling through the night, as they say, on our way to a bar where the guys own speedboats, snowmobiles, whatever else is current. I sing full-throttle: *You can take me to paradise, but then again you can be cold as ice; I'm over my head, but it sure feels nice.* I turn the rearview mirror around, check to see what's happening with the face.

Nothing good. But there you have it. It's yours at least, and your hair isn't liable to thrust itself upward into stray pointing fingers. It doesn't sound like corn husks when you brush it.

My cousin, beautiful in the dashboard light, glances over at me. She has a first name but I've always called her Wendell. She pushes it up to eighty and the song ends, a less wonderful one comes on. We're coming to the spot on the highway where the giant trees dangle their wrists over the ground. In the crotch of an elm, during daylight hours, a gnarled car is visible, wedged among the branches.

Up ahead, the cornfields are dark and rustling. The deer shifts nervously behind the curtain of weeds, waiting for its cue. The car in the tree's crotch is a warning to fast drivers, careening kids. Hidden beneath the driver's seat, way up in the branches, is a silver pocketwatch with a broken face. It had been someone's great-grandfather's, handed down and handed down, until it reached the boy who drove his car into the side of a tree. Below the drifting branches, the ground is black and loamy, moving with bugs. In the silence, stalks of corn stretch their thin, thready feet and gather in the moisture. The pocketwatch is stopped at precisely 11:47, as was the boy. Fleetwood Mac rolls around the bend and the deer springs full-blown out of the brocade trees. In the white pool of headlights, in front of a swerving audience, it does a short, stark, modern dance, and exits to the right. We recover and slow it down, shaking.

"He could have wrecked my whole front end," Wendell says. This is the farm-kid mentality. Her idea of a gorgeous deer is one that hangs upside down on the wall of the shed, a rib cage, a pair of antlers, a gamy hunk of dinner. She feels the same way about cows and pigs.

We're in the sticks. Way out here things are measured in shitloads, and every third guy you meet is named Junior. I've decided I don't even like this bar we're going to, that howling three-man band and the bathroom with no stalls, just stools. Now I'm slumped and surly, an old pose for me. That deer had legs like canes, feet like Dixie cups.

Wendell pats my knee, grinning. "Settle down," she says. "It didn't *hit* us. We're safe." She likes excitement as long as her car doesn't get hurt. I light a cigarette, begin dirtying up her ashtray, and mess with the tape until our favorite song comes on again. We're back up to eighty on the narrow highway, daring the ignorant to take a step onto the asphalt. This is Illinois, a land of lumbering raccoons, snake-tailed possums, and flat-

out running bunnies, all trying to cross the road. The interior of the car smells like leather and evergreen trees, the moon peers through the roof, and Wendell drives with one finger.

"Hey, how's my hair?" she asks suddenly. Her eyes are clear brown, her cheekbones are high and delicate, brushed with pink, her lips aren't too big or too little. She's wearing my shirt. A clump of hair has pushed itself forward in the excitement. It looks like a small, startled hand rising from the back of her head.

I make an okay sign, thumb and forefinger. The music is deafening.

Back in the cluster of trees, the deer moves into position again and the willows run their fingers along the ground. The corn whispers encouragement to itself. In the bar up ahead waitresses slam sloe-gin fizzes down on wet tables and men point pool cues at each other in the early stages of drunkenness. The singer in the three-man band whispers *test* into the microphone and rolls his eyes at the feedback. The sound guy jumps up from a table full of ladies and heads over to turn knobs.

We crunch over the parking lot gravel and wait for our song to finish. *I'm over my head, but it sure feels nice.* The bar is low and windowless, with patched siding and a kicked-in door; the lot is full of muscle cars and pickups. A man and a woman burst through the door and stand negotiating who will drive. He's got the keys but she looks fiercer. In the blinking neon our faces are malarial and buttery. As the song winds down, the drama in front of us ends. He throws the keys at her as hard as he can but she jumps nimbly out of the way and picks them up with a handful of gravel, begins pelting his back as he weaves into the darkness.

Wendell turns to me with a grin, a question on her lips. Before she can ask I reach over and press her excited hair back down.

Their house has a face on it, two windows with the shades half down, a brown slot of a door, and a glaring mouthful of railing with a few pickets missing. Pink geraniums grow like earrings on either side of the porch. It's August and the grass is golden and spiky against our ankles, the geraniums smell like dust. A row of hollyhocks stands out by the road, the flowers are upside-down ladies, red, maroon, and dried-up brown. An exploded raccoon is abuzz over on the far side of the highway and crows are dropping down from time to time to sort among the pieces. On either side of the house, fields fall away, rolling and baking in the heat.

The sisters are sitting on the stoop shelling peas, talking overtop of each other. My mother says mayonnaise goes bad in two hours in the hot sun and my aunt says bullshit. They've just driven out to the fields and left the lunches for the hired men. They argue energetically about this, until the rooster walks up and my aunt carries her bowl in the house to finish the discussion through the screen door. She and the rooster hate each other.

"He thinks you're a chicken," my mother explains. "You have to show him you won't put up with it." She picks up a stick, threatens the rooster with it, and he backs off, pretends to peck the yard. My aunt comes back out.

The front of her head is in curlers, the brush kind that hurt, and she keeps testing her hair to see if it's done. She has on a smock with big pockets and pedal pushers. Her feet are bare, one reason why the rooster is scaring her so much. My mother doesn't wear curlers because her hair is short but she has two clips crisscrossed on either side of her head, making spit curls in front of her ears. Every time a car drives by she reaches up automatically, ready to yank them out. She has on Bermuda

shorts and a wide-bottomed plaid blouse with a bow at the neck. They are both pregnant again.

We're going to be in a parade at four o'clock, Wendell and I, riding bikes without training wheels, our dolls in the baskets. We asked to have the training wheels put back on for the parade but they said no. Our older sisters are upstairs somewhere, dumping perfume on one another and trying on bracelets. They'll be in the parade, too, walking behind us and throwing their batons in the air, trying to drop them on our heads.

Wendell jumps at the rooster suddenly and he rushes us, we go off screaming in different directions while he stands there furious, shifting from one scaly foot to another, slim and tall with greasy black feathers and a yellow ruff like a collie. He can make the dirty feathers around his neck stand up and fall back down whenever he gets mad, just like flexing a muscle. Even his wives give him a wide berth, rolling their seedy eyes and murmuring. They get no rest. I haven't yet connected the chickens walking around out here with what we had for lunch, chopped up and mixed with mayonnaise.

The mothers give up and go in the house to smoke cigarettes at the kitchen table and yell at us through the windows. Wendell and I work on decorating our bikes and complaining about no training wheels.

"What about if there's a *corner?*" I say.

"I know," says Wendell. "Or if there's *dog* poop?" I don't know exactly how this relates but I shudder anyway. We shake our heads and try twisting the crepe paper into the spokes the way our mothers showed us but it doesn't work. We end up with gnarled messes and flounce into the house to discipline our dolls.

Here is the parade. Boys in cowboy getups with cap guns and rubber spurs, hats that hang from shoestrings around their necks. The girls squint against the sun and press their stiff dresses down. This is the year of the can-can slip so we all have

on good underpants without holes. Some kids have their ponies there, ornery things with rolling eyes and bared teeth, all decorated up. Two older boys with painted-on mustaches beat wildly on drums until they are stopped. Mothers spit on Kleenexes and go at the boys' faces while fathers stand around comparing what their watches say to what the sun is doing.

Two little girls wear matching dresses made from a big linen tablecloth, a white background with blue and red fruit clusters. One has a bushy stand of hair and the other a smooth pixie. Both have large bows, one crunched into the mass and the other practically taped on. The scalloped collars on their dresses are made from the border of the tablecloth, bright red with tiny blue grapes, little green stems. There are sashes tied in perfect bows, and pop-bead bracelets. Our shoes don't match.

The dolls rode over to the parade in the trunk of the car so we wouldn't wreck their outfits. They have the ability to drink water and pee it back out but they're dry now, our mothers put a stop to that. They have on dresses to match ours, with tiny scalloped collars and ribbon sashes. We set them carefully in our bike baskets with their skirts in full view. Mine's hair is messed up on one side where I put hairspray on it once. Wendell's has a chewed-up hand and nobody knows how it got that way. We stand next to our crepe-papered bikes in the sunlight, waiting for them to tell us what to do.

Our sisters have been forbidden to throw their batons until the parade starts and so they twirl them around and pretend to hurl them up in the air, give a little hop, and pretend to catch them again. They are wearing perfume and fingernail polish with their cowboy boots and shorts. They don't like us very much but we don't care.

My mother tells me to stand up straight and Wendell's mother tells her to push her hair back down. The baton twirlers get a last minute talking-to with threats. The parade

moves out ragged and wobbly, someone immediately starts crying, a pony wanders out of line and looks for some grass to chew. The main street is crowded with bystanders and parked automobiles. It is never clear what this parade is for, except to dress the children up and show them off, get the men to come in from the fields for a while.

As the parade pulls itself slowly down the street, the mothers stand with wry, proud faces and folded arms while fathers stand smoking, lifting the one-finger farmer's salute as their sons go by. Wendell and I steer carefully and watch our mothers as they move along the sidewalk, following. Tall, lanky frames and watermelon stomachs, the gray eyes and beautiful hands of the Patterson side of the family. Our dolls are behaving perfectly, staring straight ahead, slumped forward in their baskets. My sash has come untied and Wendell's underpants are showing. We don't care, they won't bother fixing us now; we're in the parade and they have to stay on the sidewalk.

The street is brilliant in the sun, and the children move in slow motion, dresses, cowboy hats, tap shoes, the long yellow teeth of the mean ponies. At the count of four, one of our sisters loses control, throws her baton high in the air and stops, one hand out to catch it when it comes back down.

For a long, gleaming moment it hangs there, a silver hyphen against the hot sky. Over the hectic heads of the children and the smooth blue-and-white blur of crepe-papered spokes and handlebar streamers, above the squinting smiles and upturned eyes, a silver baton rises miraculously, lingers for a moment against the sun, and then drops back down, into the waiting hand.

Back at the bar, someone has hold of me and I'm on the dance floor. Wendell's standing just inside the door. I'm going back-

ward swiftly, in a fast two-step, there's an arm slung across my shoulder. It's good old Ted, trying to make a girl feel welcome. The bar is as dark as a pocket and my eyes haven't adjusted yet. Ted runs me into a couple of people and I tell him his arm weighs a ton. He grins but doesn't move it. He has long legs and a drinking problem. Two ex-wives follow him everywhere, stirring up trouble.

When the song finally ends, I untangle from Ted and look for Wendell. She's got us a table back by the wall, beneath the bored head of a deer. As I pass the bar several guys in turn swivel their stools around and catch me. Blue-jeaned legs are parted, I'm pulled in, pressed against a chest, clamped. Hello, hello. I bum a cigarette from the first one and blow smoke in the face of the second when his hand crawls like a bull snake up the back of my shirt. Even way out here I'm known for being not that easy to get along with.

Wendell takes her feet off my chair and pushes a rum and Pepsi my way. She tries to tell me something over the din.

"What?" I holler back and turn my ear to her.

"I *said*, your *buddy*'s here," she yells into my hair. I pull back and look at her. She jerks a thumb upward, to the passive, suspended face of the deer. Someone has stuck a cigarette butt in one of its nostrils. I show her my middle finger and she sits back again, satisfied. Side by side at the spindly table, we drink our drinks for a while and watch the dancers go around.

Ida's out there, going to town, seventy-five if she's a day, with dyed black hair and tall, permanently arched eyebrows. From nine to midnight, even when it's just the jukebox, she takes herself around the dance floor — fox-trot, swing shuffle, two-step. She comes here every Saturday night to dance by herself while her grandson drinks Mountain Dew and plays pool in the back room. Her tennis shoes look like they're disconnected from the rest of her body. Every once in a while, she

presses one hand against her waist and closes her eyes for an instant, keeping time with her shoulders, all part of some interior dancing-drama, some memory of Pete and her, before they got old, before she up and got widowed. Apparently, they were quite a deal on the dance floor. Nobody ever bumps into her out there, even the drunkest of the drunk make a space for those shoes and that head of hair. She's dancing with a memory, putting all the rest of us to shame.

Here comes our darling Nick. Everyone's in love with him, blond hair in a ponytail and wire-rims, drives a muddy jeep. Too bad he's related to us. He sets us up with two more drinks, takes a joint out of his shirt pocket, puts it in my cigarette pack, and lays a big kiss on Wendell, flat on the lips. Right as he leaves, he zooms in on me unexpectedly. I give him one hand to shake and put the other one over my mouth. Wendell takes a drink and leans over.

"Gross," she shouts into my ear. I nod. Cousin cooties.

"I'm telling Aunt Bernie," I shout back. Aunt Bernie is his mom.

We've been sitting too long. Wendell carries her drink, I light a cigarette, and we move out into the revelers, and lose each other. The rum is a warm, dark curtain in my chest. I suddenly look better than I have in weeks, I can feel geraniums blooming in my cheeks, my mouth is genuinely smiling for once, my hair, fresh from the ironing board, falls like a smooth plank down my back. It's Saturday night and I'm three rum and Pepsis to the wind. I love this bar, the floor is a velvet trampoline, a mirrored ball revolves above the dance floor, stars move across faces and hands, everyone encountered is a close personal friend. I'm in line for the bathroom, chatting with strangers.

"I like your shirt." This from the woman behind me, she may be trying to negotiate her way up the line.

"Thanks," I tell her. She's pretty. "I like yours, too."

"Your cousin's really drunk," she says, rolling her eyes. I guess she knows me. She means Nick, not Wendell. Women are always striking up conversations about Nick.

"I know" is what I tell her. I smile when I say it and shrug, trying to indicate that she can come to family dinners with Nick as far as I'm concerned. We lapse back into silence until the door bursts open and three women come out, reeking of reefer and perfume.

I look at the woman who struck up the conversation with me. We raise our eyebrows.

"Nice perfume," she says, wrinkling her nose.

"Nice reefer," I say. I let her come in while I go and she checks her makeup and examines her teeth in the mirror. I wait for her, too, bending over at the waist, shaking the hair out, and then flipping it back. It makes it fluffier for a few minutes, before it settles back into the plank again. The bending and flipping sends the room careening for a moment, I'm in a centrifugal tube, then it halts. She wants to know who Nick's going out with.

"His dog, I think," I tell her. I'm politely not noticing her peeing. "He's got the nicest golden retriever you ever saw." I love that dog; it refuses to hunt, just walks along and stirs up ducks and pheasants, watches with surprise when they go flapping off. "That's one thing about Nick. His dog's nice." I don't think Nick ever shoots anything anyway, he just looks good in the boots and the vest.

Actually, I think Cousin Nick's going out with everyone, but I don't tell her that. She looks hopeful and sparkly and she's not nearly as drunk as me. I give her a swimmy smile on the way out and we part company forever.

The band rolls into a slow one, with a creaky metallic guitar hook and a lone warbling voice. Someone asks me to dance and

we stroll around the floor, amid the stars and the elbows. I close my eyes for a moment and it's night inside my head, there are strange arms moving me around, this way and that, feet bumping into mine. The steel guitar comes overtop of it all, climbing and dropping, locating everyone's sadness and yanking on it. In the shuffling crowd the dark curtain of rum parts for an instant, and reveals nothing. I open my eyes and look up at my partner. He's leading away, a grinning stranger, his hand strolls down and finds my back pocket, warms itself. Christ Almighty.

Ida swims through, and past, eyes blank as nickels, disembodied feet, arms like floating strings. One song ends and a new one starts up, I shake my head at my partner and he backs off with a sullen shrug. Apparently he likes this song because he begins fast-dancing by himself, looking hopefully around at the other dancers, trying to rope a stray.

This is Wendell's favorite song, *She's a good-hearted wo-man, in love with a two-timing man*. Here she is, ready to dance. I move with her back into the lumbering crowd on the dance floor, and we carve out a little spot in front of the band. *She loves him in spite of his wicked ways she don't understand*. The bar has gone friendly again while I wasn't looking, the faces of the other dancers are pink with exertion and alcohol, Nick's dancing with the bathroom girl, Ted's twirling an ex-wife, the singer in the band knocks the spit out of his harmonica and attaches it to his neck again. Look at Wendell's face. She's twenty-one and single; her hair has a story to tell. In the small sticky space in front of the band, we twirl a few times, knuckles and lifted elbows, under and over, until I get stomped on. We're singing now, recklessly, it's almost closing time and us girls are getting prettier by the moment. *Through teardrops and laughter we pass through this world hand in hand*. Of course, both Wendell and I would like to be good-hearted women but we're from the Patterson clan, and just don't have the temperament for it.

The sisters are making deviled eggs. They have on dark blue dresses with aprons and are walking around in nyloned feet. No one can find the red stuff that gets sprinkled on top of the eggs. They're tearing the cupboards apart right now, swearing to each other and shaking their heads. We all know enough to stay out of the kitchen.

We're at my grandma's house in our best dresses with towels pinned to the collars. Our older sisters are walking around with theatrical, mournful faces, bossing us like crazy, in loud disgusted whispers. They have their pockets loaded with Kleenex in preparation for making a scene. We're all going to our grandfather's funeral in fifteen minutes, as soon as the paprika gets found.

Wendell and I get to go only because we promised to act decent. No more running and sliding on the funeral-home rug. Someone has *died*, and there's a time and a place for everything. We'll both get spanked in front of everyone and put in chairs if we're not careful. And if we can't keep our gum in our mouths then we don't need it: both pieces are deposited in a held-out Kleenex on the ride over. Wendell and I are in disgrace from our behavior last night at the visitation.

"It wasn't our fault he moved," Wendell had explained, right before being swatted in the funeral-home foyer. Our grandfather had looked like a big, dead doll in a satin doll bed. We couldn't stop staring, and then suddenly, simultaneously, got spooked and ran out of the room, squealing and holding on to each other. We stayed in the foyer for the rest of the night, greeting people and taking turns sliding the rug across the glossy floor. We were a mess by the end of the evening.

Our dads have to sit in a special row of men. They're going to carry the casket to the graveyard. We file past them without looking, and the music gets louder. The casket sits like an open

suitcase up front. After we sit down in our wooden folding chairs all we can see is a nose and some glasses. That's our grandpa up there, he won't be hollering at us ever again for chewing on the collars of our dresses or for throwing hangers out the upstairs window. He won't be calling us giggleboxes anymore. He doesn't even know we're all sitting here, listening to the music and the whispers. He is in our hearts now, which makes us feel uncomfortable. Wendell and I were separated as a precautionary measure; I can just see the tips of her black shoes. They have bows on them and mine have buckles. She is swinging hers a little bit so I start to swing mine a little bit too. This is how you get into trouble, so I quit after a minute and so does she.

Pretty soon the music stops and my mother starts crying into her Kleenex. My aunt's chin turns into a walnut, and then she's crying too. Their dad is dead. Wendell puts her shoe on the back of the chair in front of her and slides it slowly down until it's resting on the floor again. I do the same thing. We're not being ornery, though. A lady starts singing a song and you can hear her breath. I can see only one inch of her face because she's standing in front of the dads. It's a song from Sunday school but she's singing it slower than we do and she's not making the hand motions. I do the hand motions myself, very small, barely moving, while she sings.

Wendell's mom leans over and tells me something. She wants me to sit on her lap. She has a nickname for me that nobody else calls me. She calls me Jody and everyone else calls me Jo. She's not crying anymore, and her arms are holding me on her lap, against her good blue dress. It's too tight in the armpits but you can't tell from looking. My mom's got Wendell.

After a while everyone starts crying, except Uncle Evan, my grandma's brother who always spits into a coffee cup and leaves it on the table for someone else to clean up. My aunt rests her chin on my head and rearranges her Kleenex so there's a

dry spot. I sit very still while the preacher talks and the mothers cry, not moving an inch, even though my arms don't have anywhere to go. Wendell keeps moving around but I don't. Actually, I don't feel very good, my stomach hurts. I'm too big to sit on a lap, my legs are stiff, and now my heart has a grandpa in it.

The fairgrounds are huge and hot, an expanse of baking bodies and an empty stage. There are guys monkeying around on the lighting scaffold, high in the air. Mostly they're fat, stoned, and intent on their tasks, but Wendell's spied one that might be okay. Ponytailed and lean, he has his T-shirt off and stuck in the waistband of his jeans. I can't look at him because he's too high up, hanging off of things that don't look reliable. Wendell trains her binoculars on him, focuses, and then sets them down. "Yuck," she reports.

We will see God this afternoon — this is an Eric Clapton concert. We're sitting on one of our grandmother's worn quilts, spread out on the ground twenty feet from the stage. "Hey, look." I show Wendell a scrap of fabric. It's blue-and-red plaid with dark green lines running through. She and I used to have short-sleeved shirts with embroidered pockets made out of that material. On the ride over here we each took a small blue pill, a mild hallucinogen, and now Wendell has to put her face about an inch away from the quilt in order to get a sense of the scrap I'm talking about.

"It used to be seersucker," she says sadly. "And now it isn't." We think that over for a few minutes, how things change, how nothing can be counted on, and then Wendell remembers something. "My shirt had a pony on the pocket and yours had a *schnauzer*." She snickers.

For some reason that irritates me no end. I hadn't thought of that schnauzer in years, and she has to bring it up today.

Thanks a whole hell of a lot. It did used to be seersucker, too, which is very strange, because now it's not. What could have happened to it? How can something go from being puckered to being unpuckered? You could see if it was the other way around, but this just doesn't make sense. My halter top keeps feeling like it's coming undone.

We put the cooler over the unsucked seersucker so we can quit thinking about it. Wendell stretches out on her back and stares at the sky. I stretch out on my stomach and stare at some grass. We are boiling hot but we don't know it, my hair is stuck to my back and Wendell's is standing straight up in a beautiful manner.

"Your hair is standing straight up in a beautiful manner," I tell her. She nods peacefully. She holds her arms up in the air and makes a *c* with each hand.

"I'm cupping clouds," she says. I try to pay closer attention to my grass, which is pretty short and worn down. It looks like it's been grazed. I read somewhere once that hysterical fans used to eat the grass where the Beatles had walked.

"Do you think Eric Clapton walked on this grass?" I ask Wendell. She looks over at me and considers. She thinks for so long that I forget the question and have to remember it again.

"No," she says finally. I feel relieved.

"Well then, I'm not eating it," I tell her flatly.

"Okay," she replies. I wish she had said "Okey-dokey" but she didn't. She said "Okay," which has an entirely different meaning.

I sit up and my halter top sags alarmingly. All I can do is hold it in place. There's nothing else to be done, I wouldn't have any idea how to retie it. Wendell is curled up in a ball next to me with her eyes shut.

"My top is falling off," I tell her. She doesn't open her eyes. I can feel sweat running down my back like ball bearings. Wendell groans.

"The clouds are cupping *me* now," she says. "Get them off." She's still got her eyes shut, making a whimpering sound. I don't know exactly what to do because I can't see any clouds on her and my shirt is falling off. I have to think for a moment. If I had just taken one bite of grass this wouldn't have happened.

A guy on the blanket next to us tries to hand me a joint. I can't take it because I'm holding my chest. He looks at me, looks at Wendell balled up on the ground, and nods knowingly. "Bummer," he proclaims.

I can't stand to have Eric Clapton see me like this. I let go of my shirt for one second and wave my arms over Wendell. My halter top miraculously stays in place. In fact, it suddenly feels too tight. "I just got the clouds off you," I inform her. She opens one eye, then the other, and sits up.

"You look cute," she tells me. She's turning pink from the afternoon sun and her hair is hectic and alive. We open beers from our cooler and start having fun.

By the time old Eric comes out, we've completely forgotten about him, so it's a pleasant surprise. We climb up on our cooler and dance around, waving our arms in the air. We're so close to the stage he is almost life-size. This is amazing. We dance and mouth the words while Eric sings tender love songs about George Harrison's wife and plays his guitar in a godlike manner.

The sky has turned navy blue. Eric stands in a spotlight on the stage. I pick him up once, like a pencil, and write my name in the air, then put him back down so he can play his guitar again. My halter top stays stationary while I dance around inside it naked. *Darling,* we sing to Eric, *you look won-der-ful tonight*. The air is full of the gyrations of six thousand people. My cousin is covered with clouds again but she doesn't seem to notice. Although it's still five months until Christmas, tiny lights wink on and off in her hair.

The tablecloth is covered with pie crumbs and empty coffee cups, a space has been cleared for the cribbage board and ashtrays. The sisters are smoking, staring at their cards, and talking about relatives. Neither of them can believe that Bernice is putting indoor-outdoor carpeting in her kitchen.

"You can't tell her a thing," my mother says. She lays down a card and moves her red peg ahead on the board.

"Shit," my aunt says softly. She stares at her cards. One of the husbands comes in for more pie. "What do I do here?" she asks him. He looks at her hand for a moment and then walks around the table to look at my mother's hand. He points to a card, which she removes and lays down. "Try that on for size," she tells my mother.

The back door flies open and two daughters enter. There is a hullabaloo. Barbie's little sister, Skipper, was sitting on the fence and accidentally fell off and got stepped on by a pig. "She's wrecked," Wendell reports. "We had to get her out with a stick." I show them the stick and Wendell shows them Skipper.

"Stay away from the pigs," my aunt says. She's looking at her cards.

"We *were* staying away from the pigs," I answer, holding up the muddy stick as evidence. "Tell them to stay away from *us*, why don't you?" My mother looks up. "Well," I say to her.

"You might find out *well*, if you're not careful," she tells me.

Wendell takes a whiff of Skipper, who is wearing what used to be a pair of pink flowered pajamas. A small bit of satin ribbon is still visible around her neck, but the rest, including her smiling face, is wet brown mud and something else. "Part of this is *poop*," Wendell hollers.

My aunt turns around finally. "Take that goddamn doll out-

side." She means business so we go upstairs, put Skipper in a shoe box, and find our Barbies.

"Mine's going to a pizza party," I say. My Barbie has a bubble haircut, red, and Wendell's has a black ponytail.

"Let's just say they're sitting home and then Ken comes over and makes them go to a nightclub," Wendell suggests. Hers doesn't have a pizza-party outfit so she never wants mine to get to wear one either.

"Mine's going to sing at the nightclub then," I warn her.

"Well, mine doesn't care," Wendell offers generously. She's eyeballing a white fur coat hanging prominently in my carrying case. Her Barbie walks over to mine. "Can I wear your fur tonight?" she asks in a falsetto.

"If I can wear your bola," my Barbie replies.

"It's boa, stupid," Wendell tells me. She digs out a pink feathered scrap, puts it in her Barbie's hand, and makes her Barbie throw it at mine.

"Let's say it's really hot out and they don't know Ken is coming over and they're just sitting around naked for a while," I suggest.

"Because they can't decide what to wear," Wendell clarifies. "All their clothes are in the dryer." She wads up all the outfits lying around and throws them under the bed.

"Oh God, it's so hot," my Barbie tells hers. "I'm going to sit at the kitchen table." Naked, she sits down in a cardboard chair at a cardboard table. Her hair is a smooth auburn circle, her eyes are covered with small black awnings, her legs are stuck straight out like broomsticks.

Black-haired, ponytailed Barbie stands on tiptoe at the cardboard sink. "I'm making us some pink squirrels," she announces. "But we better not get drunk, because Ken might come over."

Both Barbies do get drunk, and Ken does come over. He ar-

rives in an ill-fitting suit, and the heat in the Barbie house is so overwhelming that he has to remove it almost immediately.

"Hey baby," Ken says to no one in particular. The Barbies sit motionless and naked in their cardboard kitchen, waiting for orders. This is where Dirty Barbies gets murky — we aren't sure what's supposed to happen next. Whatever happens, it's Ken's fault, that's all we know.

The Barbies get tired and go lie down on their canopied bed. Ken follows them in and leans at a forty-degree angle against their cardboard dresser. He's trying to tell them he's tired, too.

"You're going to prison, buddy," Wendell finally says, exasperated. She heaves him under her bed and we get our Barbies up and dress them.

"Ken better not try anything like *that* again," ponytailed Barbie says. She's wearing a blue brocade evening gown with the white fur coat, and one cracked high-heeled shoe.

"He thinks he's funny but he's not," my Barbie replies ominously. "He's in jail and *we're* the only ones who can bail him out." She's got on a yellow satin-and-net dress with a big rip up the back, and the boa is wrapped tightly around her neck. By the time they get Ken out of jail and into his tuxedo, the whole evening is shot. The judge has to be bribed with a giant nickel that ponytailed Barbie holds in her outstretched hand.

"Crap," Wendell says when they holler at us from downstairs. I pack up my carrying case, drag it down the steps and out to the car. I keep sitting down the whole way because I'm tired.

"Get moving," my mother tells me. My aunt calls me Jody and gives me a little whack on the behind, but she doesn't mean anything by it. I climb in beside my sister and roll down the window.

"Whaaa," Wendell says to me. This is the sound her Betsy-Wetsy makes when it gets swatted for peeing.

The car pulls out onto the highway and turns toward town.

I left my Barbie's pizza-party outfit under Wendell's pillow so she could use it until next time. Too bad, I miss it already. Red tights and a striped corduroy shirt with tassels that hang down. It goes better with a bubble cut than a ponytail, really. I should never have left it.

August, early evening. We're crammed into Uncle Fred's yellow Caddie, driven by Little Freddy, our cousin. I have on a low-backed, peach-colored dress with spaghetti straps and a giant, itching wrist corsage made of greenery and tipped carnations. Wendell is wearing an ivory wedding gown with a scoop neck and a hundred buttons down the back. It's the dress our grandmother married our grandfather in and it makes Wendell look like an angel. There are guys present — my boyfriend, a sweet, quiet type named Eric, and Wendell's brand-new husband, Mitch, a mild-mannered, blue-eyed farmer who is gazing at the cornfields streaking by.

Cousin Freddy is in control at this point, possibly a big mistake. One misplaced elbow and all the windows go down at once, causing hot air to whirl around inside the Caddie, stirring up everyone's hair and causing a commotion. "Okay, okay," Freddy says in a rattled voice. He pushes another button and all the windows go back up, the commotion stops, the air conditioning comes back into play.

Wendell has a wreath of baby's breath perched on top of her head like a crown of thorns. A slight crevice has appeared in the front of her hair, the baby's breath has lifted with the landscape and sits balanced on two distinct formations. The back is untouched. She wrestles herself over to the rearview mirror and gets a glimpse.

"Oh my God, it's the Red Sea," she says. "You parted my *hair*, Freddy."

There is an audible combing noise inside the car for a mo-

ment as she tries to impose some discipline on it. Freddy looks at her in the rearview mirror. He's got Uncle Fred's five-o'clock shadow and Aunt Velma's tiny teeth, he's wearing a powder blue short-sleeved shirt and a flowery necktie, fashionably wide. "We can borrow you a rake at one of these farmhouses," he says, braking. The Caddie, dumb and obedient as a Clydesdale, slows down, makes a left and then a right, pulls onto a dirt track leading into a cornfield. Freddy gets his wedding present from under the seat, lights it, and passes it back. We pile out into the evening and stand, smoking, next to the car.

The sky is way up there, a lavender dome. There's a gorgeous glow of radiation in the spot the sun just vacated, a pale peach burst of pollution that matches my dress. The corn is waxy and dark green and goes on forever. We're standing in a postcard.

"This is my big day," Wendell mentions. The crown of thorns is resting peacefully, swifts are swooping back and forth, drinking bugs out of the sky. We're trying to keep the hems of our dresses from dragging in the dirt.

"This corn is *ready*," Mitch says quietly, to no one in particular. The stalks are taller than us by a foot, a quiet crowd of ten million, all of them watching us get high and wreck our outfits.

"Don't lean on the car," I tell Wendell. She stands in her usual slouch, one arm wrapped around her own waist, the other bringing the joint to her lips. She squints and breathes in, breathes out. "You look like Lauren Bacall only with different hair," I say.

She considers that. "You look like Barbara Hershey only with a different face," she says kindly. We beam at one another. This is Wendell's big day.

"Hey, bats," Eric says suddenly. He's looking up into the air where the swifts are plunging around. I'm very fond of him for a moment, and then I feel a yawn coming on. A breeze has

picked up and the corn is rustling, a low hiss from the crowd. We're making Wendell late to her own party.

The Caddie takes us out of the cornfield, haunch-first. Freddy steers it up to the highway, sets the cruise, and we all lean back, stare out the side windows, and watch the landscape go from corn to soybeans to cows to corn. Next thing you know we're getting out again, this time at Wendell's old house, the farm.

The wedding cake is a tiered affair with peach-colored roses and two very short people standing on top. Our mothers made the mints. This is a big outdoor reception, with a striped awning and a skinned pig. The awning is over a rented dance floor, the pig is over a bed of coals. There are as many relatives as you'd want to see in one place; the men standing around the revolving pig, the women putting serving spoons in bowls of baked beans, potato salad, things made with Jell-O, things made with whipped cream, things made with bacon bits.

Two uncles are tapping the beer keg. They keep drawing up tall glasses of foam and dumping it on the ground.

"I need a beer bad," Wendell says. She touches her head. "How's the crown?"

"Firm," I tell her. We get ourselves two glasses of foam to carry around and wander over to the food tables.

"This has prunes in it, if you can believe that," an aunt tells us, uncovering a bowl full of something pink that just came from the trunk of her car. Our mothers are standing at a long table where more women are unwrapping gifts and logging them in a book. Wendell's mother is wearing a long dress, gray silk with big peach-colored roses and green leaves down the front. My mother has on a pantsuit that everyone keeps admiring. They're both wearing corsages. "Ooh," my aunt says. A box has just been opened containing an enormous macramé plant hanger, with big red beads and two feet of thick fringe.

"Holy shit," Wendell says, taking a drink of foam.

The guests eat salads and chips and pig, the sky turns pewter, deep cobalt, then black. The band strikes up; four guys, two of them relatives. They play a fast number and everyone under the age of ten gets out there to dance. The littlest kids concentrate on trying to get it exactly right, swinging their hips and whirling their arms around. After about two songs all of them are out of control and sweating, hair stuck to their head, girls seeing who can slide the farthest on patent-leather shoes, boys taking aim and shooting each other with their index fingers without mercy. The parents have to step in, remove a few examples, and put them in chairs. One gets spanked first for calling his mother a dipshit in front of the whole crowd.

A waltz begins to play and the older couples move out onto the floor, husbands with wives, various uncles with various aunts. My own dad dances me around a few times, tells me my dress is pretty, and delivers me in front of Eric, who looks stupendously bored and not quite stoned enough. "Hey, lotta fun," he says insincerely. I make him go dance with my mom.

Wendell takes a break from talking to people and we pull up lawn chairs next to the dance floor. Her ivory dress shines in the darkness. "I keep losing my drink," she says. We share a full, warm beer that's sitting on the ground between our chairs, passing it back and forth, watching the fox-trotters.

"I wish I could do the fox-trot," I say wistfully.

She nods. "We can't do anything good," she says wearily.

"We can two-step," I answer, in our defense.

"Yeah," she says through a yawn. "But big whoop, the two-step." Two short great-aunts glide by at a smart clip and wave at us, the bride and the bridesmaid. Wendell waves back like a beauty queen on a float, I smile and twinkle my fingers. "Yee-haw," I say quietly. On the other side of the dance floor Mitch stands listening intently to one of our distant, female relatives.

He winks at us when she isn't looking and we wink back hugely. "That's my first husband, Mitch," Wendell says fondly.

The night air is damp and black against my arms, like mossy sleeves. There are stars by the millions up above our heads. Wendell and I are sitting directly under Gemini, my birth sign, the oddball twins, the split personality. Part of me wants to get up and dance, the other part wants to sit with my head tipped back. All of me wants to take off my wrist corsage.

"Nice ragweed corsage," I tell Wendell. My arm itches like fire, long red hives are marching up to my elbow. I take it off and put it under my chair.

"Give it a heave," she suggests, and I do. It lands within twenty feet of our lawn chairs. A giant calico farm cat steps out from nowhere, sniffs it, then picks it up delicately and fades back into the blackness. Under the awning the air is stained yellow, the band is playing a disco song. Our mothers are in the midst of a line dance, doing their own version of the Hustle, out of synch with everyone else. Their work is done, they've mingled, they've been fairly polite. Now they've got about twenty minutes of careening before they collapse in lawn chairs and ask people to wait on them. They're out there trying to kick and clap at the same time, without putting their drinks down. I decide I'd better join them.

My mother's cheeks are in bloom, from sloe gin and exertion, her lipstick has worn off but her corsage is still going strong, a flower the size of a punch bowl. She tries for the relaxed shuffle-kick-pause-clap of all the other line dancers but can't do it. She sets her drink down at the edge of the dance floor where it's sure to get knocked over and comes back to the line, full steam ahead. She starts doing the Bump with Wendell's mom and another aunt. Before they can get me involved, I dance myself over to the edge of the floor and step out into the darkness.

"The moms need to be spanked and put in chairs," I tell Eric,

who hands over his beer without being asked. He looks peaceful and affectionate; his hair is sticking straight up in front and there's something pink and crusty all over the front of his shirt.

"One of those kids threw a piece of cake at me," he says placidly. He's been smoking pot out in the corn with Freddy, I can tell. The band pauses between numbers and the mothers keep dancing. In the distance, two uncles stand talking, using the blue glow of a bug zapper to compare their mangled thumbnails. Up by the band, the bride is getting ready to throw the bouquet. I'm being summoned to come stand in the group of girl cousins clustered around Wendell. I walk backward until I'm past the first row of corn, Eric following amiably, pink-eyed and slap-happy. He's using a swizzle stick for a toothpick.

Inside the corn it is completely dark, the stalks stand silent, the sounds of the party are indistinct. We can hear each other breathing. There is a muffled cheering as the bouquet gets thrown, and then someone talks loud and long into the microphone, offering a toast. Eric begins nuzzling my ear and talking baby talk.

"Hey," I whisper to him.

"Mmmm?" he says.

"Have you ever seen a corn snake?"

He refuses to be intimidated. A waltz begins and we absently take up the one-two-three, one-two-three. Around us the dark stalks ripple like water, the waves of the blue Danube wash over us. "I can show *you* a corn snake," he says softly, into my hair.

Here is a scene. Two sisters talk together in low voices, one knits and the other picks lints carefully off a blanket. Their eyes meet infrequently but the conversation is the same as always.

"He's too young to retire," my mother says. "He'll be stuck to her like a burr, and then that's all you'll hear. How she can't stand having him underfoot." One of my uncles wants to retire from selling Motorola televisions and spend the rest of his years doing woodworking.

"How many pig-shaped cutting boards does anybody need?" my aunt says. She holds her knitting up to the window. "God*damn* it. I did it again." She begins unraveling the last few rows, the yarn falling into a snarl around her feet.

"Here," my mother says, holding out a hand, "give me that." She takes the ball of pale yellow yarn and slowly, patiently winds the kinked part back up. While they work, a nurse enters and reads a chart, takes a needle from a cart in the hall, and injects it into the tube leading into my mother's arm. When the door snicks shut behind her, my aunt quits unraveling long enough to get a cigarette from her purse.

"They better not catch me doing this," she says, lighting up. She's using an old pop can for an ashtray. The cigarette trembles slightly in her long fingers and her eyes find the ceiling, then the floor, then the window. She adjusts the belt on her suit, a soft green knit tunic over pants, with silver buttons and a patterned scarf at the neck. She's sitting in an orange plastic chair.

My mother is wearing a dark blue negligee with a bedjacket and thick cotton socks. She takes a puff from my aunt's cigarette and exhales slowly, making professional smoke rings. "Now I'm corrupted," she says dryly.

"If any of them walked in right now, they'd have a fit," my aunt replies uneasily. She's worried about stern daughters, crabby nurses.

"Do I give a good goddamn?" my mother asks peacefully. She's staring at the ceiling. "I don't think I do." She's drifting now, floating upward, her shot is taking effect. She gets a glimpse of something and then loses it, like a fish swimming in

and out of view in the darkness under water. She struggles to the surface. "I hope you get a girl," she says.

My aunt is knitting again, the long needles moving against each other, tying knots, casting off, creating small rosettes. Wendell is ready to have a baby any day now. "Well, she's carrying it low," my aunt answers skeptically. The room is dimming, she turns her chair more toward the window. There is a long pause, with only the needles and the tedious breath, the sterile landscape of cancer country.

"That doesn't mean anything," my mother finally replies. Her father bends over the bed to kiss her, as substantial as air; he's a ghost, they won't leave her alone. She moves slowly through the fluid and brings a thought to the surface. "We carried all of ours low, and look what we got." They swim through her lake, gray-eyed sisters, thin-legged and mouthy. They fight and hold hands, trade shoes and dresses, marry beautiful tall men, and have daughters together, two dark-eyed cousins, thin-legged and mouthy. A fish splashes, a silver arc against the blue sky, its scales like sequins. She startles awake.

"I hope you get a girl," she says again. This is all she can think to say. Her sister, in the dimness, sets down her work and comes to the bed. She bends over and pulls the blanket up, straightens it out. She can't think of what to say either. The face on the pillow is foreign to her suddenly, distant, and the weight of the long afternoon bends her in half. She leans forward wearily, and lets herself grimace.

"We got our girls we wanted so bad, didn't we?" my mother whispers to her, eyes still shut. My aunt straightens and fingers a silver button at her throat.

"Those damn brats," she comments. She presses both hands against the small of her back and shuts her eyes briefly. For an instant she sees the two original brats — wearing their droopy calico dresses, sassing their mother, carrying water up from the

pump at the home place, knocking into each other. "You were always my sister," she says softly.

My mother is completely without pain now, the lake is dark, the fish move easily out of her way. Her sister swims by and makes a statement. "I know it," she answers. She tries to think of a way to express something. Sequins fall through the water, fish scales, and a baby floats past, turned upside-down with a thumb corked in its mouth. The morphine is a thin vapor in her veins. She rouses herself.

"He did do a nice job on those Christmas trees," she says. My aunt nods. She's talking about the woodworking uncle now, who made Christmas trees for all the sisters to put in the middle of their dining-room tables.

"I told him to make me a couple more for next year," my aunt says. "My card club went nuts over it." She lights another cigarette, hating herself for it. My mother is silent, her hands cut the water smoothly, like two long knives. The little gray-eyed girls paddle and laugh. She pushes a spray of water into her sister's face and her sister pushes one back. Their hair is shining against their heads.

In the dimness of the hospital room, my aunt smokes and thinks. She doesn't see their father next to the bed, or old Aunt Grace piddling around with the flower arrangements. She sees only the still form on the bed, the half-open mouth, the coppery wig. She yawns. Wendell's stomach is out to here, she remembers, any day now. That's one piece of good news.

My mother sleeps silently while my aunt thinks. As the invisible hands tend to her, she dives and comes up, breaks free of the water. A few feet over a fish leaps again, high in the air. Her arms move lazily back and forth, holding her up, and as she watches, the fish is transformed. High above the water, it rises like a silver baton, presses itself against the blue August sky, and refuses to drop back down.

Behind the Screen

I'm looking at the backs of all their heads. They're sitting on lawn chairs in the dusk and so am I, only their lawn chairs are on the lawn while mine is on the enclosed back porch. I have to look at the backs of their heads through the screen. We're waiting for the fireworks to begin.

My sister is wearing shorts, a midriff top, and all manner of jewelry — a pop-bead necklace, a Timex wristwatch, a mood ring, and a charm bracelet that makes a busy metallic rustle every time she moves her arm, which she does frequently. On the charm bracelet, between a high-stepping majorette and a sewing machine with movable parts, is a little silver book that opens like a locket to display The Teen Commandments. Engraved in infinitesimal letters: *Don't let your parents down, they brought you up; Choose a date who would make a good mate*; and

the famous *At the first moment turn away from unclean thinking — at the first moment.* It has such an urgent tone it forces you to think uncleanly. Right now my sister is sitting in a lawn chair waiting for it to get dark. Every few minutes she raises and lowers her right arm so the charm bracelet, which I covet, clanks up to her elbow and then slides slowly and sensuously back down to her wrist. She doesn't bother turning around to see how I take this. She knows it's killing me.

They won't let me off the porch because I'm having an allergy attack. A low whistling sound emanates from my chest whenever I breathe. I can put a little or a lot of force behind it, depending on my mood. I'm allergic to ragweed and thistles and marigolds and dandelions and daisies, so we're all used to me being stuck on the porch while everyone else is having fun. Also grass; I'm allergic to grass. Right now one nostril is completely plugged up while the other runs in a steady drip.

My four-year-old brother is wearing cowboy boots and shorty pajamas, a gunbelt minus the guns, and a hat with earflaps. He's shooting each member of my family in turn with his crayon-size index fingers. He smiles at me, his little teeth glinting in the dusk. "You dead," he says.

I press my face up against the screen. It smells like dirt. I put my tongue out tentatively. It tastes like dirt. "Go to H," I say.

My mother turns her head halfway around and looks into my father's ear. "You're gonna get a whole lot sicker, miss," she tells me. Stars are beginning to be visible through the cloudy beehive of her teased hair. It's the Fourth of July 1962, and our city is having a fireworks display in the park. I have my own bowl of popcorn on the porch, and a glass of pop. The fireworks will be visible over the top of the dying elm tree in our backyard. It's impossible for me to eat the popcorn because I'm wearing a nose tourniquet, an invention I came up with myself: half of a twisted Kleenex, one end stuffed into one nostril, the

other end in the other nostril. It has a wicking effect, and saves the effort of swabbing all the time.

"I can't even taste this pop," I say to the screen, after taking a sip. They all ignore me. The family dog, Yimmer, is sitting on my father's lap, growling quietly each time my brother shoots her.

My sister takes a loud swig out of a bottle of Pepsi, wipes her mouth elaborately, and says, "Man, was that good."

I examine a series of interesting scabs on my right knee. None of them are ready to be removed, although a couple are close. "You should see these scabs," I say to the backs of their heads.

My brother marches in place, talking to himself in a stern whisper.

My mother lights another Salem and positions a beanbag ashtray on the metal arm of her chair.

My father leans down and gives Yimmer's head a kiss.

Suddenly the scruffy edges of the elm tree are illuminated. The night sky turns pale above the garage, staccato gunfire, and a torpedo of light wiggles upward, stops, and fizzles. There is a beat of silence and then a burst of cascading pink and green worms. A long sigh is heard, from my family and the family next door.

I have my forehead against the screen, breathing in the night air and the heavy, funereal scent of roses, the only flower I'm not allergic to. A noodle skids across the sky, releasing a shower of blue spangles, jewels on a black velvet bodice. Way up there is outer space. I lean back and touch my forehead; an indented grid from the screen has been pressed into it. All these fireworks are somehow scaring me. "You should see my forehead," I say to my mother's hair.

"What's wrong with it?" she asks patiently. She doesn't turn around.

"I keep pressing it on the screen," I say.

"Don't push on that screen," my father says.

"I'm not," I say.

The sky is full of missiles. All different colors come out this time, falling in slow motion, red and blue turning to orange and green. It's so beautiful, I have to close my eyes. My family joins the neighbors in oohing. Suddenly, as the delayed booms are heard, I have to lean forward and put my head on my knees, inhaling the scent of Bactine and dirt. Everything is falling away from me. I open my eyes.

Black sky, dissipating puffs of gray smoke, the barely visible edges of the elm tree. My father's hand is dark against the white of the dog's fur. My brother is aiming both forefingers at the sky. A match flares suddenly; my mother touches it to her cigarette and inhales.

I am stuck somewhere between the Fourth of July and the rest of time, the usual chaos inside my head distilled down into nothing. I put my cheek against the screen, feeling the grid. There is an uproar, gunfire, sounds from the crowd.

Shooting stars in the cold of outer space; one after another the missiles are launched until the sky is brilliant with activity and smoke. Huge arcs of pink and yellow. Orange things that fizzle for an instant and then send out sonic booms. Long terrible waterfalls of yellow and blue. In the brightness, the backs of all their heads look rapt. My brother has his hands over his ears. My sister's mouth is open. The dog has her head in my father's armpit. It goes on for minutes, the booming sounds and the brilliant light. Closing my eyes doesn't work, it makes me feel like I'm falling backward. Instead I watch their hair, all the different styles right in my own back yard, and say The Teen Commandments quietly to myself: *Avoid following the crowd; be an engine, not a caboose. Stop and think before you drink*. Gunfire, one last wild spiraling of colors, and it's over.

"I'm not going to bed," my brother says resolutely.

The dog jumps down and stretches.

I remain in my lawn chair as they all troop into their house. One of my sister's better personalities comes out and she stops to comb her fingers through my hair and carries my full popcorn bowl into the house.

"She can't eat a thing," she tells my mother piously.

"Bath," my mother says to her. I hear my sister stomp up the stairs and then I hear my brother stomp up behind her, two feet on each stair.

"I saw a goddamned mosquito in here," my mother says. There's some flailing around, the whap of the flyswatter, and then my dad says, "Ick." The freezer opens, a bowl is clattered out of the cupboard. Ice cream. There's the unscrewing sound of a jar opening. Marshmallow stuff. My head hurts. I remove my spent nose tourniquet and start twisting a new one. Before I can get it in place there is a damp trickle on my lip.

"You guys?" I say. Any minute now they're going to send me upstairs.

There's an expectant pause in the kitchen.

"This lawn chair is stuck to my legs," I tell them.

A bottle is opened and an audible swig is taken. The lighter snaps and there's silence while she exhales.

Uh-oh.

"Bath," she says.

Coyotes

A *small gesture of movement, a* hiss of grass, and he is frozen stone for an instant, yellow eyes pinned on the spot, ears cocked forward. A quick lunge of muscles and paws, a darting switchback, and suddenly a rabbit is beating itself to death inside his mouth, against his tongue. This is lunch, unexpected.

In the tall papery weeds he pants and heaves and eventually, regretfully, begins licking the red off his paws. This will lead, as always, to the licking of his whole body, the coarse mangy fur like sawgrass against his tongue. He spreads the toes of one back paw and gnaws something hard and spiny away from the pad. He shakes his head fiercely to dislodge it from his teeth and then groans, rolls over flat on his side. He is in a trance now, one lobe of the brain completely at rest, in a smooth white fog that settles completely, like bedcovers, and doesn't lift until dark. The other lobe is on edge, senses opened so wide they

collect amazing things: the screaming of unseeable insects hopping from one hair follicle to another; the droning currents emanating from power lines a quarter mile away; the throbbing of water deep beneath the ground. In the fog each paw twitches in preparation for the leap, the bite, the flat-out escaping run. Through the mist creeps a glowing, dull-witted bunny, eyes stupid, tail erect. Yellow paws pulse against the dirt as the coyote closes over its belly and suddenly the bunny is a chicken and the prized feel of it — white feathers beating softly against his muzzle — causes him, like a dog being petted, to wag heavily against the grass and bark lightly in sleeping pleasure.

In my dreams the ground murmurs over and over, until I'm ready to wake up swinging. *I am Kansas*, it says, *I am Kansas I am Kansas I am Kansas*. This is a train headed for Arizona and those are other passengers. The guy across from me has on house slippers and a hat because it's freezing in here. He's reading a book with a sprawled dead woman on the cover. Beside me, Eric is sleeping with his neck exposed and both hands lying open and empty. God. I put my own hands back into my armpits, bring my knees up, bend my head down, and try to sink back into some kind of blankness. Inside my mind a green and brown landscape appears, a mountain hillside with white-tailed deer arranged here and there, a stump, a path, a clump of rocks. Old slides from past vacations click into place and then disappear, one after another. The wheels drone. A burned forest, the sharp gaze of a fox, a pair of ponies standing at a fence, wildflowers, and broken barns; they each snap into position, linger while I look, and then make way for the next. Beneath me the gravelly ground goes on and on, explaining itself in dull tones: *I am Kansas I am Kansas I am Kansas.*

Small- to medium-size creatures creep and coil themselves over the desert floor, making their separate ways toward their separate destinies. Big creatures drive their cars along its roads and mostly don't get out, except to take leaks at the edge of the blacktop. Or point their cameras, hesitate, and give up. It looks different through the lens than through the windshield. Empty and blank and pointless.

I'm in a green tent that turned luminous a few minutes ago when the sun hit it. Eric is cooking breakfast and I'm lying in a sleeping bag not wanting to get up. It is freezing, that much is definitely true. And my shoulders hurt from too much sun and the ground is hard as a city street.

"Come on and get up," Eric calls. "It's warm out here." I peel up a corner of the green door and see him turning omelets with one gloved hand. The other is inside his coat pocket. He's got binoculars around his neck and a purple wool baseball cap on his head. He looks like a maniac.

I'm getting up.

He roams in the blistering sunlight. The sand beneath his paws feels like fire. Every two or three miles he finds a spot of shade and stretches out, squinting into the distance, panting fast and loud. A quick movement, an interruption in the blankness of the sand, and he rises and runs, ears cocked, feet springing off the sandy ground. Mice and snakes. It takes several to make a meal. If the head of the snake rises in the air, he backs off, whining and growling; if not, he pursues it, sometimes winning, sometimes not. In his dreams at night the long limber bodies of the serpents move unexpectedly at him. Awake, he bites the heels of the beasts in the pastures, on the long empty range, dodging the hooves, tasting the dirt and dung and

the coarse fringe of fur. The coyote hates horses and mules, the lowing cows, rich men and poor men. He likes mice and rats, the birds that burst forth in a glorious fan of wings, a squawk.

He roams in the blistering sunlight. His stomach gnaws and his eyes become more alert. The scent of water rises in his consciousness, he presses his nose upward and springs into his lilting trot. Around water is food. The desert gives way to the dappled green of sparse bushes, billowing grass. The coyote tilts his head sideways and uses the round dish of his upright ear to bring in any sounds along the bank. He drinks, listens again, and settles himself to wait. He scratches the area right where his heart beats. Small sounds come forward tentatively from the buzzing emptiness. The grass begins to sway as the breeze picks up. The sun is receding; it is long past dinnertime. The current carries small sticks and leaves, twirling, past his face as the coyote watches the bank, still as stone, waiting for a creature to come forth. From the cover of the wavering rushes, the rabbits press low against the ground, against the urge to run-run-run. The riverbank breathes quietly and patiently; the coyote pins his eyes on a moving reed, turns his ear, lifts his muzzle slightly. A chipmunk leaves the shelter of the grass to step forward. A cluster of oblong seeds on the moist bank has called to him and he must obey.

Inside its green skin a frog blinks, a rectangular insect with a tender belly is claimed by a sticky tongue. The chipmunk squeaks once, the coyote wags and growls as he chews, the dying sun pinkens the air.

We are under a giant balanced rock. There are trees here with bark like alligator hide. Suitcases with leaves. Their roots pop up out of the shallow soil like bent knees poking out of bath-

water. We have canteens, just like cowboys, but the water tastes old and filthy after it's been sitting in there. My shoes are covered with dust and a mile ago a small, thick rattlesnake buzzed at us from the edge of the trail. From above, this place appears as rugged badlands, big craggy pinnacles sticking up like blunt bayonets. The snake made me jumpy as all get-out but I've already filed the image of it away — recoiling on itself, the head a pulled-back wedge, its pattern subtle, smudged and blended like a charcoal drawing on the rock's surface — to be remembered later when I'm back in my own habitat, standing on a linoleum floor somewhere. What I really want to see is a javelina, but of course I won't. They're piglike things with tusks and they run in small herds, snorting and huffling over the pine needles and fallen logs at the bottom of this place. This is a bowl of mountains and greens with tender pieces of meat roaming here and there.

My thighs are on fire, from the burn of the sun and the exertion. From the lip of the bowl, up top, it looked more treacherous and lively than it turned out to be. The cleared overlook at the tip of the trail, Massai Point, is named for a Chiricahua Apache man who stole a horse out from under the droopy mustache of a settler. The startled, righteous white man gathered up some of his buddies and they stood at the point and watched for the Apache to show the top of his head. Rifles poised and scanning, they kept their eyes peeled. From the overlook there are a hundred thousand gaps and crevices between the balanced monoliths and stacked boulders. Breathing into the granite walls, hands flat and calming against the heaving sides of his new horse, he waited them out, watching the sky darken and the moon lift its face. They got tired of waiting and rode back to their settlement, miffed at the giant sheltering landscape, the defiant stone thumbs that hid wild Indians in their shadows.

This is daytime. My soap opera is on right now, somewhere. Back in Iowa. My people are roaming back and forth on the television screen, all prepared for any kind of upheaval; there are a lot of chiffon dresses and dyed-to-match shoes. I mention to Eric that my show is on. He turns with a grin and watches me ski down a dissolving patch of trail. Loose rocks roll beneath my feet as I'm carried along. This is elementary physics, ancient Egyptians used it to take house-size rocks here and there, up and down various hills. I skid one foot halfway under an overhanging rock and a curled ribbon of skin peels up my leg. Rattlers hang out under rocks, waiting for a shin to come along. Yee-ikes. I pull my lower leg back out where it belongs and start making an enormous deal out of my injury. Eric sprinkles water on it and yawns. He remembers that we're an hour off down here, the soap is already over.

The air turns tangy and alive, the sun is gone, the sky is black. Glimmers of light bristle forward in the dome above the coyote's head. He moves out. The night has a seething quality, a crisp silence that hides the tunneling of small, cowering mammals, the slumped somnolence of the wandering cattle, the wide-eyed jitters of the stick-leg deer. The moon, from the bitter cold of outer space, croons to the griddle of the desert. The coyote listens and turns to the west. An image has moved forward in his head: Out of the murk a picture comes to the forefront, melting into view. The thick, spongy edges of lightness, the dark legs and face, the palpable panic of the herd. The sheep are waiting. The moon pushes him forward from behind and snakes slide under bushes until he passes. Out of nowhere a skunk appears, startled, hunkering low with wide mirrored eyes. The coyote darts, bites, and opens the belly with one efficient fang. He drags it around in a gleeful circle, then thrusts

one shoulder at a time into the cooling wetness. It is night and feelings are rising up, like blood to a scrape.

The desert is lunar. Every so often a night bird courses low over the sand and the mice shudder, the lizards peer lidlessly around, unroll their tongues and reel them in again. The moon lowers itself, sitting for a few moments on the shoulders of a western butte, considering the lake of shadows. In its distant, porous memory, the moon can conjure up how it pulled the ice back like a bedsheet, exposing the tender ground beneath. The face on the butte is ice blue and furious, slumping beneath its shoulders infinitesimally, down and down, until it is gone and the stars are livid and blinking. The insects teem, the rodents scrabble, the night-blooming flowers push themselves open and await their guests.

We have two things going for us: a spectacular white rental car and a bag of red-hot cinnamon Fireranchers. We discuss for a fair amount of time while sucking on the Fireranchers whether it is right to "beat" a rental car more than you would beat your own car. We decide it isn't right, although we immediately follow that up by seeing how fast it can go on a stretch of gummy blacktop. It goes to one hundred and thirty miles an hour before it starts shivering.

The rental car has air conditioning but we're not using it. Instead we're keeping a spray bottle full of water in the cooler and spritzing ourselves with it every few miles. Now there is a contest to see who can put a new Firerancher in his or her mouth and not bite it for however long it takes it to disintegrate. I will lose this game and we both know it. We're playing it because we're stupendously bored but still in high spirits.

Every so often I put my foot on the dashboard for a leg inspection. My shinbone is a gentle, peeled blue. This is from when I fell down the mountain into the den of rattlesnakes.

"It wasn't a mountain, it was a path," Eric says. "And there weren't any rattlesnakes."

I spray cold water on my shin and then put my leg back down where it belongs. My whole body feels swampy. The air is a blast furnace and the windshield is a magnifying glass trained on our forearms. We are one moment from ignition. I turn the water bottle around and squirt myself flat in the face and then offer to do Eric.

"I'll do myself," he says threateningly. I hand the bottle over. It's not my style to squirt him with ice water while he's driving but predictably he falls apart for an instant and turns the bottle on me. It dries in one second from the hot breath coming through the window. We roll along in silence for awhile, sweating and thinking, working on our Fireranchers. Mine is so thin I try just resting my teeth on it to see how it feels. I bite it in half.

We are taking the low road from Tucson to a national monument on the border of Mexico. The map says we are now passing through the Comobabi Mountains, but outside the windows of our car the desert is as flat as a sheet of parchment. The saguaros have given way to brush and patches of gravelly dirt; along the highway from time to time are homemade altars. We keep passing them, eighty miles an hour. The next one we'll stop at so I can see who it's an altar to. There aren't even any jet trails out here, the sky is a long, blue yawn. Neil Young comes on the radio.

We see a hawk up ahead, standing on the hood of a broken-down car. We slow down to gaze and it stares at us. Its black-trousered legs are sturdy and long, its beak is curved. We peel off, back up to warp speed, and the landscape turns into a melting blur out the windshield.

"Look, sweetie," Eric says, turned toward me in the driver's seat.

On the very tip of his tongue is his Firerancher. Thin as tissue paper, it looks like the moon in the daytime sky. Suddenly love is looming over the car, as big and invisible as the ghost mountains of the Comobabi range. I smile at him and turn up the radio with my toes.

He snaps peevishly at his haunch, bending stiffly backward to chew the peppery trail of a flea. The walls of the den are pungent with the smell of safety and his own fur. He gives up and flops back over, closes his eyes in the dimness and begins panting. No good, he's awake now, it's time to step back out into the day. In the sunlight he blinks and stretches, fore and aft, like a collie. He shakes so hard he almost knocks himself off his feet. The sky is as blue as blue and the coyote is in a good mood.

He lifts his muzzle and takes in a long snort of air, pulling with it the invisible happenings in the vicinity. There's something big and dead looming just over the rise. The coyote yawns and his tail swings down between his back legs in its traveling position. He puts his nose to the ground and begins his afternoon expedition. Somewhere, right on the edge of what his nose is capable of, a rabbity perfume is lingering. He breaks into a lope just for the fun of it but drops back down to a trot after a hundred yards or so. The sun is pressing burning fingers into his spine. The blacktop dips into view, and as the coyote moves toward it he prepares himself for the highway's big medicine. The sandy dirt beneath his paws gives way just a bit as each foot lands and springs off, the small stones and irregularities in his path add juice to his travels but rarely pain. Under his paws it is *sand . . . sand . . . rock . . . sand . . . stick . . . sand . . . stick* and then the highway's medicine: *hard . . .*

scalding . . . scalding . . . scalding and then *gravel . . . sand . . . rock . . . sand . . . sand . . . rock . . . sand* again.

As he passes once more safely through the hard pond of highway fire the coyote is startled by something in the air, something dangerous bearing down on him. Alert and agile, he jumps to the side, cringing and whining, but it is too late. An empty bread wrapper hits him smack in the side of the head.

The landscape has changed from the invisible Comobabi Mountains of love to the barren flats of boredom and annoyance. The sun is a yellow baseball hanging over right field, the driver's side is in the shade and the passenger's side is sizzling. I decide it's my turn to drive.

Eric glances over. "Uh, doubt it," he says.

I've just noticed how his hairline has taken a daring swoop down his forehead and back up again, just like his father's. I mention this to him while inspecting my fingernails.

He smiles and addresses me by my mother's name. "I mean, honey," he corrects himself, "the kid's got the wheel and the kid's keeping it." He's leaning back in his seat, steering with one finger, brow arched. We are very bored.

The kid is a shithook, I remark.

A shithook with the *wheel*, though, he clarifies. He points out that I'm sweating a lot, more than he's ever seen me do. "Pretty hot over there, eh?"

I begin calling him Lovey, and suggest that we change drivers without stopping. He gives in reluctantly, only because he knows eventually he'll lose. If I don't get to drive pretty soon I will open my car door while we're moving and he can't stand that. He's afraid I'll get sucked out by accident and it'll be his fault for being a control freak.

You have to be going really fast for this trick, over seventy

miles an hour. Both of us recline our seats all the way down, I do the gas pedal with my left foot and hold the steering wheel steady with my left hand while Eric climbs into the back seat. I move over the gear shift and slide into his seat while he climbs over my reclined seat back into the passenger side. It's not exactly that smooth, of course, there is a lot of swerving and hollering that goes along with it. We settle in and bring our seat backs into position and open a can of malt liquor.

"Yee-haw," I say, now that I'm in the driver's seat. Eric tries to rig up a shade for his window using a white T-shirt. He can't get it to stay draped over while he rolls up the glass. I enjoy watching him do this a few times and then look sympathetic when he gives up. "Pretty hot over there, isn't it?" I ask him.

"Not really," he answers.

Twenty miles later we enter the Valley of the Ajo and head for the monument, right above the border of Mexico. The road is endless, with wavering lines of heat rising up and a mirage that looks like a silver pool always about half a mile ahead of the car. Suddenly Eric points and I press on the brake. Along the edge of the blacktop on the opposite side of the highway is a coyote, pushing a bread wrapper along with his nose. He ignores us completely, stops and puts one paw on the plastic wrapper, takes it in his teeth, and begins pulling it apart. He shakes his head like a dog. I pull off into the gravel and try to sit quietly, like I'm not a human. He's staring at me now, still nosing into the bag, gold eyes looking up from the dirty plastic.

The car is a boiling caldron. The coyote stands scruffy and skittish, like a wild dingo dog I met once, who bit everything in sight, wagging his tail like a maniac. Eric slides the camera to me and puts a hand on my arm. He whispers in my ear. I nod. I love dogs better than anything else on earth, next to cigarettes and a couple of people.

I find him in the lens, framed in a square. As I click the shutter he jumps sideways and takes off, running a few yards and then skidding to a halt, looking back over his shoulder. He's not afraid of us, he's just horsing around. In the rearview mirror he canters over the rocks, low to the ground, tail tucked. In the slide, projected on my living room wall, he will be a gray, moving blur, a running pelt. The gracious arms of an organ pipe cactus direct him up the hill, over the rise, out of the frame, and into memory.

The saguaros send out long lavender fingers into the afternoon. Grains of sand cool and then warm again as the slow sweep of the shadows moves past. Something looped and coiled unravels gradually, in no hurry, to follow the pool of purple, the spot where the shadow meets its source. It feeds a tongue out, testing the temperature of the air, and begins to wind back into the debris of the cactus again, until there is only a barely visible presence on the ground, a tangled rope with scales and eyes.

Nearly fifty feet in the air a scar, made with a pocketknife and dirty fingers, is visible on the skin of the cactus. A flicker lands on the green pinnacle and peers around, pokes the needle of its beak into the flesh, and peers again. A ridge ten miles west stands fluted and browning, like the crust of a pie, a hawk slides down a current of air and floats above it. The flicker thrusts again and shrugs the moisture down its throat.

The cactus receives the bird, tiny claws like pins, with the same indifference as it had the man with the pocketknife on the shuddering horse. Weak and boiling, he dug and dug into the spiny hide with his pocketknife. The horse died within the reach of the saguaro's shadow, descending into a dull bag that collapsed on itself, bones moving out across the desert floor in the mouths of jackals.

The man either made it or didn't. The words he spoke and the voice he spoke them in linger high above the ground nearly two hundred years later, buffeted by the hot wind, nourished by desperation and the terrible solitude. The flicker turns his head into the wind, finds the moisture again, drinks, and lifts off. The currents of air move around the top of the cactus, over the thorny scar.

Now, as then, the saguaro stands beneath the sun as the desert clock sweeps over the ground in circles, and begins the slow, tedious task of sealing its wound.

This is the campground: acres and acres of barren plots, bent and scraggy trees, stand-up grills, picnic tables, no people. One big vehicle is parked about a hundred yards away, on the other side of the bathrooms, tethered to an electrical hookup. The people won't come outside until the sun leaves, but a small apricot poodle ventures out a few times and barks at itself wildly. The door opens to let it back in, sending out a big waft of refrigerated air for the bugs and birds to enjoy.

Our tent is all set up, with a minimum of arguing. We stretch out inside it to see how long we can stand to lie there. First it gets very stuffy, then the air leaves completely. We climb out and sit in the front seat of the car, listening to the radio and eating potato chips, waiting for the sun to back off. I'm reading a book about vampires that is so graphic in various parts that I have to breathe through my mouth and stop eating chips. Eric is thumbing through an astronomy magazine. Every once in a while I'll tell him a detail from the vampire book and he'll show me his magazine, explain something about one of the pictures, a black background with white dots. We read and thumb until the landscape is a hazy 3-D postcard and the sky is a turquoise tent. Our legs decide to walk.

The Official Map and Guide stresses not once but twice that rattlesnakes are protected here. It has a curt, no-nonsense tone that indicates we'd better act right. Small quail run across the path, back and forth, stopping and starting, murmuring and pecking. In the distance one cactus stands apart, reaching at least two feet taller than any of the others, a surly foreman, the dad of the landscape. I want to go see it, see how tall it is compared to me.

Eric has a forked stick that he's using for a divining rod. "It'll come in handy for snakes," he tells me, "*and* show us where there's water." The stick suddenly lifts in the air and starts shaking, he manages to hold on and push it back down. "I accidentally pointed it towards the bathrooms," he says.

The camper people are out with their little dog. The guy has a garden hose that he's spraying the path with because he doesn't want dust from cars to get on his Astroturf rug. I feel like talking to him but he just nods without smiling and we have to keep walking. He points the hose politely in another direction until we're past, and the poodle barks and barks.

I tell Eric I wish I had a little dog like that one.

"Of course you do," he answers, "that's the one thing you're short on." Three dogs mingle and mill somewhere in the vast universe, in Iowa, wondering why we're not there petting them. I muse on this for a while. A big dog, a medium-size dog, and a charming lapdog with a mean streak.

"They don't even know we're gone," I tell Eric, "they think we went in the other room and just haven't come back yet." The minds of dogs interest me, the way they never bother to anticipate problems.

By the time we get to the tall cactus the light has softened to a benign burn, a warm pat on the head. We both look great all of a sudden, stained brown with pink auras. Eric sets down his stick and moves back to get the whole cactus in the frame, with

me standing at the base for comparison. At the very top of the saguaro a crista has formed over some kind of damage. The scar blooms out, hard and dark green, like the tiny head on a giant. I step over the debris at the base and arrange myself with arms out, bent at the elbow. The cactus is very old and very tall; up close it is hard and weathered and looks important; a cactus emeritus.

I stand in the soft, end-of-day shadow and have my picture taken. It feels like being on Mars here, the light is strange, these green men stand all over the terrain.

Ninety-three million miles due west, the sun continues to shoot off its bottle rockets. The desert has edged away now, out of range. At the foot of the saguaro, a snake, without moving anything but the thread of tongue, gently touches shoe leather, considers it, and decides no.

The nervous birds are gone from the ground now, it is night. The coyote runs in a mile-wide circle, at a lope, thirty miles an hour. There is nothing else moving. The moon bounces in the sky, over his right shoulder, now behind. A rock rises, a cholla extends soft elbows in his path, a dry husk stares up from the ground. There is nothing. The moon is a wide, mottled face, the countenance of an enraged idiot. The coyote runs and runs, not gasping, until there is something.

Three mule deer spring and run in various directions, bounding, flinging their hooves in the air. He picks one and chases halfheartedly for a distance, hearing his own feet, feeling the moon. They reassemble farther out, staring at him through the dimness, long ears moving back and forth like wings, each face small and wary. The one he chased turns first and takes up its occupation again: finding forage and trying not to die. He holds the moment until he can stay still no longer

and begins running again, away from the sky. The ground is silver, the rocks are gleaming. There is nothing.

We play euchre and hearts, drink beer, rearrange the lantern thirty times. Finally we put it under the picnic table and it illuminates our legs and shorts, blows the whistle on a large furred spider.

"It's got knees," I marvel. Actually, it has sort of a face, too, attached to a slender neck. I decide to sit on top of the table for a while.

"Let me get my spider stick," Eric says. He holds the tines of the divining rod and gently points the way for the spider. It scuttles a few feet and then pauses, goes back into a trance. "Get along, buddy," he urges, giving it a prod. It does several push-ups, puts a leg in the air, and then moves of its own volition out from under the table and into the darkness.

We play a few more hands of hearts, until I realize that we both want me to win and I still can't manage it. The whole desert is disappointed. We fold our hands and practice being bored for a while. Our dogs are sleeping at home, two of them nose to nose and snoring, one off by herself, flat on her side, dreaming of me. The stars are no match for the wash of the moon, the night air is navy blue and coolish against our skin.

The camper people are out of it. Their colored lanterns are dark now and the TV is on inside, the glow of Letterman and his guests reflected in the window. I can see a head framed in the light, surrounded by a frizz of hair. It's the poodle, looking at stars.

We clear the table and spread out a sleeping bag on it, flannel side up. This is the best way to watch the sky. Eric has his red flashlight and charts, I have my sweatshirt zipped and a Walkman with two pairs of headphones. It's his turn to choose

a tape so I'm waiting for something discordant and spooky but when he pushes the button it's one of my favorites. *Thank you,* I mouth to him. He smiles, closes his eyes, and takes my hand. Side by side. He moves into the solitude of headphones and constellations. I am perched on planet Earth, Milky Way galaxy, who knows what universe. Way up there, satellites are parked with their motors running, and vivid rings of plasma do laps around Saturn. Way down here, there is only the terrible arch of the sky, the sagging moon, and nothing else.

The earphones make my head feel like a hollow tube, full of horns and drums and a voice that echoes like green glass. I am alone inside my own skin and the edges of everything have begun to darken slightly, curling and browning, the beginnings of disintegration. Inside my chest a heart begins knocking to get out. I am alone down here, and up there, clinging to the spoke of a satellite, looking upward at the dark velvet, and downward at the dark velvet.

There is nothing.

Pockmarked and surly, the moon steps back and drops the curtain, darkens the theater for the stars. The clock is halted, the desert gives up its heat. A finger-size lizard with infrared spots and oval eyes finds itself, one second too late, in the damp cotton of a mouth. Power lines gleam and bounce their signals on the ground, startling the brain waves of small mammals, putting thoughts in their heads. Something swims through the medium of sand and surfaces, pinches hard and holds on.

In the endless black of deep space a small comet hurtles along, tossing iceballs and dirt behind it, on a perpetual path, around and around and around, pointless and energetic. Propelled by the force of its combustion, the comet passes within

a light year of Sirius, burning out of control. Under the press of gravity and air, inside the earth's atmosphere, the coyote reads the signals in the ground, whirls, stops, and sprays a bush. He begins loping again, without awareness, the desire widening, a dark basin, until he cries as he runs, low and controlled. They are somewhere.

The moon is gone and Eric has fallen asleep beside me. Planets and stars. I know only the ones that everyone knows: the sun, the moon, the dippers, Gemini and Cancer. They move into formation, still and distant as dead relatives, outlining the shape of my mother's mouth. Nothing moves. Inside my head images emerge and retreat, emerge and retreat. I have to open my eyes. In the vivid blackness overhead a diamond falls through the sky, trailing its image, a split-instant of activity. By the time I realize I've seen it, the sky has recovered. I can't breathe in this emptiness. I turn on my side on the hard picnic table and look at Eric.

He is awake, watching me. He knows the desert is making me sad, that I have these moments; he smiles and moves up close. I can feel the sky on my face, the warm flannel of the desert floor below. I can feel the face of the man beside me. In the silence of the monument he begins whispering the names of the constellations while I listen: Cygnus the Swan, Pegasus the Horse, Canis Major the Great Dog, Cassiopeia, Arcturus.

I am on planet Earth.

They are near. He pulls in the scent with loud snorts, running from bush to rock to bush again. This is a clearing, a high naked spot. On the distant rise, just ahead, waiting, they are still invisible, but the scent rises in the air around him, palpa-

ble as mist. He opens his mouth wide and stands frozen, ears back, eyes pressed shut. The dirt beneath his pads is hard and dry, devoid, the moon is gone.

As the mist rises around him, the sound comes forth, pulled from tendon and muscle. It pushes itself through his lungs and into the night, a long trembling wail, dying slowly, drifting finally, without his help, dissipating. Still frozen, he listens for a moment to the roaring silence, waiting, and slowly the sound moves back toward him, fainter, broken into parts like music. Many voices.

They are ahead of him, in the high clearing where the deer sometimes sleep, pausing to listen, ready to bring him in with the radar of their voices. He begins running again and gravity relinquishes its hold. The terrain becomes buoyant and he soars low over the ground, like a night bird, a skipped stone.

The tent is completely dark. I am floating on the ocean in a canoe, each dip of the oar pours out a panful of light, beneath the surface small silver minnows hover like aircraft. My big collie roams along the shore, following the boat, whining low in her throat, stamping her white paws against the sand. I row toward the beach, casting light behind me, and she begins to bark.

I am awake suddenly in the darkness. Outside the tent is the padding of feet, around and around, a swift turning, a pause. There is something in our campsite, trying to get our food. Eric startles and wakes, I touch his hair, breathe into his ear. The paws turn again, there is loud panting, the low whine, and then a series of barks and yelps, a prolonged terrible howl. It is deafening and wild, I can feel him out there, conjuring hysteria out of the dark. A long, plaintive keening, and suddenly it ends, drifting off, carried away from us. We are breathing low and shallow, resting on our elbows.

When the reply comes he joins in, barking first and then crying, pitched high then low, the howl of loneliness and communion. It is lunar and eerie, the pleading of the cold, dead moon to the blue and green revolving earth, the call of sister stars across years of space, the cry of a child who has lost her mother. Now it is coming from every side, the beautiful wailing; they are swarming over us, gray and brown ghosts, distant relatives.

In our green cocoon, we move closer to each other, hands, faces, knees. The walls of the tent press down like skin, the ground presses up like bone. The coyote is gone, suddenly, the air thins out and becomes ours again. Inside the narrow landscape of the tent, hills and valleys realign, adjust themselves, realign again with whispers.

The coyote runs, straining to reach the others, a quarter mile away, over the crest of the ridge. They are waiting for him in the darkness, in the burning desert with its lifted arms of cactus. In the dark tent, on my smooth ocean, inside my mind, he is there already, gray and golden like the desert, like the moon, moving among them in the clearing, feeling the thrust of snouts, the padding of many paws, the push of love.

Against the Grain

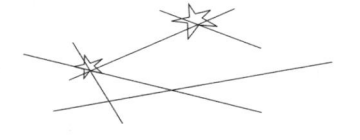

*It's okay to be married to a per*fectionist, at least for a while. Just don't try to remodel a house with one, is all I can say. This is what he'll do: set you up with practice boards and nails to make sure you have the technique completely down before you attend to the task at hand, which he has suggested would be the best task for you at this particular time in your training. You sigh and jokingly threaten him with the hammer but because you aren't adept at pulling nails from ceiling trim you grudgingly work on the practice boards until you can almost remove a nail without splitting the wood all to hell. It makes your knees hurt to crouch that way so you take a doughnut break, staring out the dirty window at the neighbor's house across the way. The perfectionist comes in on his way from a completed task to a waiting, un-begun one. He notices you standing there and grins.

"It doesn't get done that way, does it?" he kids you.

You feel revitalized from the jelly filling and pour a tepid cup of coffee from the thermos, head back in, crouch some more. The pieces of trim are in pretty good shape, long stately things that will nestle up against the ceiling, hopefully hiding the uneven line between wallpaper and paint. The perfectionist is feeling very sensitive about that particular uneven line, since he tried and tried to make it straight. You assured him over lunch the previous day and again over dinner that the line would be covered up by the lovely trim. You, in fact, feel encouraged knowing that an uneven, almost jaggedy, edge will be hiding in the house. You tell the perfectionist this in a joking way and he stares at you for a long moment and then smiles uncertainly.

In the other room you can hear him giving explicit directions to his brother-in-law, who owes you guys a big favor for helping him put an oak floor in his den last summer. The perfectionist convinced him to go ahead and sand and refinish all the floors in the house while he was at it. After all, he explained, you might as well do it right. Then it's done and you can feel good about it. You know? His own sister didn't speak to the perfectionist for about three weeks after that, until the job was done and her furniture was back in place. He kept advising her to try another way whenever she got frustrated and started sanding wildly against the grain. Unfortunately, she knew that "try another way" is what they used to say to the retarded citizens at the sheltered workshop where he worked after college.

"I'm not retarded, pal," she told him.

No matter how hard you try, the long, lovely pieces of trim start out fine and end up with these odd-looking splits and splinters. He's whistling in the other room. You try a different technique than he showed you and suddenly the longest piece has become divorced from itself. Oh dear.

"Well," says the perfectionist, standing in the doorway. "We're having trouble, I see." He sets down his chisel and shows you once again how to tease the nail from the wood. "You can't just go nuts on it," he explains. "You can't *wrestle* it."

Carefully and efficiently, he sets himself to the task. Within fifteen minutes the wood is free of the nails, which are stacked, mostly unbent and ready to be used again, on a windowsill. You open the can of spackle with a screwdriver and begin the tedious job of filling all the little holes left behind. He's behind you before you know it.

His hair is tufted up in back from the hat he's been wearing and his pants have plaster dust on the knees. He has the sweetest face of any man you've ever seen. He smiles. "Just be sure not to glob it on," he says gently, and then retreats again, into the rest of the house, which is structurally unsound but possibly fixable, just like you.

The Fourth State of Matter

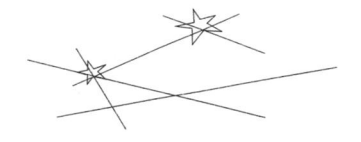

T*he collie wakes me up about* three times a night, summoning me from a great distance as I row my boat through a dim, complicated dream. She's on the shoreline, barking. Wake up. She's staring at me with her head slightly tipped to the side, long nose, gazing eyes, toenails clenched to get a purchase on the wood floor. We used to call her the face of love.

She totters on her broomstick legs into the hallway and over the doorsill into the kitchen, makes a sharp left at the refrigerator — careful, almost went down — then a straightaway to the door. I sleep on my feet, in the cold of the doorway, waiting. Here she comes. Lift her down the two steps. She pees and then stands, Lassie in a ratty coat, gazing out at the yard.

In the porchlight the trees shiver, the squirrels turn over in their sleep. The Milky Way is a long smear on the sky, like something erased on a chalkboard. Over the neighbor's house,

Mars flashes white, then red, then white again. Jupiter is hidden among the anonymous blinks and glitterings. It has a moon with sulfur-spewing volcanoes and a beautiful name: Io. I learned it at work, from the group of men who surround me there. Space physicists, guys who spend days on end with their heads poked through the fabric of the sky, listening to the sounds of the universe. Guys whose own lives are ticking like alarm clocks getting ready to go off, although none of us is aware of it yet.

The collie turns and looks, waits to be carried up the two steps. Inside the house, she drops like a shoe onto her blanket, a thud, an adjustment. I've climbed back under my covers already but her leg's stuck underneath her, we can't get comfortable. I fix the leg, she rolls over and sleeps. Two hours later I wake up again and she's gazing at me in the darkness. The face of love. She wants to go out again. I give her a boost, balance her on her legs. Right on time: 3:40 A.M.

There are squirrels living in the spare bedroom upstairs. Three dogs also live in this house, but they were invited. I keep the door of the spare bedroom shut at all times, because of the squirrels and because that's where the vanished husband's belongings are stored. Two of the dogs — the smart little brown mutt and the Labrador — spend hours sitting patiently outside the door, waiting for it to be opened so they can dismantle the squirrels. The collie can no longer make it up the stairs, so she lies at the bottom and snores or stares in an interested manner at the furniture around her.

I can take almost anything at this point. For instance, that my vanished husband is neither here nor there; he's reduced himself to a troubled voice on the telephone three or four times a day.

Or that the dog at the bottom of the stairs keeps having mild

strokes which cause her to tilt her head inquisitively and also to fall over. She drinks prodigious amounts of water and pees great volumes onto the folded blankets where she sleeps. Each time this happens I stand her up, dry her off, put fresh blankets underneath her, carry the peed-on blankets down to the basement, stuff them into the washer and then into the dryer. By the time I bring them back upstairs they are needed again. The first few times this happened I found the dog trying to stand up, gazing with frantic concern at her own rear. I praised her and patted her head and gave her treats until she settled down. Now I know whenever it happens because I hear her tail thumping against the floor in anticipation of reward. In retraining her I've somehow retrained myself, bustling cheerfully down to the basement, arms drenched in urine, the task of doing load after load of laundry strangely satisfying. She is Pavlov and I am her dog.

I'm fine about the vanished husband's boxes stored in the spare bedroom. For now the boxes and the phone calls persuade me that things could turn around at any moment. The boxes are filled with thirteen years of his pack-rattedness: statistics textbooks that still harbor an air of desperation, smarmy suitcoats from the Goodwill, various old Halloween masks and one giant black papier-mâché thing that was supposed to be Elvis's hair but didn't turn out. A collection of ancient Rolling Stones T-shirts. You know he's turning over a new leaf when he leaves the Rolling Stones behind.

What I can't take are the squirrels. They come alive at night, throwing terrible parties in the spare bedroom, making thumps and crashes. Occasionally a high-pitched squeal is heard amid bumps and the sound of scrabbling toenails. I've taken to sleeping downstairs, on the blue vinyl dog couch, the sheets slipping off, my skin stuck to the cushions. This is an affront to two of the dogs, who know the couch belongs to them;

as soon as I settle in they creep up and find their places between my knees and elbows.

I'm on the couch because the dog on the blanket gets worried at night. During the day she sleeps the catnappy sleep of the elderly, but when it gets dark her eyes open and she is agitated, trying to stand whenever I leave the room, settling down only when I'm next to her. We are in this together, the dying game, and I read for hours in the evening, one foot on her back, getting up only to open a new can of beer or take peed-on blankets to the basement. At some point I stretch out on the vinyl couch and close my eyes, one hand hanging down, touching her side. By morning the dog-arm has become a nerveless club that doesn't come around until noon. My friends think I'm nuts.

One night, for hours, the dog won't lie down, stands braced on her rickety legs in the middle of the living room, looking at me and slowly wagging her tail. Each time I get her situated on her blankets and try to stretch out on the couch she stands up, looks at me, wags her tail. I call my office pal, Mary, and wake her up. *"I'm weary,"* I say, in italics.

Mary listens, sympathetic, on the other end. "Oh my God," she finally says, "*what* are you going to do?"

I calm down immediately. "Exactly what I'm doing," I tell her. The dog finally parks herself with a thump on the stack of damp blankets. She sets her nose down and tips her eyes up to watch me. We all sleep then, for a bit, while the squirrels sort through the boxes overhead and the dog on the blanket keeps nervous watch.

I've called in tired to work. It's midmorning and I'm shuffling around in my long underwear, smoking cigarettes and drinking coffee. The whole house is bathed in sunlight and the faint

odor of used diapers. The collie is on her blanket, taking one of her vampirish daytime naps. The other two dogs are being mild-mannered and charming. I nudge the collie with my foot.

"Wake up and smell zee bacons," I say. She startles awake, lifts her nose groggily, and falls back asleep. I get ready for the office.

"I'm leaving and I'm never coming back," I say while putting on my coat. I use my mother's aggrieved, underappreciated tone. The little brown dog wags her tail, transferring her gaze from me to the table, which is the last place she remembers seeing toast. The collie continues her ghoulish sleep, eyes partially open, teeth exposed, while the Labrador, who understands English, begins howling miserably. She wins the toast sweepstakes and is chewing loudly when I leave, the little dog barking ferociously at her.

Work is its usual comforting green-corridored self. There are three blinks on the answering machine, the first from an author who speaks very slowly, like a kindergarten teacher, asking about reprints. "What am I, the village idiot?" I ask the room, taking down his number in large backward characters. The second and third blinks are from my husband, the across-town apartment dweller.

The first makes my heart lurch in a hopeful way. "I have to talk to you right *now*," he says grimly. "Where *are* you? I can never find you."

"Try calling your own house," I say to the machine. In the second message he has composed himself.

"I'm *fine* now," he says firmly. "Disregard previous message and don't call me back, please; I have meetings." Click, dial tone, rewind.

I feel crestfallen, the leaping heart settles back into its hole

in my chest. I say damn it out loud, just as Chris strides into the office.

"What?" he asks defensively. He tries to think if he's done anything wrong recently. He checks the table for work; none there. He's on top of it. We have a genial relationship these days, reading the paper together in the mornings, congratulating ourselves on each issue of the journal. It's a space physics quarterly and he's the editor and I'm the managing editor. I know nothing about the science part; my job is to shepherd the manuscripts through the review process and create a journal out of the acceptable ones.

Christoph Goertz. He's hip in a professorial kind of way, tall and lanky and white-haired, forty-seven years old, with an elegant trace of accent from his native Germany. He has a great dog, a giant black outlaw named Mica who runs through the streets of Iowa City at night, inspecting garbage. She's big and friendly but a bad judge of character and frequently runs right into the arms of the dog catcher. Chris is always bailing her out.

"They don't understand dogs," he says.

I spend more time with Chris than I ever did with my husband. The morning I told him I was being dumped he was genuinely perplexed.

"He's leaving *you?*" he asked.

Chris was drinking coffee, sitting at his table in front of the chalkboard. Behind his head was a chalk drawing of a hip, professorial man holding a coffee cup. It was a collaborative effort; I drew the man and Chris framed him, using brown chalk and a straightedge. The two-dimensional man and the three-dimensional man stared at me intently.

"He's leaving *you?*" And for an instant I saw myself from their vantage point across the room — Jo Ann — and a small bubble of self-esteem percolated up from the depths. Chris shrugged. "You'll do fine," he said.

During my current turmoils, I've come to think of work as my own kind of zen practice, the constant barrage of paper hypnotic and soothing. Chris lets me work an erratic, eccentric schedule, which gives me time to pursue my nonexistent writing career. In return I update his publications list for him and listen to stories about outer space.

Besides being an editor and a teacher, he's the head of a theoretical plasma physics team made up of graduate students and research scientists. During the summers he travels all over the world telling people about the magnetospheres of various planets, and when he comes back he brings me presents — a small bronze box from Africa with an alligator embossed on the top, a big piece of amber from Poland with the wings of flies preserved inside it, and, once, a set of delicate, horrifying bracelets made from the hide of an elephant.

Currently he is obsessed with the dust in the plasma of Saturn's rings. Plasma is the fourth state of matter. You've got your solid, your liquid, your gas, and then your plasma. In outer space there's the plasmasphere and the plasmapause. I like to avoid the math when I can and put a layperson's spin on these things.

"Plasma is blood," I told him.

"Exactly," he agreed, removing the comics page and handing it to me.

Mostly we have those kinds of conversations around the office, but today he's caught me at a weak moment, tucking my heart back inside my chest. I decide to be cavalier.

"I wish my *dog* was out tearing up the town and my *husband* was home peeing on a blanket," I say.

Chris thinks the dog thing has gone far enough. "Why are you letting this go on?" he asks solemnly.

"I'm not *letting* it, that's why," I tell him. There are stacks of manuscripts everywhere and he has all the pens over on his side of the room. "It just *is*, is all. Throw me a pen." He does, I

miss it, stoop to pick it up, and when I straighten up again I might be crying.

You have control over this, he explains in his professor voice. You can decide how long she suffers.

This makes my heart pound. Absolutely not, I cannot do it. And then I weaken and say what I really want. For her to go to sleep and not wake up, just slip out of her skin and into the other world.

"Exactly," he says.

I have an ex–beauty queen coming over to get rid of the squirrels for me. She has long red hair and a smile that can stop trucks. I've seen her wrestle goats, scare off a giant snake, and express a dog's anal glands, all in one afternoon. I told her on the phone that a family of squirrels is living in the upstairs of my house and there's nothing I can do about it.

"They're making a monkey out of me," I said.

So Caroline climbs in her car and drives across half the state, pulls up in front of my house, and gets out carrying zucchinis, cigarettes, and a pair of big leather gloves. I'm sitting outside with my sweet old dog, who lurches to her feet, staggers three steps, sits down, and falls over. Caroline starts crying.

"Don't try to give me zucchini," I tell her.

We sit companionably on the front stoop for a while, staring at the dog and smoking cigarettes. One time I went to Caroline's house and she was nursing a dead cat that was still breathing. At some point that afternoon I saw her spoon baby food into its mouth and as soon as she turned away the whole pureed mess plopped back out. A day later she took it to the vet and had it euthanized. I remind her of this.

"You'll do it when you do it," she says firmly.

I pick the collie up like a fifty-pound bag of sticks and feathers, stagger inside, place her on the damp blankets, and put the

other two nutcases in the backyard. From upstairs comes a crash and a shriek. Caroline stares up at the ceiling.

"It's like having the Wallendas stay at your house," I say cheerfully. All of a sudden I feel fond of the squirrels and fond of Caroline and fond of myself for heroically calling her to help me. The phone rings four times. It's the husband, and his voice over the answering machine sounds frantic. He pleads with whoever Jo Ann is to pick up the phone.

"Please? I think I might be freaking out," he says. "Am I ruining my life here, or what? Am I making a *mistake?* Jo?" He breathes raggedly and sniffs into the receiver for a moment, then hangs up with a muffled clatter.

Caroline stares at the machine like it's a copperhead.

"Holy fuckoly," she says, shaking her head. "You're *living* with this crap?"

"He wants me to reassure him that he's strong enough to leave me," I tell her. "Else he won't have fun on his bike ride. And guess what; I'm too tired to." Except that now I can see him in his dank little apartment, wringing his hands and staring out the windows. He's wearing his Sunday hairdo with a baseball cap trying to scrunch it down. In his rickety dresser is the new package of condoms he accidentally showed me last week.

Caroline lights another cigarette. The dog pees and thumps her tail.

I need to call him back because he's suffering.

"You call him back and I'm forced to kill you," Caroline says. She exhales smoke and points to the phone. "That is evil shit," she says.

I tend to agree. It's blanket time. I roll the collie off onto the floor and put the fresh ones down, roll her back. She stares at me with the face of love. I get her a treat, which she chews with gusto and then goes back to sleep. I carry the blankets down to

the basement and stuff them into the machine, trudge back up the stairs. Caroline has finished smoking her medicine and is wearing the leather gloves which go all the way to her elbows. She's staring at the ceiling with determination.

The plan is that I'm supposed to separate one from the herd and get it in a corner. Caroline will take it from there. Unfortunately, my nerves are shot, and when I'm in the room with her and the squirrels are running around all I can do is scream. I'm not even afraid of them, but my screaming button is stuck on and the only way to turn it off is to leave the room.

"How are you doing?" I ask from the other side of the door. All I can hear is Caroline crashing around and swearing. Suddenly there is a high-pitched screech that doesn't end. The door opens and Caroline falls out into the hall, with a gray squirrel stuck to her glove. Brief pandemonium and then she clatters down the stairs and out the front door and returns looking triumphant.

The collie appears at the foot of the stairs with her head cocked and her ears up. She looks like a puppy for an instant, and then her feet start to slide. I run down and catch her and carry her upstairs so she can watch the show. They careen around the room, tearing the ancient wallpaper off the walls. The last one is a baby, so we keep it for a few minutes, looking at its little feet and its little tail. We show it to the collie, who stands up immediately and tries to get it.

Caroline patches the hole where they got in, cutting wood with a power saw down in the basement. She comes up wearing a toolbelt and lugging a ladder. I've seen a scrapbook of photos of her wearing evening gowns with a banner across her chest and a crown on her head. Curled hair, lipstick. She climbs down and puts the tools away. We eat nachos.

"I only make food that's boiled or melted these days," I tell her.

"I know," she replies.

We smoke cigarettes and think. The phone rings again but whoever it is hangs up.

"Is it him?" she asks.

"Nope."

The collie sleeps on her blankets while the other two dogs sit next to Caroline on the couch. She's looking through their ears for mites. At some point she gestures to the sleeping dog on the blanket and remarks that it seems like just two days ago she was a puppy.

"She was never a puppy," I say. "She's always been older than me."

When they say good-bye, she holds the collie's long nose in one hand and kisses her on the forehead; the collie stares back at her gravely. Caroline is crying when she leaves, a combination of squirrel adrenaline, and sadness. I cry, too, although I don't feel particularly bad about anything. I hand her the zucchini through the window and she pulls away from the curb.

The house is starting to get dark in that terrible early-evening twilit way. I turn on lights, get a cigarette, and go upstairs to the former squirrel room. The black dog comes with me and circles the room, snorting loudly, nose to floor. There is a spot of turmoil in an open box — they made a nest in some old disco shirts from the seventies. I suspect that's where the baby one slept. The mean landlady has evicted them.

Downstairs, I turn the lights back off and let evening have its way with me. Waves of pre-nighttime nervousness are coming from the collie's blanket. I sit next to her in the dimness, touching her ears, and listen for feet at the top of the stairs.

They're speaking in physics so I'm left out of the conversation. Chris apologetically erases one of the pictures I've drawn on the

blackboard and replaces it with a curving blue arrow surrounded by radiating chalk waves of green.

"If it's plasma, make it in red," I suggest helpfully. We're all smoking illegally in the journal office with the door closed and the window open. We're having a plasma party.

"We aren't discussing *plas*ma," Bob says condescendingly. He's smoking a horrendously smelly pipe. The longer he stays in here the more it feels like I'm breathing small daggers in through my nose. He and I don't get along; each of us thinks the other needs to be taken down a peg. Once we had a hissing match in the hallway which ended with him suggesting that I could be fired, which drove me to tell him he was *already* fired, and both of us stomped into our offices and slammed our doors.

"I had to fire Bob," I tell Chris later.

"I heard," he says noncommittally. Bob is his best friend. They spend at least half of each day standing in front of chalkboards, writing equations and arguing about outer space. Then they write theoretical papers about what they come up with. They're actually quite a big deal in the space physics community, but around here they're just two guys who keep erasing my pictures.

Someone knocks on the door and we put our cigarettes out. Bob hides his pipe in the palm of his hand and opens the door.

It's Gang Lu, one of their students. Everyone lights up again. Gang Lu stands stiffly talking to Chris while Bob holds a match to his pipe and puffs fiercely; nose daggers waft up and out, right in my direction. I give him a sugary smile and he gives me one back. Unimaginable, really, that less than two months from now one of his colleagues from abroad, a woman with delicate, birdlike features, will appear at the door to my office and identify herself as a friend of Bob's. When she asks, I take her down the hall to the room with the long table and then to his empty

office. I do this without saying anything because there's nothing to say, and she takes it all in with small, serious nods until the moment she sees his blackboard covered with scribbles and arrows and equations. At that point her face loosens and she starts to cry in long ragged sobs. An hour later I go back and the office is empty. When I erase the blackboard finally, I can see where she laid her hands carefully, where the numbers are ghostly and blurred.

Bob blows his smoke discreetly in my direction and waits for Chris to finish talking to Gang Lu, who is answering questions in a monotone — yes or no, or I don't know. Another Chinese student named Shan lets himself in after knocking lightly. He nods and smiles at me and then stands at a respectful distance, waiting to ask Chris a question.

It's like a physics conference in here. I wish they'd all leave so I could make my usual midafternoon spate of personal calls. I begin thumbing through papers in a businesslike way.

Bob pokes at his pipe with a bent paper clip. Shan yawns hugely and then looks embarrassed. Chris erases what he put on the blackboard and tries unsuccessfully to redraw my pecking parakeet. "I don't know how it goes," he says to me.

Gang Lu looks around the room idly with expressionless eyes. He's sick of physics and sick of the buffoons who practice it. The tall glacial German, Chris, who tells him what to do; the crass idiot Bob who talks to him like he is a dog; the student Shan whose ideas about plasma physics are treated with reverence and praised at every meeting. The woman who puts her feet on the desk and dismisses him with her eyes. Gang Lu no longer spends his evenings in the computer lab, running simulations and thinking about magnetic forces and invisible particles; he now spends them at the firing range, learning to hit a moving target with the gun he purchased last spring. He pictures himself holding the gun with both hands, arms straight

out and steady; Clint Eastwood, only smarter. Clint Eastwood as a rocket scientist.

He stares at each person in turn, trying to gauge how much respect each of them has for him. One by one. Behind black-rimmed glasses, he counts with his eyes. In each case the verdict is clear: not enough.

The collie fell down the basement stairs. I don't know if she was disoriented and looking for me or what. But when I was at work she used her long nose like a lever and got the door to the basement open and tried to go down there except her legs wouldn't do it and she fell. I found her sleeping on the concrete floor in an unnatural position, one leg still awkwardly resting on the last step. I repositioned the leg and sat down next to her and petted her. We used to play a game called Maserati, where I'd grab her nose like a gearshift and put her through all the gears, first second third fourth, until we were going a hundred miles an hour through town. She thought it was funny.

Now I'm at work but this morning there's nothing to do, and every time I turn around I see her sprawled, eyes mute, leg bent upward. We're breaking each other's hearts. I draw a picture of her on the blackboard using brown chalk. I make *X*s where her eyes should be. Chris walks in with the morning paper and a cup of coffee. He looks around the clean office.

"Why are you here when there's no work to do?" he asks.

"I'm hiding from my life, what else," I tell him. This sounds perfectly reasonable to him. He gives me part of the paper.

His mother is visiting from Germany, a robust woman of eighty who is depressed and hoping to be cheered up. In the last year she has lost her one-hundred-year-old mother and her husband of sixty years. She mostly can't be cheered up, but she likes going to art galleries so Chris has been driving her around

the Midwest, to our best cities, showing her what kind of art Americans like to look at.

"How's your mom?" I ask him.

He shrugs and makes a flat-handed so-so motion.

We read, smoke, drink coffee, and yawn. I decide to go home.

"Good idea," he says encouragingly.

It's November 1, 1991, the last day of the first part of my life. Before I leave I pick up the eraser and stand in front of the collie's picture on the blackboard, thinking. I can feel him watching me, drinking his coffee. He's wearing a gold shirt and blue jeans and a gray cardigan sweater. He is tall and lanky and white-haired, forty seven years old. He has a wife named Ulrike, a daughter named Karein, and a son named Goran. A dog named Mica. A mother named Ursula. A friend named me.

I erase the *X*s.

Down the hall, Linhua Shan feeds numbers into a computer and watches as a graph is formed. The computer screen is brilliant blue, and the lines appear in red and yellow and green. Four keystrokes and the green becomes purple. More keystrokes and the blue background fades to the azure of a summer sky. The wave lines arc over it, crossing against one another. He asks the computer to print, and while it chugs along he pulls up a golf game on the screen and tees off.

One room over, at a desk, Gang Lu works on a letter to his sister in China. *The study of physics is more and more disappointing,* he tells her. *Modern physics is self-delusion* and *all my life I have been honest and straightforward, and I have most of all detested cunning, fawning sycophants and dishonest bureaucrats who think they are always right in everything.* Delicate Chinese characters all over a page. She was a kind and gentle sister, and he thanks her for that. He's going to kill himself. *You yourself should not be too sad about it, for at least I have found a few*

traveling companions to accompany me to the grave. Inside the coat on the back of his chair are a .38-caliber handgun and a .22-caliber revolver. They're heavier than they look and weigh the pockets down. *My beloved elder sister, I take my eternal leave of you.*

The collie's eyes are almond-shaped; I draw them in with brown chalk and put a white bone next to her feet.

"That's better," Chris says kindly.

Before I leave the building I pass Gang Lu in the hallway and say hello. He has a letter in his hand and he's wearing his coat. He doesn't answer and I don't expect him to. At the end of the hallway are the double doors leading to the rest of my life. I push them open and walk through.

Friday afternoon seminar, everyone is glazed over, listening as someone explains something unexplainable at the head of the long table. Gang Lu stands up and leaves the room abruptly; goes down one floor to see if the chairman, Dwight, is sitting in his office. He is. The door is open. Gang Lu turns and walks back up the stairs and enters the meeting room again. Chris Goertz is sitting near the door and takes the first bullet in the back of the head. There is a loud popping sound and then blue smoke. Shan gets the second bullet in the forehead, the lenses of his glasses shatter. More smoke and the room rings with the popping. Bob Smith tries to crawl beneath the table. Gang Lu takes two steps, holds his arms straight out, and levels the gun with both hands. Bob looks up. The third bullet in the right hand, the fourth in the chest. Smoke. Elbows and legs, people trying to get out of the way and then out of the room.

Gang Lu walks quickly down the stairs, dispelling spent cartridges and loading new ones. From the doorway of Dwight's office: the fifth bullet in the head, the sixth strays, the sev-

enth also in the head. A slumping. More smoke and ringing. Through the cloud an image comes forward — Bob Smith, hit in the chest, hit in the hand, still alive. Back up the stairs. Two scientists, young men, crouched over Bob, loosening his clothes, talking to him. From where he lies, Bob can see his best friend still sitting upright in a chair, head thrown back at an unnatural angle. Everything is broken and red. The two young scientists leave the room at gunpoint. Bob closes his eyes. The eighth and ninth bullets in his head. As Bob dies, Chris Goertz's body settles in his chair, a long sigh escapes his throat. Reload. Two more for Chris, one for Shan. Exit the building, cross two streets, run across the green, into building number two and upstairs.

The administrator, Anne Cleary, is summoned from her office by the receptionist. She speaks to him for a few seconds, he produces the gun and shoots her in the face. The receptionist, a young student working as a temp, is just beginning to stand when he shoots her in the mouth. He dispels the spent cartridges in the stairwell, loads new ones. Reaches the top of the steps, looks around. Is disoriented suddenly. The ringing and the smoke and the dissatisfaction of not checking all the names off the list. A slamming and a running sound, the shout of police. He walks into an empty classroom, takes off his coat, folds it carefully and puts it over the back of the chair. Checks his watch; twelve minutes since it began. Places the barrel against his right temple. Fires.

The first call comes at four o'clock. I'm reading on the bench in the kitchen, one foot on a sleeping dog's back. It's Mary, calling from work. There's been some kind of disturbance in the building, a rumor that Dwight was shot; cops are running through the halls carrying rifles. They're evacuating the building and she's coming over.

Dwight, a tall likable oddball who cut off his ponytail when they made him chair of the department. Greets everyone with a famous booming hello in the morning, studies plasma, just like Chris and Bob. Chris lives two and half blocks from the physics building; he'll be home by now if they've evacuated. I dial his house and his mother answers. She tells me that Chris won't be home until five o'clock, and then they're going to a play. Ulrike, her daughter-in-law, is coming back from a trip to Chicago and will join them. She wants to know why I'm looking for Chris; isn't he where I am?

No, I'm at home and I just had to ask him something. Could he please call me when he comes in.

She tells me that Chris showed her a drawing I made of him sitting at his desk behind a stack of manuscripts. She's so pleased to meet Chris's friends, and the Midwest is lovely, really, except it's very brown, isn't it?

It *is* very brown. We hang up.

The Midwest is very brown. The phone rings. It's a physicist. His wife, a friend of mine, is on the extension. Well, he's not sure, but it's possible that I should brace myself for bad news. I've already heard, I tell him, something happened to Dwight. There's a long pause and then his wife says, Jo Ann. It's possible that Chris was involved.

I think she means Chris shot Dwight. No, she says gently, killed too.

Mary is here. I tell them not to worry and hang up. I have two cigarettes going. Mary takes one and smokes it. She's not looking at me. I tell her about the phone call.

"They're out of it," I say. "They thought Chris was involved."

She repeats what they said: I think you should brace yourself for bad news. Pours whiskey in a coffee cup.

For a few minutes I can't sit down, I can't stand up. I can only smoke. The phone rings. Another physicist tells me there's

some bad news. He mentions Chris and Bob and I tell him I don't want to talk right now. He says okay but to be prepared because it's going to be on the news any minute. It's 4:45.

"Now they're trying to stir Bob into the stew," I tell Mary. She nods; she's heard this, too. I have the distinct feeling there is something going on that I can either understand or not understand. There's a choice to be made.

"I don't understand," I tell Mary.

We sit in the darkening living room, smoking and sipping our cups of whiskey. Inside my head I keep thinking *Uh-oh,* over and over. I'm in a rattled condition; I can't calm down and figure this out.

"I think we should brace ourselves in case something bad has happened," I say to Mary. She nods. "Just in case. It won't hurt to be braced." She nods again. I realize that I don't know what *braced* means. You hear it all the time but that doesn't mean it makes sense. Whiskey is supposed to be bracing but what it is is awful. I want either tea or beer, no whiskey. Mary nods and heads into the kitchen.

Within an hour there are seven women in the dim living room, sitting. Switching back and forth between CNN and the special reports by the local news. There is something terrifying about the quality of the light and the way voices are echoing in the room. The phone never stops ringing, ever since the story hit the national news. Physics, University of Iowa, dead people. Names not yet released. Everyone I've ever known is checking in to see if I'm still alive. California calls, New York calls, Florida calls, Ohio calls twice. All the guests at a party my husband is having call, one after the other, to ask how I'm doing. Each time, fifty times, I think it might be Chris and then it isn't.

It occurs to me once that I could call his house and talk to him directly, find out exactly what happened. Fear that his

mother would answer prevents me from doing it. By this time I am getting reconciled to the fact that Shan, Gang Lu, and Dwight were killed. Also an administrator and her office assistant. The Channel 9 newslady keeps saying there are six dead and two in critical condition. They're not saying who did the shooting. The names will be released at nine o'clock. Eventually I sacrifice all of them except Chris and Bob; they are the ones in critical condition, which is certainly not hopeless. At some point I go into the study to get away from the terrible dimness in the living room, all those eyes, all that calmness in the face of chaos. The collie tries to stand up but someone stops her with a handful of Fritos.

The study is small and cold after I shut the door, but more brightly lit than the living room. I can't remember what anything means. The phone rings and I pick up the extension and listen. My friend Michael is calling from Illinois for the second time. He asks Shirley if I'm holding up okay. Shirley says it's hard to tell. I go back into the living room.

The newslady breaks in at nine o'clock, and of course they drag it out as long as they can. I've already figured out that if they go in alphabetical order Chris will come first. Goertz, Lu, Nicholson, Shan, Smith. His name will come on first. She drones on, dead University of Iowa professors, lone gunman named Gang Lu.

Gang Lu. Lone gunman. Before I have a chance to absorb that she says, The dead are.

Chris's picture.

Oh no, oh God. I lean against Mary's chair and then leave the room abruptly. I have to stand in the bathroom for a while and look at myself in the mirror. I'm still Jo Ann, white face and dark hair. I have earrings on, tiny wrenches that hang from wires. In the living room she's pronouncing all the other names. The two critically wounded are the administrator and

her assistant, Miya Sioson. The administrator is already dead for all practical purposes, although they won't disconnect the machines until the following afternoon. The student receptionist will survive but will never again be able to move more than her head. She was in Gang Lu's path and he shot her in the mouth and the bullet lodged in the top of her spine and not only will she never dance again, she'll never walk or write or spend a day alone. She got to keep her head but lost her body. The final victim is Chris's mother, who will weather it all with a dignified face and an erect spine, then return to Germany and kill herself without further words or fanfare.

I tell the white face in the mirror that Gang Lu did this, wrecked everything and killed all those people. It seems as ludicrous as everything else. I can't get my mind to work right, I'm still operating on yesterday's facts; today hasn't jelled yet. "It's a good thing none of this happened," I say to my face. A knock on the door and I open it.

The collie is swaying on her feet, toenails clenched to keep from sliding on the wood floor. Julene's hesitant face. "She wanted to come visit you," she tells me. I bring her in and close the door. We sit by the tub. She lifts her long nose to my face and I take her muzzle and we move through the gears slowly, first second third fourth, all the way through town, until what happened has happened and we know it has happened. We return to the living room. The second wave of calls is starting to come in, from those who just saw the faces on the news. Shirley screens. A knock comes on the door. Julene settles the dog down again on her blanket. It's the husband at the door, looking frantic. He hugs me hard but I'm made of cement, arms stuck in a down position.

The women immediately clear out, taking their leave, looking at the floor. Suddenly it's only me and him, sitting in our living room on a Friday night, just like always. I realize it took

quite a bit of courage for him to come to the house when he did, facing all those women who think he's the Antichrist. The dogs are crowded against him on the couch and he's wearing a shirt I've never seen before. He's here to help me get through this. Me. He knows how awful this must be. Awful. He knows how I felt about Chris. Past tense. I have to put my hands over my face for a minute.

We sit silently in our living room. He watches the mute television screen and I watch him. The planes and ridges of his face are more familiar to me than my own. I understand that he wishes even more than I do that he still loved me. When he looks over at me, it's with an expression I've seen before. It's the way he looks at the dog on the blanket.

I get his coat and follow him out into the cold November night. There are stars and stars and stars. The sky is full of dead men, drifting in the blackness like helium balloons. My mother floats past in a hospital gown, trailing tubes. I go back inside where the heat is.

The house is empty and dim, full of dogs and cigarette butts. The collie has peed again. The television is flickering *Special Report* across the screen and I turn it off before the pictures appear. I bring blankets up, fresh and warm from the dryer.

After all the commotion the living room feels cavernous and dead. A branch scrapes against the house and for a brief instant I feel a surge of hope. They might have come back. And I stand at the foot of the stairs staring up into the darkness, listening for the sounds of their little squirrel feet. Silence. No matter how much you miss them. They never come back once they're gone.

I wake her up three times between midnight and dawn. She doesn't usually sleep this soundly but all the chaos and com-

pany in the house tonight have made her more tired than usual. The Lab wakes and drowsily begins licking her lower region. She stops and stares at me, trying to make out my face in the dark, then gives up and sleeps. The brown dog is flat on her back with her paws limp, wedged between me and the back of the couch.

I've propped myself so I'll be able to see when dawn starts to arrive. For now there are still planets and stars. Above the black branches of a maple is the dog star, Sirius, my personal favorite. The dusty rings of Saturn. Io, Jupiter's moon.

When I think I can't bear it for one more minute I reach down and nudge her gently with my dog-arm. She rises slowly, faltering, and stands over me in the darkness. My peer, my colleague. In a few hours the world will resume itself, but for now we're in a pocket of silence. We're in the plasmapause, a place of equilibrium, where the forces of the Earth meet the forces of the sun. I imagine it as a place of silence, where the particles of dust stop spinning and hang motionless in deep space.

Around my neck is the stone he brought me from Poland. I hold it out. *Like this?* I ask. Shards of fly wings, suspended in amber.

Exactly, he says.

Bulldozing the Baby

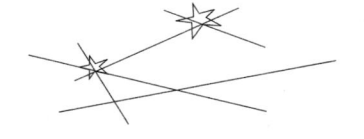

A*t age three, my most successful* relationship was with Hal, a boy doll. He had molded brown hair, a smiling vinyl face, and two outfits. One was actually his birthday suit, a stuffed body made of pink cloth with vinyl hands and feet attached. Clothes encumbered me; I liked the feeling of air on skin, and when left alone for more than five minutes, I'd routinely strip us down to our most basic outfits and we'd go outside to sit on the front stoop. Hal's other outfit was a plaid flannel shirt with pearl buttons and yellow pants with flannel cuffs. He had black feet molded in the shape of shoes.

The gorgeous thing about Hal was that not only was he my friend, he was also my slave. I made the majority of our decisions, including the bathtub one, which in retrospect was the beginning of the end. Our bath routine was like this: My mother would pick me up and stand me in the tub — I had fat,

willful legs, and I wouldn't bend them while she was touching me — then while I was settling into the water and coordinating the bathtub toys, she'd undress Hal and sit him down on the toilet tank to watch me.

"Tell Jo-Jo she is *not* to stand up in the tub," she'd say to Hal, before leaving us to our own devices. I found it unnerving to have her speak directly to him; didn't she know he was a doll? Plus, Hal couldn't stop me from doing anything. The moment she left I'd stand up and sit back down whenever I felt like it. Hal's job was to watch.

The bathtub toys were dull in an indestructible kind of way. You could drown them or bounce them off the ceiling and they were still unbreakable plastic in primary colors. Hal, however, was both filthy and destructible; my mother had proved it by trying to scour his head with an S.O.S. pad — he now had a small bald patch on the crown of his head, just like a real guy.

I decided on impulse to bring Hal into the tub with me, just to see what would happen. First he floated, then when I pressed on his stomach he submerged, smiling placidly. It was at that exact moment that the spark went out of him — he became waterlogged in an unflattering way and all I could do was put him back up, dripping, on the toilet tank. He sat more slumpedly, and the pink cloth of his stuffed body had a gray cast to it. Something had gone wrong with my experiment.

My mother came in and tried to wash my hair. She'd given up reasoning with me long ago, had adopted a style that married brute force with loud comforting comments. "You're such a good girl," she lied, struggling to hold my head in the water. Soap was lapping onto my face. I shrieked and tried to shake my head; a wave washed over my mouth. "One more time and then we're done," she said resolutely, sitting me back up with one viselike hand and squirting soap on my head with the other. I looked her in the eye and shrieked again. My father came and stood in the door of the bathroom, watching.

"What're you doing to her?" he asked my mother.

"She's doing it to *me*," my mother replied grimly. She gestured with her head. "Look at Hal."

Crap. Now I'd have to listen to that. I stepped up my end of the struggle.

"Oh dear," my father said. Hal was collapsed on himself, dripping slightly. My father rolled him in a towel and wrung him a couple of times. I screamed; they were trying to kill us.

"*Shut up*," my mother said. She stood me up and began brass-knuckling my head with a towel. When she was done she swatted my wet rear. It made a loud insulting noise without exactly hurting. I collapsed on the bath mat, wailing, while she strode off to find my jammies.

The bathroom ceiling had sparkles on it. The dog-in-the-boat stain was still there. Hal was wadded up inside a towel on the floor. I unrolled him and we lay on the bath mat together, panting quietly. They had manhandled us.

My mother has hung Hal upside down on the clothesline. I'm spending the morning in the sandbox to be near him, using an old comb to make furrows and lines which I then plant blades of grass in. I'm making a farm. Every once in a while I use the comb on my own hair, and warm sand falls down the back of my shirt. Hal is watching from upside down, clothespins pinched into his calves, vinyl hands dangling near his ears.

"*I am not hurting him*," my mother said dangerously as she pinned him up there. I better not pull a trick like that again or somebody's in trouble. I try to reach the measuring cup and my leg makes the grass fall over. I have to stand up and stomp on it carefully and then sit back down and start over, combing in the rows. Once I find a caterpillar and hold it up to show Hal. He can't see too good upside down. The caterpillar won't get off my finger so I scrape it onto the sand and use my scoop to

throw it out on the ground, along with a considerable amount of sand.

I have on blue sunglasses with wiener dogs on the frames. I can pull up my shirt and fill my belly button with sand except if I do she'll dig it out with the washcloth tonight. I'm starting to learn cause and effect. Hal in the bathtub means Hal up in the air. He still doesn't have his clothes on. I climb out of the sandbox and sit down on the ground to take my sandals off. I put my sunglasses on top of them and stand back up. After I push my shorts and underwear down I have to sit again in order to pull them off my feet. The shirt gets stuck on my head and I can't see. After a frantic second I get it off but it yanks my nose. The barrettes slid out of my hair while the shirt was going past; I put one inside each sandal. I get up and sit on the edge of the sandbox to rest.

A bee is on the hollyhock by the fence. It steps into the flower and walks around, then steps out again, flies to the sandbox, and hangs in the air in front of my face, buzzing. I shake my head at it and it hovers for another instant and then takes off again, flies to Hal, and lights on his hanging hand.

Injury laid right over top of insult. I start screaming.

When she comes out we look at each other for a long moment, then she sighs, reaches up, releases the clothespins, lets him drop, then catches him before he hits the ground. She hands him over and stoops to collect my clothes while I put my sunglasses back on. I follow her to the back door, carrying Hal by the feet. His shoes are warm from the sun and he smiles as I drag his face along through the grass and then — bump, bump — up the two steps and into the house.

Hal's body has become lumpy, with protrusions of wadded stuffing in some spots and absolutely nothing in others. My mother tries to fix him each morning by squeezing him like a

tube of toothpaste, forcing the stuffing from his lower body into his upper body. A gritty, sandlike substance is coming through his pores. He's still smiling. Hal and I are the only ones who don't care about personal appearances.

"She tried to give him a bath," my mother tells my aunt, who is holding Hal and looking at him through the bottoms of her bifocals. They're trying to figure out if he can be given a torso transplant. My aunt runs her thumb over his bald spot.

"The paint's wearing off his head," she says definitively. "Throw him out and get her a new one." Thus spake Bernice.

"No," I say, shaking my head vigorously. I get right up in Aunt Bernie's face. I shake my head again, harder. She holds Hal out of my reach. I do one short bloodcurdling scream and she hands him over.

My mother, the one who is not taking credit for the bald spot on his head, lights a cigarette nervously and exhales. Bernie is the oldest of five brothers and sisters. My own big sister Linda is playing jacks on the kitchen floor and every time I move she calls out *She's getting my jacks.* My mother believes her. One more time and I'm going to be sat right down in a chair. Aunt Bernie is still waiting for a reply. Her eyebrows are in the middle of her forehead.

"Listen," my mother tells her. "She will scream until we're *all* in the asylum, you included." Bernie snorts, takes a cigarette and lights it. Smoke pours out her nose.

"She may run *you*," Bernie says dryly, "but she doesn't run *me*." Her own daughters are in the living room standing in separate corners. The crime was cursing. It's time for Hal's thumb to be sucked.

"She's got that thing in her *mouth*," Bernie says.

"Don't put that in your mouth," my mother tells me in a stagey, I'm-the-mother voice. I stare at her until she reaches over and gives his hand a yank. It doesn't move.

"She's *biting* on it," Bernie says.

"I don't know what's got into her today," my mother says nervously. She lights another cigarette and gives me a desperate glare. Linda's rubber ball bounces one, two, three, four times. Hal's hand drops back down to his side. "Okay then," my mother says.

When they put me down for my nap Bernie looks around the bedroom and says she doesn't know why they've got me in a crib. "It's either a crib or a leash," my mother says shortly. When they leave I cry the minimum amount and then put my feet through the bars. Hal is lying with his head on the pillow and the blanket up to his chin. I put him down at the bottom where he belongs and then I go down there with him. The ceiling is white and has sparkles just like in the bathroom. If I pee in this bed it doesn't matter but I don't have to pee right now. I put my face next to Hal's and close my eyes. The ceiling sparkles appear against my eyelids, like stars. Hal's got his arm under me.

In my sleep I show my girl cousins how to tie shoes, just like my dad showed me. Make a bunny, cross over, push one ear through, and pull. It's supposed to be a bow but it unravels, just like always. *I can't do it*. My girl cousins disappear and in their place is Bernice, who points to the corner. I shake my head. She takes the manual, grasp-and-steer approach. *This is **not** a good idea*, my mother whispers. I'm in the corner all alone and I can't feel Hal's arm in my back. Wherever I am, that's where Hal's supposed to be. I turn around and around, but the corner is completely empty. All that's in it is me.

Under the sofa: quite a bit of dirt, several jacks, a book called *The Wait for Me Kitten*, a ballpoint pen, and the crust off a peanut butter sandwich. No Hal. To look behind the refrigerator you have to put your cheek against the kitchen wall. All that's back there is dirt. The broom closet doesn't even have a

broom in it, just the vacuum cleaner. Under Linda's bed are about ten sandwich crusts, a clear plastic coin purse with an empty lipstick tube inside, the usual dirt, and a strange piece of red felt that looks like the tongue of a stuffed animal. The bedroom closets yield nothing but shoes. Hal wouldn't be able to go out to the sandbox by himself because he can't walk. Nevertheless, I open the back screen door and call to him.

Nothing from Hal, but in the kitchen my mother drops what she's doing and moves directly to the telephone. She dials with a pencil, puts a cigarette in her mouth, fishes around in her pocket for a lighter, finds it, snaps it open, lights the cigarette, and says into the receiver Let me talk to your mom.

The kitchen counter can be gotten to by way of a red step stool; you can climb up there while your mother is in the other room and eat chocolate chips out of the cupboard. You can also stand in the sink and look at the whole backyard through the window. She stops me before I make it up to the counter. She's carrying the phone, the receiver pinned to her shoulder. The other arm picks me off the stool and sets me on the floor. I point to the cupboards.

"He's not up there," she says shortly.

She knows something.

Back in the living room I watch her as she finishes the call and hangs up. She leans back in her chair, lights another cigarette, and blows large ragged smoke rings up to the ceiling. Even when I lie down on the floor right at her feet she won't look at me. From upside down she doesn't resemble herself; she could be a lady from anywhere.

I gently kick the rungs of her chair, once, twice. Her eyes flicker downward for an instant, and then back up. She checks her watch, and then a second later checks it again.

Any minute now our menfolk should be coming home.

From the kitchen come the sounds of sizzling and whispering. Fried chicken and a mother and father. From outside, the rhythmic thump and scrape of a game of jacks being played on the front stoop. Linda and her best friend, Pattyann. In the living room is the sound of a thumb being sucked. My mother has brought out Petie, a stuffed dog with a missing tongue, to sit with me. We're on the sofa, being quiet and waiting. My mother peeks her head out of the kitchen and then summons my father.

"She's back to sucking her t-h-u-m," she says.

"B," my father tells her.

"What?" she says.

"There's a *b* on it," he explains.

"What did I say?" she asks.

"'T-h-u-m,'" he says.

"Either way," she answers.

She's wiping her hands on a dish towel and he's holding a spatula. They're looking at me. Two thumps, a scrape, and Linda tells Pattyann she's a cheater. I use my foot to move Petie down to the floor where he belongs. They consider me and I consider them. My mother is the first to fold.

"Jesus H.," she says, disappearing into the kitchen.

My father brings a pencil and a piece of paper over to the coffee table. We're going to draw pictures. I climb down off the couch and stand watching.

"You don't want to step on Petie, do you?" he asks me. Petie is underneath my feet.

I take the thumb out of my mouth and nod, then put it back in.

He draws a triangle with a beak. "That's a bird," he says, and offers me the pencil.

I can draw pretty hard as long as the pencil doesn't break. When I'm done the whole paper is covered with a picture, and

the bird is nowhere in sight. My father licks one finger and rubs the extra pencil marks off the coffee table.

"Jo-Jo made a gorgeous picture," he calls to my mother. He considers it carefully, turning the paper sideways and then back.

"Is it a house?" he asks me. "Is it a dog? Is it Mommy?"

No, no, and no.

My mother comes in and stands over us. She looks at the picture and then at me.

"Hal?" she asks.

I take my thumb out just long enough to nod.

"This is truly unbelievable," my mother says. She's sitting in the rocking chair with her shoes off, smoking. My father is walking back and forth across the living room, singing. Each time he gets to the fringe on the rug he turns around and walks to the other fringe. The song is one he made up, called "Bye Oh Baby," and usually I hum along but not tonight. I can't actually cry anymore but I can still make the crying noise. He's patting me on the back and I'm patting him on the back. We're walking the floor with each other.

"She's a sandbag," he tells my mother as we go past.

"Tell me about it," she answers.

Linda appears suddenly, squinting in the light. She has her nightgown on backward and her hair is messed up from being asleep. She shields her eyes with one hand and stares at us all. "Can we have pancakes in the morning?" she asks the room.

"I'm going to pancake somebody right now," my mother says, preparing to stand up. Linda stomps back the way she came.

"I'd like to pancake *Bernice*," my father says darkly. He moves me to the other shoulder, turns, and walks. My hand is

tired of patting, I'm just watching the rug go by. Three more times and he walks me over to the rocking chair and points me at my mother.

"She asleep?" he whispers.

My mother and I are looking at each other. "You asleep?" she asks.

I shake my head.

She sighs, stands up, goes to the telephone table, dials, and scratches her head with a pencil while she waits. "Wake up and smell the hysteria," she says into the receiver, and then carries the phone out to the kitchen. My father switches shoulders again and we sit down to rock.

When my mother comes back in she's carrying a bottle of beer. She's glad we're sitting down. Bernie and the monsters stopped at the Dairy Queen out on Route 50 to get ice cream cones on their way home.

"You *bet* they did," my father says, rocking. His shirt smells good.

There was no reason to cart the d-o-l-l in question all the way home, so he was placed in a t-r-a-s-h b-i-n at said Dairy Queen. Under the awning, next to the counter. That would have been approximately three o'clock, and it would be now, oh, twelve-thirty.

My father groans. "Shit," he says.

The chair is rocking and rocking.

My mother lifts her beer bottle by the neck and takes a sip. The chances are slim to none but maybe Roy Rogers should get on Trigger and ride out there. Dale Evans will stay here with her beer.

Rocking and rocking.

My eyes won't open, but I'm still wide-awake. I go back up in the air with my eyes closed and then down the hallway and to the right. My arms flop when he puts me down, but I'm not

asleep. He leaves and comes back with Petie and I try to make the crying noise but nothing comes out.

After he closes the door, I struggle up just long enough to force Petie through the bars and onto the floor where he belongs.

"My pancakes have bonanas in them," Linda tells me. She's wearing shorts, a midriff top, and an Easter hat, pointing her fork at me. I'm sitting in the big-girl chair with a dish towel tied around me so I don't climb down. My pancakes are clean.

"Jo-Jo can have all the bananas she likes," my mother says. "But they don't interest her." She's drinking coffee and yawning, tapping a cigarette against her wrist. She can't find her lighter this morning.

"That's because her doll is gone and she misses him," Linda recites sadly. "Even though our dad went to find him he wasn't there because he probably went to the dump which we're all sad about but there's nothing we can do." She forks in a mouthful of pancake, chews thoughtfully, and swallows. "And now she keeps thinking, 'Where is my *doll?* Where is my *poor doll?* What will I *do* without my *doll?*'" She takes a long drink of milk and looks at my mother. "Right?"

"Right," my mother says dryly. She gets up and lights her cigarette using a burner on the stove. Linda starts to speak again, fork in the air, but she's halted with a look and a pointed finger.

I can't eat pancakes that don't taste good. I push the plate away and lean over as far as the dish towel will allow, put my cheek on the tablecloth, and close my eyes. Now they're gone and it's pure dark. My thumb tastes like syrup.

She's talking to her girlfriend on the phone and polishing the spoons at the same time. I'm sitting on the footstool which I've

pushed in front of the picture window. Linda walks by on her way outside, carrying a plastic bowl which she holds way up in the air as she passes.

"I've got a norange," she tells me.

And I have a pop bead that rolled out from under the footstool. It fits perfectly in my nose but we're not doing that. I'm just holding it.

"You didn't ruin it," my mother says. "Fill it with water, put in a tablespoon cream of tartar, and then boil the hell out of it. You'll take all that black off there." She listens for a minute, polishing. "Well, you can be the bad housewife and I'll be the bad mother." She listens again. "Sitting at the window, staring out," she says in a low voice. "I don't know what to do next." More listening and then she laughs. I put my forehead and both my hands against the glass. Behind me is the sound of snapping fingers. She can snap her fingers so loud it scares you. I climb down off the footstool to get my bead and then climb back up again. She snaps again, twice, and I have to carry the bead over and deposit it in her hand. She puts it in the pocket of her pants and we stare at each other. "Maybe he ought to be cooking for *you*, since he's the big expert," she says. She feels my forehead, runs one hand quickly down the back of my shorts, turns me around, and points me at the stool. "I sprinkle potato chips over the top before I put it in," she says.

The front sidewalk has a hopscotch picture on it but Linda and Pattyann aren't out there. I don't know where a dump is, and I don't know how long it takes to get back from one. A car pulls up to the curb, stops, and one of my girl cousins gets out holding a sack. Aunt Bernie and my other cousin stay in the car.

My mother hangs up the phone and goes to the door while Bernice and I watch each other through the glass. "We went to the store and this is for Jo-Jo," my cousin says when she hands the sack over. She's been crying. "*We* didn't get anything!" she bursts out.

My mother sends her into the kitchen for cookies. "One for you, one for your sister, and none for your mom," she tells her. She holds up the sack and calls, "You didn't have to do this!" to Bernie, who rolls down her window.

"You're raising a brat!" she hollers.

My mother laughs and shakes her fist in the air. The girl cousin goes back down the sidewalk and triumphantly shows her mother the cookies before getting in. They pull away from the curb and my mother waves as they head down the street, then says, "I'd like to slap that mouth right off her face."

Linda and Pattyann come into view on the other side of the street. They look both ways and then hop across the street on one foot.

"I can't *wait* to see what's in here," my mother says brightly, setting the sack on the coffee table. She checks all her pockets, looking for her lighter, then puts a cigarette in her mouth and heads to the kitchen to light it on the stove.

They got that sack at the store. Outside, a lady is walking by with a dog, and Linda and Pattyann pet the dog so fervently the lady has to pull him away and keep going. The sack is folded over at the top and it's pretty big but not that big. Linda and Pattyann start playing hopscotch on the front sidewalk, using soda crackers for markers.

My mother is all excited about the sack. She sits down with her ashtray and pats the couch next to her. I climb up and then lie down with my eyes closed. She can't figure out why we aren't more curious about our new present. It must be something very special or they wouldn't have brought it all the way over here. You know, there just might be something inside that will make Jo-Jo forget her troubles. So. Is somebody ready to go down for her nap, or is she ready to *sit up here right now* and see what's in the sack?

It's a box with a picture of girl on it. She's wearing an apron over her dress and a pearl necklace. Her hair is curled and she

has lipstick on. Inside the box are a broom, a dustpan, and a vacuum cleaner.

"Christ," my mother snorts. She puts her cigarette out, pulls me onto her lap, and rests her chin on my head. "Poor Jo-Jo," she says quietly.

They are miniature, and the vacuum cleaner has a pretend cord and a pretend knob to turn it on and off. The broom is yellow, the dustpan is pink, and the vacuum cleaner is orange with a pink and yellow striped handle.

They're so glamorous I can barely look at them.

"She spent the whole afternoon cleaning under the beds," my mother tells my father. They're sharing a beer in the living room. My hair is wet from the bath and I have my cowgirl jammies on. Linda is in the bathtub now, singing a loud, monotonous song about not getting a new toy.

My mother is sewing a button on my father's shirt while he's still wearing it. "I was having this terrible feeling," she says, "that she'd be this forty-year-old woman, going around telling people that we took her d-o-l-l away from her." She leans down to bite off the thread.

My father tests his new button and it works perfectly. "In three days she won't remember she even *knew* that d-o-l-l," he predicts.

They stop talking and, in unison, lift their feet so I can vacuum under them.

The Family Hour

If she has to come up here we're both going to regret it. It's ten o'clock at night and there has been a territorial dispute over where the line down the middle of the bed really is. After a short skirmish we have yelled downstairs to the mediator. From the top of the stairs all we can see is my father's bare feet crossed on the white divan and a corner of my mother's newspaper. They're drinking beer and eating popcorn. Linda pins my arms behind my back and I bite her. There are screaming noises.

She's had it. Once more and it's going to be the belt.

This surprises us and we tiptoe back into the bedroom. My mother's spanking abilities scare her and so she has a ratio of about one spank per forty threats. We always know where we happen to be along the spanking continuum. That's why we can't believe she's going straight for the belt. We're more afraid

of her hand than the belt, because the belt is a cloth one from a housedress, while her hand is made of granite. But still, this is erratic behavior on her part, and we don't care for it.

Once we're back in the bedroom with the door closed, I say, "I'll give *her* the belt." Linda opens the door again and points her face down the hall toward the stairs.

"Mother?" she calls. "Jo Ann just said something you might want to hear."

There's a thud from downstairs and the sound of foot stomping. Linda slams the door shut and leaps for the bed; we hide under the covers, breathing into our nightgowns, but nothing happens. She faked us out.

The border dispute has to be settled with what is known as a foot-feet fight. This is where you lie on your back and put the soles of your feet against the soles of your sister's feet and then push with all your weak might until she gets tired of it and shoves you off the bed. There are rules to foot-feet fighting, but they are frequently defied, and then someone gets hurt, usually from being rocketed off the bed backward and onto the floor (me). On this occasion what goes wrong is that my own right foot slips from its station on her left foot and propels itself forward until it is stopped by her eye socket. She rolls herself up into a ball.

"That didn't hurt," I say immediately. She's got her head under a pillow, crying furiously and trying to kick me. I carefully get out of the way of her legs until she has me wadded up at the foot of the bed. Her sobs now have an alarming, forlorn quality, and it isn't like her to muffle them. I try a different approach: I start crying, too.

Eventually we fall asleep and roll as we always do into the demilitarized zone down the center of the bed. When I wake in the morning she's sitting in the rocking chair with her ankles crossed, virtuously reading her science book. I go back under

the covers immediately. She has the most pronounced black eye I've ever seen, even on TV. I'm a dead man.

We dress ourselves slowly, not looking at one another; her underwear says Friday, mine says Wednesday, but today it doesn't matter who is right. White knee socks, navy blue knee socks, a gray skirt, a plaid one. Blouses. Teeth, faces, hair.

On the third step from the bottom we stop and look at ourselves in the hallway mirror. I've got my barrette in wrong. Linda has her mohair sweater buttoned over her shoulders like a cape, the way the girls in her class do it. Her face is thin on one side and fat on the other. The fat side is purple. I move slightly so that my own reflection goes into the bevel of the mirror, distorting my nose and one eye until I look like the monster that I am. It's time to sit down.

"Oh no you don't," she says firmly, lifting me by the collar of my shirt, steering me into the kitchen ahead of her. My mother is at the table, looking into a magnifying mirror, putting on makeup. A cigarette is going in the ashtray. My father is cracking our morning eggs into a bowl, dish towel tied around his waist, a spatula in his back pocket. He's singing the "I'm a Bum" song that drives my mother nuts. She's turning the radio up right at the moment we step into her line of view. The announcer makes a staticky squawk and then disappears into silence. My father sets his spoon down. My mother puts her glasses on.

Linda steps forward, Jo Ann steps backward.

I am immediately dispatched to the living room, where I can hear every word but not defend myself by looking stricken. In the kitchen my father whistles long and appreciatively until my mother tells him to shut up. "*Look* at this," she cries. I know just what she's doing: turning Linda's face back and forth, back and forth. I pick up some knitting from its basket and before I realize it I've unraveled a row and a half. My heart starts

pounding. I'm a maniac, kicking people in the head and unraveling knitting.

"We *want* the truth," my mother says, in a voice that ensures she will never get it. A pause, an inhalation, an exhalation, and then the story unfolds. It has a complicated plot that is difficult but not impossible to follow, and several very dramatic things occur, but the gist is this: the bathroom doorknob poked her in the eye. It's a play with several acts but only one actress; my name is never mentioned. I hope he puts the eggs on pretty soon because I'm suddenly hungry. I begin fiddling with my barrette, trying to fix it.

"The doorknob would come up to about *here,*" my mother says. I imagine she's pointing to my sister's stomach.

"Well, it didn't," Linda responds flatly. "It came up to *here,* as a matter of fact."

There is a long, stand-off silence in which all you can hear is Linda thinking.

"I had to pee so bad I was bending *over,*" she says firmly. Brilliant. This is why she's the older sister and I'm the younger one.

Snap. Crack. My mother's lighter and my father's eggs. I don't see why I'm quarantined in the living room when I didn't do anything.

"Can someone please fix my bar*rette?*" I call out.

Right before we file out the door for school, my mother calls me over. She takes off her glasses to get a better bead on me. "Do *you* have any idea why your sister has a black eye?" she asks.

I hesitate. You hate to say it, but when it's the truth, it's the truth. She *never* looks where she's going.

In addition to Linda and me, there's a brother, a strange little guy named Bradley, obsessed with his own cowboy boots. He

paces around and around the house, staring at his feet and humming the G.I. Joe song from the television commercial. He is the ringleader of a neighborhood gang of tiny boys, four-year-olds, who throw dirt and beat each other with sticks all day long. In the evenings he comes to dinner with an imaginary friend named Charcoal.

"Charcoal really needs a bath," my mother says, spooning Spaghettios onto his plate. His hands are perfectly clean right up to the wrists and the center of his face is cleared so we can see what he looks like. The rest of him is dirt.

"Charcoal was locked in the garage all day," he replies. My mother made fried chicken for dinner, but Brad will only eat food prepared by Chef Boyardee.

Across the table from me, Linda pushes a mouthful of potatoes past her teeth and lips until it's hanging there, making me sick. I will only eat potatoes in the form of french fries, and that's because I don't know that french fries *are* potatoes. I have a weak stomach. The second I open my mouth to complain, she sucks it back in and swallows, touches a napkin to her lips, and goes for a preemptive strike.

"Jo Ann is making me sick," she tells my mother. Everyone stops eating and looks at me. I'm searching my chicken leg for the big rubbery string. If I get that string in my mouth, dinner is over.

"I can't find it," I say. The fork won't do what I want it to, and chicken juice is getting on my hands. *Quit looking at me.* My mother reaches over and takes the chicken leg, drops it on my father's plate.

"Find the string for her," she tells him shortly. He looks at her, looks at the leg, and finally picks it up. He begins hacking at it amiably, gazing around the table in benign spirits. He's not paying attention to what he's supposed to be doing; the leg slips suddenly out of his grasp and, in the ensuing clatter, milk is dumped over and my father's plate is flooded.

"Well, I'll be," he says slowly, watching with surprise as his beans and potatoes become islands. A full minute passes while we wait for my mother to do something about it. Eventually she gets up from the table, takes his plate, scrapes it into the dog's bowl, gets another plate from the cupboard and hurls some food onto it. While she's doing all this, my father is sitting with his elbows on the table and his face in his hands.

By the time she puts the new plate of food down in front of him, he's asleep. She shoves him and he comes to with a snort. He no longer has the amiable slap-happy look that offends her; now he looks belligerent. She tells him he's a sorry excuse for a man, which causes him to shrug.

"Who do you think you are?" she asks him. She has her face right up in his. "Dean Martin? Because he's nothing but a lush, too."

My father not only drinks like Dean Martin, but he actually looks like him. They sing alike, too, Dean on TV, and my father when he's shaving. He can't help but like Dean Martin, because they have so much in common. Somehow, though, the word lush hits him the wrong way and he guffaws instead of fighting back. My mother quickly corrects herself.

"He's a *drunk*," she says.

My father doesn't like that one bit. He tries to counter it by insulting Carol Burnett but my mother cuts him off. You don't see Carol Burnett standing there with a drink in her hand; she actually puts on a *show*. Usually I try to think of other things when they fight like this at the dinner table, like how to swallow. But by using television personalities, they're holding my interest. My favorite show is *That Girl*, but I'm one hundred percent sure they aren't going to mention her.

Linda ignores them completely, staring instead at me, willing me to look. I can see out of the corner of my eye what appears to be a Ping-Pong ball coming out of her mouth.

Next to me, Brad is a country unto himself, quietly stirring his Spaghettios and taking occasional peeks under the table at his cowboy boots. His mouth is orange.

Dinner ends when my father gets indignant and tries to stand up. He falls backward into the wall and the big ceramic salad fork drops from its hook and shatters. My mother can't have anything nice; the minute she gets something decent, it's ruined. She works all day and then comes home and makes a beautiful meal like this, and the dog is the only one who will eat it.

Soon there are distant unrestful snores coming from upstairs; from the sewing room the furious, intermittent buzz of the Singer 9000. In the living room, Brad and Charcoal play a friendly game of cards. "When I go like this, it means you lose," the visible one tells the invisible one.

This is our house in Moline, Illinois, a big white clapboard that needs new gutters. There's a little garage out back, and in the corner of the garage is an old cupboard. Inside it are cans of paint, folded rags, tools for cleaning fish, an old dog brush, and a bottle of vodka in a brown paper sack.

Here in the kitchen, African violets bloom wildly on the windowsill, hopped-up with fertilizer. The radio on the counter plays a new Beatles song and the girls take a break from clearing the table to clutch their hearts and listen. Tuesday night at the Beard household, and it's business as usual: Linda washes, Jo Ann dries.

Yimmer the dog is missing. She spends most of her time shedding on the furniture, or balanced on her back legs at the end of her chain, barking at the house. Right now, the last time any of us can remember seeing her was hours ago, at lunch, when she coughed up part of a garter snake on the living room rug.

My father is also missing, which has led the authorities — my mother and her girlfriend — to believe they are together.

"It isn't enough that he goes to the tavern in broad daylight," my mother says to Helen. Her mouth is full of pins. "He's got to advertise it to the neighbors." Popular thinking places Yimmer at the crime scene, a white dog against a brown brick establishment, fodder for local dinner table discussion tonight.

"If there's a garter snake in this neighborhood, then I'm moving," Helen tells her. They're making sheers for Helen's dining room, so she can open her drapes without the whole world looking in. They keep taking the pins out of their mouths in order to smoke, and then putting them back in. As soon as they get the hard part done they plan to switch from iced tea to beer.

All three kids have been dispatched to find the dog on our own block, but I have come back early, due to the bogus nature of the mission. We all know where she is. I'm trying to get my parakeet to look at me. No matter where I stand, next to his cage, he turns around in a single hopping motion and looks the other way.

"I think this bird is mad at me," I say. He wants me to put my finger in there so he can peck it. The back door slams and the refrigerator opens.

"Get out of there," my mother says through her pins.

Linda flops down on the sofa and opens her book, taking small bites off a radish. "She's putting her fingers in the birdcage," she tells my mother.

"I forgot," I say quickly.

"Well, he'll be happy to remind you," my mother says.

"Linda's eating a radish without washing it," I report.

"I wish I had about eight more just like them," my mother tells Helen. She goes to the back door and calls for Brad, very,

very loudly, in a voice designed to scare all neighborhood children, then stops at the refrigerator and gets two cans of beer.

It takes Brad a full ten minutes to report in, and when he does, it turns out he forgot his mission altogether and was making a campfire in the middle of the alley.

"We're rubbing the sticks together and then we're going to cook things over it," he tells my mother. His mouth is still vivid from lunch and he has his T-shirt on inside out. Helen is charmed by him and exclaims over the idea of a campfire in the alley. He glances at her. "Don't worry," he explains, "it's all pretend."

What about the dog?

"Huh?" he says.

The tavern is several long blocks away. The girls are to get their shoes on and go over there with the leash and see if the dog is waiting outside. If she is, they are to put the leash on her and bring her home. If it turns out they can do that without fighting, then they won't get beat to a pulp when they get back.

Helen thinks this is funny and so does my mother.

Two things we are never, under any circumstances, to do. Ride double on a bike and ride a bike on Nineteenth Avenue. Riding double means the person in control isn't, and if she ever catches one of her kids doing it, that's it for the bike; sold. Nineteenth Avenue is at the end of our street, a double-laned thoroughfare with no stoplights, lined with parked cars and carpeted with the pelts of squirrels and stray cats. We aren't even allowed to cross it on foot.

Linda's bike is new and almost too tall for her. We wheel it behind the garage and I climb on the back fender. I've got the dog leash wrapped conveniently around my neck. She gets on and we wobble for a distance, recover momentarily, and then fall over.

This time I sit on the handlebars, which is more comfortable, except Linda can't see around my head and if I shift my weight we swerve harshly. We veer past the campfire crew, who are sitting on the ground holding long sticks over a pile of short sticks; Brad's face is a blur of startlement, but he can be counted on to forget it as soon as we've crossed his line of vision. I'm balancing us by using my legs as rudders and keeping my head to the side so Linda can see where she's going.

Directly to Nineteenth Avenue and a right-hand swerve, out into the stream of Saturday afternoon cars. I bank my legs going around the turn and then am forced to retract them altogether, due to the close nature of the parked cars to my right and the whizzing cars to my left. Once my feet are settled on the front fender, I have to sit straight in order not to fall off, and once I sit straight, Linda can't see. Wobbling begins to occur almost immediately, along with shouting. I'm trying to tell her where to steer and she's trying to tell me she can't. Somebody's mother gets into the act by yelling at us out the window of a car going the other direction. Cars are honking and careening out around us, causing mayhem.

Up ahead there's a gap in the parked cars. A little street. I can't tell if she plans to take it or not, but I'm going for it. I bank my legs again and the traffic arcs out around us; Linda tries to compensate by leaning in the other direction. She uses her forehead to butt me between the shoulder blades.

No.

Yes.

Around the corner, clipping a parked car.

Sewer grate. *Here comes a sewer grate.*

Hard to describe how skinny my legs are, except to say that one of them fit perfectly down the sewer grate. I'm wearing the bike like a cape on my head and shoulders; Linda is in a heap with the wind knocked out of her. Her lips are moving but the sound is missing.

My leg is in the sewer.

One end of the handlebars is jammed into the grate and the front wheel, now curved like a potato chip, is pinning my head down. Six feet away, Nineteenth Avenue roars dynamically. Below the street, the air is cool and damp, like air-conditioning.

MY LEG IS IN THE SEWER.

Linda is up, making a bleating sound and circling her bike. Okay, she can't believe this. This is a practically *new* bike. This bike is now *ruined*. If it isn't ruined, you could've fooled *her*.

MY LEG IS IN THE SEWER.

She grabs the handlebar and tries to twist it out of the grate. When she lets go, my chin is pressed to the ground. I can now see the undercarriages of cars whizzing past, six feet away. The first one that decides to turn the corner will smash me like a garbage can lid. The direness of the situation dawns on both of us at the same moment. Linda steps discreetly onto the curb and starts walking backward.

DON'T LEAVE ME HERE.

"I'm not," she says, and then turns and starts running. She stops at the end of the block and begins limping, holding her elbows, until she's out of view.

This is more of an alley than an actual street, and the houses look like nobody's home. I try hollering as loud as I can, but Nineteenth Avenue drowns me out. Now my throat hurts. I'm going to be killed, and the only people I know in heaven are my grandfather and an old dog named Mike, who *got hit by a car*.

Help! Help! Help!

Nobody helps you when you need help. When your sister left you trapped in the sewer and your dad is at the tavern, drinking with the dog. Screaming doesn't work but I can't stop doing it. Nobody is helping me!

Oh, wait. Here they come. My mother and Helen, walking briskly, Linda hanging back a few paces, nursing herself. Helen points and suddenly my mother breaks into a run. I've

never seen her run before! She gets larger and larger, her mouth a stark gash across her face, until she's just a pair of feet, the bike is wrenched out of the grate and thrown on the curb, I'm lifted, turned, and pulled. Up and out.

Well. That was easier than it looked.

Helen unwinds the leash from my neck, picks the gravel out of my shinbone, and tugs my shorts back around where they belong. She brushes the seat harder than she needs to, but I'm not in a position to say anything. My mother is sitting on the curb with her head on her knees, panting quietly and weeping.

Linda is just arriving on the scene. "Well, *that* was a close one," she says. "Just the kind of situation you read about, where a kid is riding her sister's bike and gets too close to Nineteenth Avenue." She's talking directly to Helen. My mother looks up.

"Get home," she says.

Linda is in for it.

"The both of you," she tells me.

We try to wheel the bike but it won't. Linda picks up the front end and I pick up the back end. At the end of the street we have to set it down for a second. My mother and Helen are still back there, sitting on the curb. My mother is talking and Helen is shaking her head.

My sewer leg is still cool to the touch. We pick up the bike and carry it another half block before resting. My mother and Helen are a ways behind, walking slowly.

"I think she's laughing," I tell Linda.

She sets down her end, fiddles with her shoelace, looks backward under her armpit, and then picks up the bike again. We resume walking. "I think she's crying."

She may be right. Either thing is possible.

We stow the bike in the garage for our dad to look at once he sobers up. Tomorrow, or a week from tomorrow, hard to say.

In the house, we divide up. I take a can of Pledge into the living room and start polishing the furniture; Linda runs dishwater and briskly begins dumping glasses and spoons into it. This place is a mess. My parakeet is asleep on his perch. I stick my finger through the bars and he's on it in an instant, biting into my knuckle with his beak. The door slams and I race back to my Pledge and spray it dramatically on the coffee table, all around the plastic flower arrangement.

Yimmer trots into the living room, leash trailing. She inspects the spot where she threw up earlier and then goes back into the kitchen for a long drink. My mother and Helen must have swung by the tavern on their way back. Well, that's a relief; one of the boozehounds is home.

The other one, lacking a leash, is always harder to retrieve.

I'm reading a book called *I Was Murdered*, a mysterious ghost story about a lady who can't rest until her killer is found. The cover has a picture of a typewriter, with two bloody hands typing the title on a piece of paper. I got it out of the neighbor's trash, along with some comic books that I already read. I'm partial to ghost stories, but this is nothing like the ones at the school library, where the ghosts invariably turn out to be real people guarding buried treasure. This book has a severed head in a refrigerator and other goings-on that I'm way too young to read about. That's the main reason I can't stop.

My sister is watching *The Man from U.N.C.L.E.* and putting on clear fingernail polish. She's quote babysitting unquote while my parents are over at the tavern. She made Brad go to bed a half hour ago but we can still hear him up there, punching his inflatable clown, which hits the floor and bobs back up again repeatedly. Sometimes he steps on the clown's head for a while to keep him down, and then there's silence. We don't care what he does, as long as he does it up there.

My book has me terrified. I want a bottle of pop really bad but it's in the refrigerator. I can picture it in there keeping a severed head company, blood dripping, pooling up on the Tupperware containers, seeping into the vegetable bin. My mother should watch me better and not let me read books like this, but if I do, my sister should go out to the refrigerator during a commercial and get my pop for me.

"Are you *kidding?*" she says, insulted.

This is grounds for a fight but before I can formulate my opening arguments, the sound of a key in the back door startles us both. *Man from U.N.C.L.E.* is followed by *Mission Impossible* is followed by *Creature Feature.* We're supposed to be able to watch all of them before our parents come home. It's getting so you can't count on anything around here.

My mother comes in and peruses the situation briefly, then listens at the stairs. Brad has fallen suddenly silent up there. I can tell by her face there won't be any *Creature Feature,* and popcorn is out of the question. Linda is watching her show intently, looking neither left nor right. I put my book down and watch it, too.

"This is a *great* show," I say to the room.

Out in the kitchen, my father is opening cupboards and getting spoons. When he opens the refrigerator there's a long moment of silence and then he shuts it again. I guess there was no head in there. A minute later he appears with ice cream, a bowl for Linda, a bowl for me, and a giant mixing bowl of it for himself. He joins us for the last fifteen minutes of *The Man from U.N.C.L.E.,* acting very impressed when Illya Kuryakin shoots a guy using his ballpoint pen for a gun. Yimmer is sitting on his lap.

"Is this the one where he has a telephone in his shoe?" he asks me.

"*Get Smart,*" I tell him. This confuses him for a moment and

then he understands, and nods. It's been about two months since he's had a drink. Every night he sits in here while we watch TV, reading his bird books and talking to us. At first we didn't like it, but now we do.

My mother is in the kitchen alone, chipping the polish off her nails and smoking. I put the ice cream dishes in the sink and drift toward the refrigerator, where my bottle of pop is waiting.

"No you don't," she says curtly.

Nothing is fair around here. I can't decide whether to argue or not. The only light is coming from the living room, and she has her glasses off. Her eyes look weak and vulnerable, but her lips look like blades.

"He embarrassed me to death tonight," she says.

Uh-oh. Why did I come out here; what was I thinking?

"In front of everyone," she continues. "Embarrassed. To *death*."

She looks pretty alive to me, but if the truth be known, I've been embarrassed by him myself. Slumped and staggering, or sleeping all night in the passenger seat of the car, parked in the driveway, because he can't manage the back steps. Disappearing into the garage at odd times during the day, sipping from a sack and staring at the back of the house through the dark doorway, thinking no one can see him. We see him.

"There we all are," she says in a low voice. "Playing cards, trying to have *fun*, drinking a few cocktails, and he sits there for two hours drinking *orange juice*. Holier than thou; won't even have a drink on a Saturday night when we're at a *tavern*."

I think about this, standing on one foot. The dark kitchen, her cigarette going, the bitten-off words. It's hard to know what expression to put on my face. From the living room comes the sound of a fuse burning and then a theme song starts up.

"*Mission Impossible* is on," I tell her. She turns back to her

ashtray and I return to the sofa. Linda is explaining the gist of the show to my dad.

"They all have different identities, and they have impossible missions," she tells him.

"I see," he says agreeably. "All different identities and missions."

"Impossible ones," she stresses.

"They aren't *impossible*, the people just think they are," I explain.

"They *seem* impossible, until the different-identity guys take over," he clarifies. "Is that it?"

We nod. He's drinking a glass of milk.

"Want me to get you a bottle of beer?" I ask him. Linda swivels her head around to stare at me but my dad keeps watching the television. After a minute he shakes his head no.

I want to go back to my book and leave them to their show, my mother to her dark kitchen, but I can't. My words are still hanging in the air of the living room, drowning out the TV. My dad is staring at *Mission Impossible* but he's no longer watching it.

Eventually, he shifts his weight and Yimmer stands up on his lap. She turns around and stares him in the face with her ears folded back and her tail going. He kisses her on the forehead, sets her on the floor, and stands up. Out to the kitchen. The refrigerator door opens, closes.

Yimmer's ears go up as she listens. Linda looks at me and I look at my book. Then the familiar, inevitable sound of a bottle being opened.

There's going to be a style show at school, something the PTA dreamed up. My mother is sewing three matching outfits and we have to be in it. Every time I think about it I feel sick; the

dress she's making for me has the wrong kind of sleeves and she's threatening to give me a permanent. The last time she gave me a permanent only one side of it took, and I looked like I had a bush stuck to my head.

"You're not going to be in a style show with stringy hair," she tells me. She's working on a little shirt for Brad made of the same material as my dress and Linda's.

"Why don't you put puffy sleeves on *him* for a change?" I ask her. He's in the kitchen, eating a post-dinner bowl of cornflakes.

"No!" he calls out, alarmed.

"If I hear another word about sleeves, you won't *be* in a style show," she says to me.

"Sleeves," I reply.

Brad's in the doorway with a dripping spoon. She shows him his shirt with its long sleeves attached. It's getting cowboy fringe on the yoke. He goes back in the kitchen.

Linda is doing her homework at the same big table where my mother is sewing. Neither of them is interested in talking to me. The pattern for our dresses shows a picture of two girls, a younger one with short curly hair and puffy sleeves, an older one with long swingy hair and a little cape.

"You should make Linda wear this cape," I say to my mother. Linda looks up.

"You'll both have the cape," my mother says firmly.

A cape! Oh my God.

Linda starts poking herself in the head with the eraser on her pencil. She can't do her math and she's starting to get hysterical. My dad is the only one who can do math around here and we have no idea where he is. He didn't show up for dinner again, and it's a sore subject with my mother.

"Let me see," she tells Linda. This won't work. My mother can always get the answers but she figures it out in her head in-

stead of on the paper. They make us figure it out on the paper to keep our parents from doing it for us at night when we're having hysterics.

"That's *old math*, Mother," Linda says desperately. "Do it in *new math*."

"Oh, *new math*," my mother says. "What a load of bullshit." She goes back to her sewing.

One time when Linda was three she shoved a tiny toy train up her nose to see how far it would go. It went quite a ways and she had to have it removed at the hospital. My mother has never gotten over this, and in our house, Life Savers and dry cleaning bags are treated like loaded handguns. So when Brad makes a choking noise out in the kitchen all hell breaks loose here in the dining room. My mother leaps up, throwing the shirt one way and the fringe the other, Linda drops her pencil, Yimmer barks.

Brad appears in the doorway, enormous-eyed. He points back to the kitchen with his spoon and then pushes past my mother into the living room where he turns and points again, then buries his shocked face in a sofa pillow. There's something in the kitchen! The rest of us crowd through the doorway to see.

Nothing.

My mother screams. I look around wildly and then I see it. Through the glass of the back door, framed by my grandmother's lace curtains, a face wearing a creature-feature mask. Black hair, forehead, two stunned eyes, and then the rest is blood. It looks like my dad. He fumbles for the doorknob but can't see through the mask, his hand slips and he cries out, something slides from his mouth and lands on his shirtfront; a wad of blood. My mother springs forward, opens the door, and we get the full picture. His clothes are frozen to his body and over it all, shirt, sport coat, trousers, is dark blood, coming

from his mouth. Some of it is frozen and some of it is fresh. He can't move at all and when Linda and my mother try to pull him inside he groans and resists.

We get him up over the threshold, my mother on one side, Linda and me on the other, and then try to sit him in a chair in the middle of the kitchen. His legs won't bend. He groans again and then, with a noise like cracking ice, sits. My mother opens the oven door and turns it up to five hundred. She wants to look inside his mouth but he won't let her, so she gets a clean dish towel, wets it under the faucet, and starts wiping the blood from his face while Linda and I try to remove his shoes. The laces are stiff but the shoes come off okay. When we peel the socks away, his feet look like long yellow boats. My mother gasps when she sees them, then hands each of us a towel and tells us to rub. When we do, he makes the groaning noise again so we stop. She resituates him so he's closer to the oven, and then fills a dishpan with tepid water. When she sets his feet in it he makes a moaning sound.

Still working on his face, she tells me to go to the phone. I do. She tells me the number to dial and what to say. My aunt answers.

"It's Jo," I say.

"Well, hi Jo," she answers cheerfully.

"My mom needs you right now," I recite.

There is no pause. She's on her way. Twenty minutes.

The oven is blasting heat out into the kitchen. As my father thaws, the story comes out. It's hard to understand what he's saying, his words are slurred and when he talks blood dribbles out, over his chin and onto his soaked shirt. He wrecked the car.

Oh! my mother cries. The beautiful new Impala! Gold with gold interior!

He was drinking with Charlie at Silver's.

Silver's! Down in the west *end?* Silver's!

Left and started driving back, was coming around the viaduct, something happened.

The *viaduct!* At the slough? Clear down *there?* Oh my God!

She's walking in circles, frantic, stopping to clear the blood from his mouth. *The slough!* Linda is gone, somehow, it's only me in here with them.

Lost control and the car went down over the embankment into the water.

Into the *water?* Oh my dear goddamned *God!*

When he opened his eyes he was underwater and the window wouldn't roll down.

My mother is moaning and twisting the bloody dish towel.

He got it down finally and swam to shore, started walking, and came home.

You *walked?* From the *viaduct?* Five *miles?*

The kitchen is baking hot, but it's November outside. When I traipsed the four blocks to school this morning I had on my winter coat, a scarf, a hat, and mittens. And I was still cold. Suddenly my mother stops.

"Where's Charlie?" she asks him. Charlie is his drinking buddy.

He doesn't know.

Where is Charlie? Was he in the car?

He can't remember. My mother's face is stark white. Linda appears in the doorway. With her eyes on my father, she reaches out for me and we hold onto each other while my mother fumbles the phone book out of the drawer and begins clawing through it. She finds the number and dials. Someone answers.

"You S.O.B.," she says into the receiver and hangs up.

I guess he was home. The back door opens and my aunt comes in. When she sees my father she starts weeping with her hand over her mouth. Like everyone else, she's fond of my dad,

she just wishes he would behave better. My mother tells her the story in terse words while my father dozes off, his head falling forward on his chest. He jerks awake and groans. Linda takes his feet out of the water and dries them.

"We love you, Dad," she whispers. He groans again as she tries to put dry socks on his poor feet. She stops and looks at me.

"We love you, Dad," I whisper. I help get the socks on and then we step back and wait until my aunt sends us into the living room. They're going to take him to the hospital.

From the sofa, arms around each other, we listen to the sounds from the kitchen, grunts and cries as they get him to his feet. My aunt appears in the doorway with her purse over her arm.

"Where's Brad?" she asks us.

Linda is mute. "Upstairs," I say.

"Jody, you go check on him," she tells me. "And I'll be back here as soon as we get your dad taken care of." She disappears again and there's a series of muffled cries as they ease him through the door and down the back steps. Linda and I each take our arms back and sit quietly, side by side on the sofa. Finally I have to speak.

"What was in his mouth?" I ask her.

"Everything but teeth," she replies.

His teeth are gone! His beautiful teeth that he smiles with.

The kitchen has to be cleaned up. There are bloody towels all over the floor and the oven is still blasting out heat. Linda will do that while I go upstairs to find Brad. She stands up wearily and doesn't move until I give her a push from behind. The steps go on and on forever until I'm finally at the top. The only light on upstairs is in the bathroom. Brad is in there, throwing up. I listen for a moment, until it's silent, and then push the door open. He's sitting on the floor next to the toilet,

a dripping washcloth in his hand. I take it from him and wring it out. All around the toilet are chewed cornflakes and old Spaghettios.

"I can't find Charcoal!" he tells me. "He saw Dad and runned away!" I give the washcloth back and tell him to stay there, I'll go look for Charcoal.

I close the door behind me and stand for a moment in the dark upstairs hallway. I can hear Linda in the kitchen, moving things around, running water in the sink. In the morning, down at the slough, we'll watch them lift our gold Impala, dripping, from the icy water. By then we'll know that four of his ribs were broken on impact, and my mother will show us the terrible gouges on the steering wheel where his front teeth hit and were driven up into his head, behind his nose, perilously close to his brain. She'll tell us how the surgeon had to go in with a scalpel and remove them, one by one, while he thrashed, too drunk to be put under. His anesthesiologists were named Jack and Bud, she'll say grimly, drawing on her cigarette. Jack Daniel's and Budweiser.

I wait in the dark hall, counting to twenty, and then to fifty. I push the door open and go back in the bathroom.

"I found good old Charcoal," I say.

Brad looks up at me from his spot on the floor. He's been rubbing the washcloth across his brow and his hair is standing up in front. He stares at the air next to my shoulder for a moment, searching. Suddenly relief floods across his face.

"Hi," he says.

Waiting

H*e places himself in the gentle* curve of the kidney-shaped desk. It is reddish mahogany, gleaming with Pledge and elbow grease. My sister can't take her eyes off the desk, because she's been looking for one like that at yard sales and estate sales and Saturday morning auctions for months. I, on the other hand, am captivated by the little guy sitting at the desk. He's in a somber profession, a low-voiced talker, a sympathizer, a crooning gentleman, here to make it all less of a hassle. He shuffles papers, twists the top of his thin gold pen and the ballpoint moves gently into place. He looks like he's been carefully dusted with talc — his head is bald and pink but it is not gleaming or garish in any way. Instead it has a matte surface, and the white hair around the bottom half of his head is straight and coarse. His shirt is white and the tips of the collar are crisp as notebook paper. Beneath

his chin and above the snowy embankment of his shirtfront rides a bowtie, black with a pattern of small golden shields. It manages to be both pert and dignified, cheerful if you feel like being cheerful, or old-fashioned and somber if you're bummed.

Linda suddenly gets the hiccups and doesn't try to hide it. Each time she hiccups he touches his ear or clicks his gold pen. His earlobes are amazingly long and thick for such a little old man. Linda hiccups loudly and begins weeping. I give her the usual sympathetic glance and pat her hand, he gently leans forward and indicates with a gesture the box of tissues on the corner of the desk. She takes one and hiccups into her hand, subdued. She is over it already, I can tell. I try to catch her eye to point out the combed tufts emerging from his ears. He smiles a dim and sincere smile, finds the floor with his tiny feet, rises. He comes out from around the kidney-shaped desk and prepares his face for the task at hand. We move in behind him and trail down the carpeted hallway of the mansion, Linda noticing the wainscoting and chandeliers, me watching the back of his neck. He opens the door with a miniature flourish and moves back demurely. We step past him and into the room full of coffins.

The best ones are wood, rubbed to the sheen of the mahogany desk, lined with soft padding, intricate tucks and pleats and folds. All that effort. Linda runs her hand along the surface of one, pokes the satin pillow delicately with one finger. It has the kind of brass handles you find on an old-fashioned sideboard. "This one looks like a yacht," she remarks.

I glance at Mr. Larson but he's looking studiously at the tips of his shoes, rocking himself gently forward and backward, waiting. Somewhere deep within the house something flushes, long tubes feed fluids into and out of stiffening lumps.

"I can't do this," I tell them. He reaches behind the door for a folding chair and as he pulls it out the seat falls smoothly into

place with a satisfying click. I sit down while Mr. Larson pads down the hall to get me a glass of water. He is accommodating and resourceful but clearly unimpressed, like a plumber in the presence of a medium clog. While he's gone Linda takes my hair in her hands and winds it softly, lets it drop. She points to the hull of a metal-sided casket.

"I like that one," she says. She wanders over and peers inside, touches the lid. She turns after a moment. "Can you keep doing this or do you need to leave?"

I shrug. Better now than later, which could end up being Christmas morning. The casket she's touching looks like the *Titanic,* gunmetal gray, waiting to be launched.

"What a waste, don't you think? All those gorgeous trees being chopped down just to get planted all over again," she said. "Here comes your guy."

He crouches to hand me the cup of water, hands on knees, wrinkled-up brow. It tastes like water from a bathroom sink.

"We think we might get her a metal one," I tell him, rising. "We like the wooden ones but they're too nice to put in the ground." I look to Linda and she nods in support.

"Plus," she says, "you know." She thinks for a second while we wait and then it comes back to her. "They go in a *vault,*" she finishes. "So who cares." She looks at him probingly. Her eyes have soft blue pouches underneath and she's getting a dangerous air about her.

"We have to get going anyway," I tell him. "We have to get back before she wonders where we are."

In her hospital bed, bent like a branch against the pain, she watches the clock, anticipates the arrival of a daughter. *Where have you been?* Her voice vanished three days ago, leaving eyes and hands for communicating. *I've been here all alone, no one would stay in the room with me, you're the only one and you left.* This is my shift alone with her. The afternoon pulls itself along.

On the rolling lunch tray is a plate of Christmas cookies dec-

orated with glaring Santas and crooked reindeer shapes. One kind has maroon jelly poured into a reservoir in the center and I take a small bite. I have a thing about red jelly but creaky old Velma Edwards made it so I'm willing to give it a shot. Ready, aim, it lands with a crumbling thud in the wastebasket. My mother rolls her gray, diminishing eyes and gives an invisible smirk. Linda has eaten almost all the good ones, left the jelly and green sugar for me. *Where did you girls go?* She has a clear tube poked up her nose nowadays, connected to an oxygen tank like an astronaut prepared to leave the ship. There is absolute silence, the clank and squeak of the hospital giving way for a moment as an angel passes over, wings beating. The instant passes and the hospital resumes itself, a cart bumps, a nurse calls out loudly, rudely, somewhere down the hall. In the room Coke seethes as I pour it into a glass. *Where did you girls go? Why did both of you need to go at once, leaving me here by myself?* I get a picture of her long ago, shopping, eating lunch in the mezzanine at McCabe's, picking out school clothes. Tall and thin in a beautiful suit; lemon meringue pie and coffee. The slide changes and the tufted ears of tiny Mr. Larson click into view. *Why did both of you have to go at once?* I rise to the occasion. Now-now, I point out, it's awful close to Christmas to be asking those kinds of questions.

Her eyes move past me, over my head, and I feel suddenly the tepid breath of Barnelle. He's a swashbuckler today, actually wearing one of those head things, like a doctor in the movies. It is a flat metallic disk connected to a band and he lifts it off and shoves it into the pocket of his suitcoat. The hair over the top of his head is a delicate auburn doily. He pats it down, using the palm of his hand, pushing the tattered strands back in place, willing them to stay there. He's wearing a plastic Santa Claus face on his lapel. He smiles at her, he has always acted as though he loves her and regrets this. He acknowledges

me with a tilt of the head, some kind of invisible language that works, lifts her wrist and counts the pulse, corpuscles stepping through from her hand to her arm, one by one, like soldiers heading back to camp. He finishes and says Hello, girls in a sweet, cheerful voice and then pulls the string on his Santa Claus. The nose lights up and beams across the bedcovers. Barnelle is sending us a signal, Santa's nose twinkling like Mars. It's four o'clock and I'm ready to do something else for a while. My legs want to walk, my eyes keep finding the window.

"I saw Barn-door," Linda announces. She is back, ready for her shift, standing in the doorway with snow melting on her coat collar. "He was climbing into his gold-plated Cadillac, hightailing it home." Linda hates Barnelle with a rare enthusiasm, able to tick off his crimes on the fingers of both hands. She passes the plate where the rejected Christmas cookies used to be. "God, you'll eat *any*thing," she remarks cheerfully. She's leaving tracks all over the clean floor, in meandering circles. She's been wrapping Christmas presents for her kids, I know, and her eyes look better. She crinkles them at me sympathetically. "Was Barn-door open?" she asks. This is rhetorical. Over on the bed the gray eyes are closed. Linda wants to know how it's going, how she's doing, but the eyes might open again unexpectedly. We tiptoe out.

"I stopped at home and went through her closet," Linda tells me. Nowadays she and I speak of the house where we grew up as home, we forget for long hours the places we live now, which have cupboards with our spices and canned peas, dressers with our clothes. When an aunt or our brother relieves us at the hospital we drive over there for some empty time, some quiet, and sit at her kitchen table with the carvings of childhood forks in its surface, stand drinking coffee right on the worn spot where she stood to stuff chickens, weave the crusts on pies. Home, we say to each other, drawing those

dented walls around us like a wool blanket, two little girls in matching nightgowns, pinching and elbowing, acting hateful, getting yelled at. She was browsing, trying to find something to bury her in.

I stretch and yawn, shake it off, tell her about Barnelle's Santa.

"Gawd," she drawls. "Did he let on when or anything?" She squints when she asks this, afraid to know, afraid not to. Barnelle has predicted two days, which will land us right smack on Christmas. We have told each other ironically, Why not? and marvel at how the universe is dribbling us like a basketball and then shooting us into the air.

"He couldn't," I tell her, "because she was alert. And I couldn't follow him out because she already got on me about leaving with you this morning. She wanted to know where we went." We both shiver at that and then in turn begin crying, the ugly kind, where you turn your clenched face to the wall until it passes. A nurse comes forward, silent, and touches our shoulders. This nurse told me yesterday she hadn't finished her shopping, still had crowds and the hectic traffic at the mall to contend with. Last week, when she could sit upright and talk a little, my mother had given me her wedding ring for Christmas.

There is slush and cold air all up and down the hall. When I go back in to get my coat her eyes are open, talking even though no one can hear. *You girls left me again.* Linda is behind me, getting her needlepoint out, untangling skeins of bright yarn. I pull on my gloves slowly, pushing each finger down meticulously, getting my keys ready for the cold, avoiding her eyes. Behind me Linda says, Hey, remembering something. She digs around in her coat pocket.

"Look, Ma," she says softly, moving toward the bed. I step backward into the doorway, halfway gone. Linda holds a sprig

of plastic mistletoe in the air above my mother's head. She whispers something I can't hear and bends down. I'm gone.

Suddenly I have this notion that she needs to wear flannel against her skin. I stop at a department store and join the current of tinkling people, Christmas shoppers. Music rains down and a clerk comes forward to ask if she can help. She has lost the heel to one pump and is trying to compensate by walking on tiptoe with that foot. She leads me to lingerie and begins thumbing patiently through nightgowns on a rack, showing me things. I tell her that it needs to be worn beneath a blouse. This confuses her and she thinks wearily for a second, one finger to her lip, one heel up in thin air. She produces an expensive long-underwear shirt made of raw silk, a tiny pink satin flower on the scooped neckline. I buy it even though I'm not sure anymore why I'm here, what I'm doing. I decide I might as well go back, only two days left.

I run into Barnelle in the main lobby, he's got his small son with him. I feel bad that he can't get any rest, can't be left alone for five minutes. He speaks frankly to me while his son attempts to tie his shoes together. He says quite honestly that he has gotten very attached to her and I say I have too, actually. He hugs me then, hard, his arms like a big pair of forceps. He lets go and one hand scans his head, searching out the wandering hairs, laying them flat. I've seen him on a bench before, reading X rays and shaking his head, biting his nails. He bends down now and unties the laces before he takes a step, his son disappointed but philosophical. There are Christmas presents waiting at home.

The room is darkening, Linda is asleep in the chair, knees drawn up like a shield, hands circling her stockinged feet. I can't tell what's happening on the bed until I turn on the light.

Her eyes are opened wide, frightened, helpless. *You left me, you girls, and here I am in the dark!* Darkness has a personality now, a power. I understand this very well, quilted satin pressing down in the velvet blackness, brushing the nose, the face. I turn on all the lights but Linda continues to sleep soundly until I bump her chair with my foot. She stretches her legs out and groans, gives me a dirty look, and I give her one back. I hold two fingers up to remind her of how much longer she needs to keep this up, to pay attention. She holds up one finger, guess which one, to remind me of who's the oldest, who's the boss. I would love more than anything to slap her.

I go to the cafeteria for a strawberry shake instead, which I can eat in front of her. On the way back up I land in an elevator with ten Christmas carolers. They seem like churchy types, the men are all shaved within an inch of their lives and the women look good-natured and opinionated. Two of them are quietly trying to harmonize on something I've never heard before, something Latin-sounding and mournful. A couple others practice scales and end up sounding out of tune. They get out on my floor and consult a list, everyone trying to get his or her head in there and direct the way. They end up following me, trying to stay a few paces behind. They are going where I'm going.

I close the door behind me and motion my sister over, whisper to her while the eyes on the bed try to make out what I'm saying. Quietly behind me, behind the oak of the door, their voices join together, hesitantly at first and then, gaining momentum, confidently. They are taking care to remember they are in a hospital, there are sick people here, but they love these songs, I can tell. One of the guys has a lilting baritone and one of the women a high vibrato. Linda hesitates and then opens the door, gestures for them to step in. We move to the head of the bed and stand like cops with our arms folded, trying to

smile. They finish one song and all look expectantly at the lady with the vibrato. She says, Three, and they begin to sing "White Christmas." This is our mother's favorite, she used to put Bing Crosby on the turntable when we all sat down for Christmas Eve dinner. It was part of the feast, like the white candles, the clean linen tablecloth, the gleaming china. As she passed the first bowl and our father stood to carve they would sing it together, one at each end of the table, softly serenading their children. Our father, in fact, had a wonderful strong baritone just like someone in the crowd of carolers. Suddenly regret is swelling in the room like the voices of the choir. As she lies in the bed she weeps, for Bing, for the melting, shimmering candles, the filigree on the holiday tablecloth. She is an unwilling astronaut, bumping against the thick glass of the ship, her line tangling lazily in zero gravity, face mask fogged with fear. My sister reaches across, over the bed, and we both embrace the mother, holding her on earth, pulling her onto the ship, breathing our oxygen into her line. Ten hours later she is dead.

Oh God, it is bitterly cold. The snow is crusted over into shocked mounds, hard as Styrofoam. My fingers are burning twigs inside my gloves, my toes ache like amputations. The heater fan in Linda's car screamed until we had to turn it off and give ourselves over to the freezing-freezing cold. Old man Larson is offering something warm in delicate cups. My poor fingers. It is morning now and he is drinking his own cup of something hot. I guess it's coffee, although I can almost see through to the bottom of the cup. He tips the cup to his little-guy lips but refrains from raising a pinky — he couldn't care less about cheering me up. He's in the morning-after mode right now; he's not looking directly at either of us and he has

cleared his throat several hollow times. Linda sits up straighter and visibly tries to pay better attention. She shakes her head and clears her own throat one, two, three times in a row. Now Larson is glaring at her, his eyes vivid blue on a yellow background.

I look away. I can feel her gazing at my ear. I look back. Then she winks and he sees and now it's even more tense.

We have selected the *Titanic* with ivory satin and the vault with the million-year guarantee of no seepage. He has accepted with grace both the outfit we've brought on a wire hanger and the prescription bottle full of safety pins, all sizes, that we think he'll need to make her clothes fit her now. Linda thought he probably had special clamps for that sort of thing but we decided it would be better if he used the safety pins from her junk drawer. He looked at them for a long second and then set them on the corner of the kidney-shaped desk. I've given up on the long-underwear idea. Actually, I'm wearing it myself because of how cold it is outside.

In a brown paper sack sitting next to my chair, between Linda and me, is her wig. We hate to give it over, both of us have held it in our laps at different times during the last few hours. It is too morbid, though, even for us. She takes it out of the bag quickly and shows it to Larson, puts it back in. She told me in the car she was going to try and scare him with it, but I guess she changed her mind.

He informs us that the flowers have started to arrive, invites us to come back and see how they have begun to arrange them on stands and in clusters. We rise and leave the pale gray suit on its hanger, the wig crouching in its sack, the bottle of pins from the top left kitchen drawer. My sister touches the mahogany desk like it's a tree in the forest. As we match his tiny steps down the wainscoted hall we have no idea, at this minute, that he is an artist, a gentleman. We have no idea as we move

toward the scent of the flowers and the Christmas greens that he will continue on through his beautiful house, leaving us behind to read cards and talk. He will go through two more rooms, down a set of stairs to a place where she lies. While we linger, rubbing our hands and whispering to each other, the grandson who is minding us watches the wall and chews gum. At this moment we don't know that downstairs he is working magic, that he will present to us a woman who looks rested.

That's how I will get to see her last, in her pale gray wool suit and pink blouse, her glasses resting on her nose as though she's just dropped off for a minute; her cheeks will be okay again. The clothes will fit perfectly, as though she hadn't lost a pound. Before the crowd arrives, when it's just me and my sister and an aunt, he will reach in his pocket and bring forth the bottle of pins, half gone.

Her hands are the only wrong thing. They look strange to me and I can't figure out why until Linda picks up my hand and shows me: Her wedding ring is on my finger; I forgot she gave it to me. The hands begin to look more normal to me now, and the silence of the room gives way to the breathing of the sisters, the coldness of the kissed hands, and the empty air that says *You girls, you girls.*

Out There

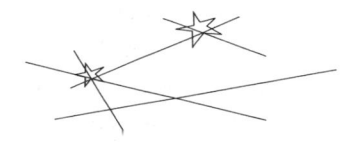

It isn't even eight A.M. and I'm hot. My rear end is welded to the seat just like it was yesterday. I'm fifty miles from the motel and about a thousand and a half from home, in a little white Mazda with 140,000 miles on it and no rust. I'm all alone in Alabama, with only a cooler and a tape deck for company. It's already in the high 80s. Yesterday, coming up from the keys through Florida, I had a day-long anxiety attack that I decided last night was really heat prostration. I was a cinder with a brain; I was actually whimpering. I kept thinking I saw alligators at the edge of the highway.

There were about four hundred exploded armadillos, too, but I got used to them. They were real, and real dead. The alligators weren't real or dead, but they may have been after me. I'm running away from running away from home.

I bolted four weeks ago, leaving my husband to tend the

dogs and tool around town on his bicycle. He doesn't love me anymore, it's both trite and true. He does love himself, though. He's begun wearing cologne and staring into the mirror for long minutes, trying out smiles. He's become a politician. After thirteen years he came to realize that the more successful he got, the less he loved me. That's how he put it, late one night. He won that screaming match. He said, gently and sadly, "I feel sort of embarrassed of you."

I said, "Of what? The way I look? The way I act?"

And he said, softly, "Everything, sort of."

And it was true. Well, I decided to take a trip to Florida. I sat on my haunches in Key West for four weeks, writing and seething and striking up conversations with strangers. I had my thirty-fifth birthday there, weeping into a basket of shrimp. I drank beer and had long involved dreams about cigarettes, I wrote nearly fifty pages on my novel. It's in my trunk at this very moment, dead and decomposing. Boy, do I need a cup of coffee.

There's not much happening this early in the morning. The highway looks interminable again. So far, no alligators. I have a box of seashells in my back seat and I reach back and get a fluted one, pale gray with a pearly interior, to put on the dashboard. I can do everything while I'm driving. At the end of this trip I will have driven 3,999 miles all alone, me and the windshield, me and the radio, me and the creepy alligators. Don't ask me why I didn't get that last mile in, driving around the block a few times or getting a tiny bit lost once. I didn't though, and there you have it. Four thousand sounds like a lot more than 3,999 does; I feel sort of embarrassed for myself.

My window is broken, the crank fell off in Tallahassee on the way down. In order to roll it up or down I have to put the crank back on and turn it slowly and carefully, using one hand to push up the glass. So, mostly I leave it down. I baked like a

biscuit yesterday, my left arm is so brown it looks like a branch. Today I'm wearing a long-sleeved white shirt to protect myself. I compromised on wearing long sleeves by going naked underneath it. It's actually cooler this way, compared to yesterday when I drove in my swimming suit top with my hair stuck up like a fountain on top of my head. Plus, I'm having a nervous breakdown. I've got that wild-eyed look.

A little four-lane blacktop running through the Alabama countryside, that's what I'm on. It's pretty, too, better than Florida, which was billboards and condos built on old dump sites. This is like driving between rolling emerald carpets. You can't see the two lanes going in the opposite direction because there's a screen of trees. I'm starting to get in a good mood again. The best was Georgia, coming down. Willow trees and red dirt and snakes stretched out alongside the road. I kept thinking, That looks like a *rope,* and then it would be a huge snake. A few miles later I would think, That looks like a *snake,* and it would be some snarl of something dropped off a truck.

Little convenience store, stuck out in the middle of nothing, a stain on the carpet. I'm gassing it up, getting some coffee. My white shirt is gaping open and I have nothing on underneath it, but who cares, I'll never see these people again. What do I care what Alabama thinks about me. This is a new and unusual attitude for me. I'm practicing being snotty, in anticipation of being dumped by my husband when I get back to Iowa.

I swagger from the gas pump to the store, I don't even care if my boobs are roaming around inside my shirt, if my hair is a freaky snarl, if I look defiant and uppity. There's nothing to be embarrassed of. I bring my coffee cup along and fill it at the counter. Various men, oldish and grungy, sit at tables eating eggs with wadded-up toast. They stare at me carefully while they chew. I ignore them and pay the woman at the counter. She's smoking a cigarette so I envy her.

"Great day, huh?" I ask her. She counts out my change.

"It is, honey," she says. She reaches for her cigarette and takes a puff, blows it up above my head. "Wish I wudn't in *here*."

"Well, it's getting hotter by the minute," I tell her. I've adopted an accent in just four weeks, an intermittent drawl that makes me think I'm not who everyone thinks I am.

"Y'all think this's hot?" she says idly. "*This* ain't hot."

When I leave, the men are still staring at me in a sullen way. I get in, rearrange all my junk so I have everything handy that I need, choose a Neil Young tape and pop it in the deck, fasten the belt, and then move back out on the highway. Back to the emerald carpet and the road home. Iowa is creeping toward me like a panther.

All I do is sing when I drive. Sing and drink: coffee, Coke, water, juice, coffee. And think. I sing and drink and think. On the way down I would sing, drink, think, and weep uncontrollably, but I'm past that now. Now I suffer bouts of free-floating hostility, which is much better. I plan to use it when I get home.

A car swings up alongside me so I pause in my singing until it goes past. People who sing in their cars always cheer me up, but I'd rather not be caught doing it. On the road, we're all singing, picking our noses, embarrassing ourselves wildly; it gets tiresome. I pause and hum, but the car sticks alongside me so I glance over. It's a guy. He grins and makes a lewd gesture with his mouth. I don't even want to say what it is, it's that disgusting. Tongue darting in and out, quickly. A python testing its food.

I hate this kind of thing. Who do they think they are, these men? I've had my fill of it. I give him the finger, slowly and deliberately. He picked the wrong day to mess with me, I think to myself. I take a sip of coffee.

He's still there.

I glance over briefly and he's making the gesture with his tongue again. I can't believe this. He's from the convenience store, I realize. He has on a fishing hat with lures stuck in it. I saw him back there, but I can't remember if he was sitting with the other men or by himself. He's big, overweight, and dirty, wearing a thin unbuttoned shirt and the terrible fishing hat. His passenger-side window is down. He begins screaming at me.

He followed me from that convenience store. The road is endless, in front there is nothing, no cars, no anything, behind is the same. Just road and grass and trees. The other two lanes are still invisible behind their screen of trees. I'm all alone out here. With him. He's screaming and screaming at me, reaching out his right arm like he's throttling me. I speed up. He speeds up, too, next to me. We're only a few feet apart, my window won't roll up.

He's got slobber on his face and there's no one in either direction. I slam on my brakes and for an instant he's ahead of me, I can breathe, then he slams on his brakes and we're next to each other again. I can't even repeat what he's screaming at me. He's telling me, amid the hot wind and poor Neil Young, what he wants to do to me. He wants to kill me. He's screaming and screaming, I can't look over.

I stare straight ahead through the windshield, hands at ten and two. The front end of his car is moving into my lane. He's saying he'll cut me with a knife, how he'll do it, all that. I can't listen. The front end of his Impala is about four inches from my white Mazda, my little car. This is really my husband's car, my beloved's. My Volkswagen died a lingering death a few months ago. There is no husband, there is no Volkswagen, there is nothing. There isn't even a Jo Ann right now. Whatever I am is sitting here clenched, hands on the wheel, I've stopped being her,

now I'm something else. I'm absolutely terrified. He won't stop screaming it, over and over, what he's going to do.

I refuse to give him an inch. I will not move one inch over. If I do he'll have me off the road in an instant. I will not move. I speed up, he speeds up, I slow down, he slows down, I can see him out of the corner of my eye, driving with one hand, reaching like he's grabbing me with the other. "You whore," he screams at me. "I'll *kill* you, I'll *kill* you, I'll *kill* you . . . "

He'll kill me.

If I give him an inch, he'll shove me off the road and get his hands on me, then the end will begin in some unimaginable, unspeakable style that will be all his. I'll be an actor in his drama. We're going too fast, I've got the pedal pressed up to 80 and it's wobbling, his old Impala can probably go 140 on a straightaway like this. There will be blood, he won't want me to die quickly.

I will not lose control, I will ride it out, I cannot let him push me over onto the gravel. His car noses less than two inches from mine; I'm getting rattled. My God, he can almost reach me through his window, he's moved over in his seat, driving just with the left hand, the right is grabbing the hot air. I move over to the edge of my seat, toward the center of the car, carefully, without swerving.

In the rearview mirror a speck appears. Don't look, watch your front end. I glance up again; it's a truck. He can't get me. It's a trucker. Without looking at him I jerk my thumb backward to show him. He screams and screams and screams. He's not leaving. Suddenly a road appears on the right, a dirty and rutted thing leading off into the trees. He hits the brakes, drops behind, and takes it. In my rearview mirror I see that the license plate on the front of his car is buried in dried mud. That road is where he was hoping to push me. He wanted to push my car off the highway and get me on that road. He was hop-

ing to kill me. He was hoping to do what maniacs, furious men, do to women alongside roads, in woods. I can't stop pressing too hard on the gas pedal. I'm at 85 now, and my leg is shaking uncontrollably, coffee is spilled all over the passenger seat, the atlas is wet, Neil Young is still howling on the tape deck. By force of will, I slow down to 65, eject the tape, and wait for the truck to overtake me. When it does, when it comes up alongside me, I don't look over at all, I keep my eyes straight ahead. As it moves in front of me I speed up enough to stay two car lengths behind it. It says *England* on the back, ornate red letters outlined in black. England.

That guy chased me on purpose, he *hated* me, with more passion than anyone has ever felt for me. Ever. Out there are all those decomposing bodies, all those disappeared daughters, discovered by joggers and hunters, their bodies long abandoned, the memory of final desperate moments lingering on the leaves, the trees, the mindless stumps and mushrooms. Images taped to tollbooth windows, faces pressed into the dirt alongside a path somewhere.

I want out of Alabama, I want to be in England. The air is still a blast furnace. I want to roll my window up, but I'd have to stop and get the crank out and lift it by hand. I'm too scared. He's out there still, waiting behind the screen of trees. I have to follow England until I'm out of Alabama. Green car, old Impala, unreadable license plate, lots of rust. Seat covers made out of that spongy stuff, something standing on the dashboard, a coffee cup or a sad Jesus. The fishing hat with a sweat ring around it right above the brim. Lures with feathers and barbs. I've never been so close to so much hatred in my whole life. *He wanted to kill me*. Think of England, with its white cows and broken-toothed farmers and dark green pastures. Think of the Beatles. I'm hugging the truck so closely now I'm almost under it. Me, of all people, he wanted to kill. Me.

Everywhere I go I'm finding out new things about myself. Each way I turn, there it is. It's Jo Ann he wanted to kill.

By noon I want to kill him. I took a right somewhere and got onto the interstate, had the nerve to pee in a rest area, adrenaline running like an engine inside me, my keys threaded through my fingers in case anyone tried anything. I didn't do anything to earn it, I realize. His anger. I didn't do anything. Unless you count giving him the finger, which I don't. *He* earned that.

As it turned out, my husband couldn't bring himself to leave me when I got back to Iowa, so I waited awhile, and watched, then disentangled myself. History: We each got ten photo albums and six trays of slides. We took a lot of pictures in thirteen years. In the early years he looks stoned and contented, distant; in the later years he looks straight and slightly worried. In that last year he only appears by chance, near the edges, a blur of suffering, almost out of frame.

Just before we split, when we were driving somewhere, I told him about the guy in the green car. "Wow," he said. Then he turned up the radio, checked his image in the rearview mirror, and smiled sincerely at the passing landscape.

The Boys of My Youth

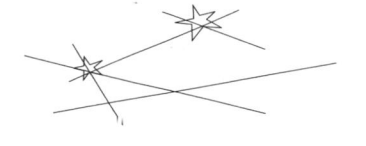

W*e adore Dave Anderson. He plays* basketball in his driveway for hours each day, dribble, fake-out, shoot, dribble some more. He has smooth brown hair cut straight across his forehead, like the Dave Clark Five Dave. We watch him until we're so bored we're falling asleep, then we call him up. It's like a commercial during a TV show. His mom hollers at him, he sets the ball down, steadies it with his foot, opens the screen door, and gives it a kick back against the house so it shuts with a flat slam. The last thing we see is tennis-shoe rubber. We always hang up after he says hello, and then a minute later he's back out, drinking a bottle of Pepsi that he holds by the neck, walking around the court, dribbling in slow motion. He has no idea it's us.

We're not even boy-crazy, just bored, watching him from Elizabeth's bedroom window. She has antiqued French Provin-

cial furniture and a princess telephone. The room is a converted front porch, with floor-to-ceiling windows and a barricaded door we use as an escape hatch on summer nights.

We're reclining on the canopied bed, Elizabeth holding back the curtains with her toes so we can watch him without sitting up. We're getting ready to dial him again, although we just did this less than an hour ago.

"She won't call him in," I predict. Dave's mother has a good sense of humor but it's wearing thin.

"This time I'm telling her who it is," Elizabeth says, dialing with a pencil. There's a chance she'll panic and hand the phone to me so I roll off the bed and stand up for a while, out of range. I have my hair in two pigtails, thin ones, and I try to fluff them up a little bit.

"You just wrecked them," Elizabeth informs me, and then suddenly looks alert. "Hello? Is Dave there?" A moment of silence while she listens. "Could you just tell him it's Brenda?" Brenda is the name of the most popular ninth-grader. We're seventh-graders. Brenda wouldn't be caught dead doing what we're doing.

"She's getting him!" Elizabeth freaks out, tries to force the phone on me. I won't take it and the receiver lies on the bed while we gesture to each other silently. Finally I hold it and we both listen, breathing steadily while he says his Hello? Hello? Just when we think he's getting ready to hang up he says, in a controlled ninth-grader voice, *"I know who this is."*

I jam the receiver back on its cradle and we go nuts, leaping off the bed and running into each other. We pull the curtains shut and overlap them, Elizabeth gets a bobby pin from her dresser and pins them shut. We sit on the floor panting and staring at each other, wild-eyed and no longer bored.

My best friend Elizabeth is tall, with lanky blond hair that looks like straw, a long thin face, and black-rimmed glasses in front of green eyes. These are her pre-beautiful days. I'm short and skinny with a pale face and limp brown hair. People are always asking me if I feel well.

We met in French class, taught by Mrs. McLaughlin, the wife of Mr. McLaughlin, who teaches civics. She's the cheerleading coach, if that gives you any idea, snake-thin with a lantern jaw and hair teased into a brown bubble. She's a monster, although her husband is likable enough.

We all had to take French names, chosen from a list that got passed around the first day. We sat in alphabetical order and my last name starts with a *B* so I got a good one: Colette. Elizabeth, unfortunately, ended up with Georgette, because she comes at the end of the alphabet. In retrospect, I kind of like the name Georgette, but at the time it was the kiss of death. It sounds like the parents were hoping for a boy.

First week of junior high, everyone is terrified of their lockers and the hall monitors. It's the year of the tent dress and loud prints, so all the girls look like small hot-air balloons. Fishnet stockings are not allowed, and dresses can be no shorter than two inches above the knee. People are getting busted left and right for that one, sent to the main office where they have to kneel next to a yardstick. If your dress is too short you get sent home, no discussion.

"What if you just happen to *grow?*" Betsy Thomason asks hotly as she's sent from the room by Mrs. McLaughlin.

"I'd suggest you not," Mrs. McLaughlin replies lightly. She rolls her eyes at us in a conspiratorial way, says something in French, and we all titter uncertainly. She's wearing a pale green mohair suit, cinnamon hose, and dark green lizard skin high heels. She weighs about ninety-eight pounds, smells like cigarette smoke, her lipstick goes up above her top lip an eighth of

an inch. The cheerleaders sit on her desk before class starts and trade jokes with her; they call her Mrs. Mick. Everyone else is utterly terrified of her. Suddenly she stops horsing around and looks directly at me, Colette.

"Ou est la bibliothèque?" she asks. I stare at her blankly, with a roaring in my ears. I'm so thin my nylons collect in pools at the knees and ankles, I'm wearing a pink plaid dress made out of spongy material, my hair is shoulder-length and supposedly curled into a flip. It's so fine that my ears stick out on either side of my head. Everyone is turned toward me.

I tilt my head to the side and pretend I can almost think of it. The roaring is louder, like seashells are clamped to my head, my heart is clattering. *Ou est la bibliothèque* . . . I've heard that somewhere before. Chances are it was last night, listening to my French dialogue record.

"Colette?" she says. *"Ou est la bibliothèque, s'il vous plait?"*

Now, *s'il vous plait* I've heard of. It means either please or thank you. I somehow manage to disengage myself, and join the other students and Mrs. McLaughlin as they stare at poor Colette, who is thinking with her head tipped to the side, her hair resting on her shoulders in horizontal sausages.

Mrs. McLaughlin finally makes a French-sounding noise of disgust and moves on. As her eyes scan the crowd, I enter my body again, and tug on my dress. She fixes her pewter gaze on the girl sitting in the last seat in the last row. This girl has straw-colored hair falling forward and bangs that come straight down and then swerve to the right. She is looking at the wall next to her intently.

"Georgette?" Mrs. McLaughlin says. *"Ou est la bibliothèque?"* Georgette continues to watch the wall, but her left cheek, the visible one, slowly turns red beneath its curtain of hair. Seconds tick past and then she whispers something.

"*Pardon,* Georgette?" Mrs. McLaughlin moves down the aisle to get a better view.

"Près d'ici," Georgette says softly. Then a little louder, *"Près d'ici."*

"If you were in France, no one would be able to understand you," Mrs. McLaughlin says shortly. "Take your hand away from your mouth and roll your *r*." She waits.

"Okay," Georgette says desperately; she holds her hands away from her mouth but they hover in the air about six inches above her desk. *"Okay, pway dee-cee."*

Mrs. McLaughlin lets out a genuine laugh, for an instant you can see how Mr. McLaughlin might have ended up marrying her. Then her eyes crinkle at the corners and she exclaims meanly, "You sound like Porky the Pig!" She laughs again, and then says, *"Pway d'ici,"* in a sputtering fat-cheeked way.

Georgette allows her hands to come back up to her face. She pushes her glasses up and stares once again intently at the wall. The minute hand crawls around the face of the clock, others are called on, dialogue is read out of the book, words are written on the board. At some point I look over at Georgette just as she looks at me. I shake my head, almost imperceptibly, in disbelief; she widens her eyes for an instant, mimicking a look of abject terror.

"That was ninth grade, not seventh," Elizabeth says. "We were already friends when that happened." She's at her office in downtown Chicago, talking to me on the WATS line. "You wouldn't believe what my desk looks like right now."

I would because I've witnessed it. She's an editor, and there are manuscripts stacked everywhere and yellow notes with *Urgent* scrawled across them stuck to the carpet. Her office is a wall that's a window surrounded by three orange head-high partitions. The view is of Lake Michigan, and at least in the summer it's spectacular, white triangles of boat sails and a

stretching blue horizon. Thumbtacked to the partition next to her desk is a photograph of her and me at age twelve, wearing matching lime green shorts (stretchy) and dark green men's T-shirts (baggy). We both have our hair in braids, mine as slim as snakes, hers thick and bushy. We've got variegated green yarn tied in bows at the ends. We're draped across her canopy bed, listening to records and enjoying our outfits.

"They're actually making me work," she says disconsolately. I can hear her rifling through papers. I'm at work, too, and I'm an editor, too. My office is in a small town in Iowa, and it's neat and tidy in a very annoying way, according to my co-workers. There's a picture on my bulletin board of the two of us when we were in love with Dave Anderson. We are lying backward against the sloping front terrace of her yard, we have on light blue shorts (stretchy) and dark blue men's T-shirts (baggy); we're using our bodies to form the letter D. I pass this tidbit along to Elizabeth.

"He must've thought we were nuts," she replies. "What did we have on?"

I tell her. "Did we shoplift those shorts?" she asks.

We never shoplifted anything; we were too scared. "I think I did, didn't I?" she says uncertainly. "Like underpants or something, and you were chicken?" That rings a bell with me, but I can't quite place it. So, if we didn't meet in French class, then how did we meet?

She thinks for a minute. "I have no idea," she says. "We just *met*, that's how we met." More paper rifling. "I'll try to remember and then call you after lunch. I have to proofread this thing this afternoon." She can proof a manuscript and talk on the phone at the same time; so can I. In school, we had a policy of never studying unless it was absolutely necessary, and still got high-to-mediocre grades. This convinced us that we were smarter than the average citizen, and actually, we're still think-

ing that way. It might be one of the reasons our husbands divorced us.

We're in our late thirties, childless, and were flung at the same time out of our marriages and back into teenagehood. We spend an hour on the telephone each week talking about boys and clothes. We alternate between hating our exes in a robust, vociferous style, and lying paralyzed on our living room floors sobbing.

"Of *course* you're lying on the floor," I tell her consolingly. It's a Tuesday morning and I'm ready to leave for work. She just called me from her house in Chicago; she's in her underwear, stretched out full length alongside her coffee table. She's just realized that the husband who recently left her really *did* recently leave her. "I didn't believe it was actually happening," she says into the receiver. She's completely stuffed up and having an asthma attack at the same time. I can hear her spraying her inhaler every few minutes. Talking about her divorce is making me think of my own, and I feel like I suddenly need my inhaler, too. I set the phone down quietly while she's weeping and run into the bathroom to retrieve it.

"I'm having an asthma attack," I tell her.

"Welcome to the *club*," she replies. "The *divorce* club." She's coming out of it a little.

"Can you get up yet?" I ask her. She thinks maybe she can, so I direct her into her bedroom where she starts going through the clothes in her closet. She's on the cordless phone and we have to talk around a big annoying hiss in the background. She picks out something to wear and gets dressed, putting the phone down once to pull a shirt over her head. I keep taking short, recreational hits from my inhaler as I talk her through it. Faint voices distinguish themselves inside the phone hiss, the content is blurred but emotion comes through. The voices rise and fall.

"Who *are* those people?" she asks once, cheerfully. The crisis has passed.

Fall of our eighth-grade year, her sister-in-law has come to stay with them for a while. She's from Thailand, her name is Jinn, and she has a flat, beautiful face and black hair that reaches to her waist in long oily ropes. She is nine months pregnant and perpetually drowsy, alternating her time between sleeping on the living room couch, watching television, and cooking outlandish food that no one else will touch. She eats sitting at the kitchen table with her eyes closed, wielding chopsticks expertly and humming a song called "Kowloon Hong Kong" that she plays over and over on the hi-fi. The woman on the record jacket looks like Jinn, with a large paper flower behind one ear and black hair wound up and held in place with pointy sticks. Her voice is high and lilting, and basically off-key. We know all the words, even though they aren't in our language. I'm not sure what Jinn is doing here, I've never asked. Elizabeth's stepbrother is in the service, and stares out at everyone from a lacy metal frame on top of the television. He's round-faced and wears a white hat and a navy blue coat with ribbons on the lapel. His cheeks are pink and airbrushed and the whites of his eyes have been enhanced. If the baby turns out to be a boy it will be named Hugh, after him; if it's a girl it will be named Angelique, after a character on *Dark Shadows,* which we all watch religiously each afternoon at three. It comes on right before *The Addams Family,* a show that Jinn dismisses with a grunt and a wave of the hand before turning over on the couch and returning to an unconscious state. She speaks English just fine, but it hardly ever occurs to us to talk to her. We treat her like one of the cats, minus the torture. We ignore her unless she can do us a favor.

Sunday afternoon, family cookout at Blackhawk State Park, Elizabeth and I spend our time looking for boys and trying to act like we're not with her parents. Jinn sits at the picnic table reading a magazine from Thailand full of hieroglyphics and cigarette advertisements. Elizabeth's stepfather turns pieces of chicken on the grill. He has a friendly disposition, warm brown eyes, and a slight limp left over from a stroke. Elizabeth's mother is a little less personable, as are all our friends' mothers. Everyone I know has a mother who operates on the fringes of what's appropriate. Elizabeth's mother, Doris, was especially excitable, and relied on us to calm her down.

"Shut up, Mother," Elizabeth would tell her. Most of the time Doris would shut up, but occasionally it struck her the wrong way and all manner of hell would break loose. One time she chased Elizabeth into the bathtub and then threw a pop bottle at her. It broke and glass went everywhere except on Elizabeth, who nevertheless screamed bloody murder and threatened to call the police. I snuck home during that one, and Jinn put a pillow over her head. Afterward Doris took to her bed with a bad back and had to be waited on for a week. Elizabeth was supposedly grounded, which, in practice, meant she wasn't.

So, the picnic. Elizabeth and I entertain ourselves by putting Styrofoam cups on the ends of sticks and holding them like marshmallows over the burning coals. They melt and run fantastically, forming odd arty-looking shapes that impress us. We give each one a name and make plans to spray-paint them when we get home. A rowboat full of boys goes by out in the water and we find a reason to wander down there, where we look upriver and downriver but see no other likely suspects. Suddenly we are being summoned, and quickly, from the picnic area. We head back up at an obedient trot and discover that Jinn has gone into labor sometime after the meal. She didn't say anything, but stopped reading her magazine and began hold-

ing her stomach. Pretty soon she was groaning, a big splash occurred, and then everyone was in a hurry.

They made us put our art-cups in the trunk along with all the other crammed-in picnic stuff. Jinn sat in the front seat between Elizabeth's parents, and Elizabeth and I had the back seat to ourselves. Her father actually laid rubber leaving the parking lot but then settled down and drove responsibly through the streets of our city. Most of the way Jinn was silent but every once in a while she would gasp out a long word in Thai that sounded like swearing because it started with an *f*.

None of us were trying to comfort her. Elizabeth and I were slightly out of control, hanging our heads out the car windows and silently screaming *We're having a baby!* to each other. Her dad said, in a cheerful voice, "Make way, we're coming through," every time a stoplight appeared up ahead, while her mom kept murmuring, "How are we doing," and casting sidelong glances at Jinn, who had her eyes closed and was saying the Thai swear word quietly over and over. Suddenly she made an *oof* noise, like someone had punched her, and then produced a muffled scream. Doris glanced at us in the back seat, where we had quieted down and were coming to the mutual, silent conclusion that we'd never have children.

Jinn screamed again, a short burst, and Elizabeth said, "*Mom,*" two syllables, in an accusing voice.

"*We're doing the best we can do,*" Doris said in a defensive voice. You could tell she thought this was all her fault, and that Elizabeth agreed. I stared out my car window and watched houses going by at a steady clip, refusing to let the sound coming from Jinn get from my ears to my brain. Soon enough we were at the door of the emergency room, and the two females in the front seat got out and went in, Jinn with one hand on her back and one clamped to her mouth, Doris looking frazzled and unprepared.

I got dropped off at my house and Elizabeth and her stepdad went home to theirs.

"Well, I just saw somebody having a *baby,*" I reported to my mother. "Right at the *picnic.*" She finds this news highly interesting but I don't have much more to say. My older sister follows me upstairs and I tell her everything. "The entire back of her dress was *soaked,*" I say. I shudder. "She was in agony, *screaming,* but don't tell Mom." Our mother isn't keen on extremes of any sort, or on foreigners. For that matter, she doesn't care much for Elizabeth's family, because she thinks they're different from us. The only difference I can see is that the dad isn't an alcoholic, but I don't mention that to her. She's known for getting in bad moods and grounding people for no reason. In the particular case of my older sister who has a mouth on her, my mother is prone to face slaps at odd moments. My sister takes it standing up, sometimes saying "*That* didn't hurt" before stomping upstairs and throwing my clothes all over the place.

Later in the evening Elizabeth telephones. "I can't talk," she says, "because we might get a call from the hospital." Nevertheless, we spend forty minutes on a review of the afternoon, the boys in the rowboat getting as much airtime as the pregnant lady in the car.

The next morning Elizabeth shows up at the usual time to walk to school with me. I see her coming up the back walk with her head down, yellow hair covering her face. She looks mad.

I ask her if the baby got born. She pushes past me and goes into the living room, sits on the couch and presses her face into the back of it. She starts crying loudly and can't stop.

"It *died,*" she says furiously, "and it was a *girl.*" At this she begins afresh, with her hands over her cheeks and her mouth a grimace.

My mother is in the kitchen eating oatmeal before work, my dad is shaving using the mirror hanging on the kitchen door.

He stops whistling and takes himself upstairs, my mother comes in the living room and looks at Elizabeth.

"Oh Liz, that's awful," she says. She feels truly bad, I can tell, but she also figures it was to be expected, I can tell that too. I feel somber and useless, I've never seen Elizabeth cry like that, even after the pop-bottle-in-the-tub business. This is something only the moms can handle; mine calls hers, Elizabeth gets sent back home, and I go off to school alone, in a stupid dress that doesn't look right.

Later we talk about it between ourselves, but we don't say a word to Jinn. She goes on, shell-shocked, her beautiful face flat as a photograph and expressionless. She continues to watch *Dark Shadows* and listen to "Kowloon Hong Kong," she continues to doze at the kitchen table and on the couch, she glides through the rooms of the apartment in her flowered housecoat as she always did, as visible and invisible as one of the cats.

Eighth grade, spring, between classes. The hallway is damp and swampy, loud with clanging lockers and the clamor of overstimulation; popular kids are being hailed, unpopular ones hooted at. A drinking fountain, a line in front of it, me in an impossibly short skirt and white knee socks. The dress code has been lifted for three months now, the boys wear pants as tight as long-line girdles and the girls wear hip-hugger skirts that are less than a foot long. Getting a drink at the fountain involves a cross between kneeling and squatting. The boy in front of me suddenly steps to the side, turns on the fountain, and with a sweep of his left hand says, "After you, my dear." I die, recover, squat/kneel, drink, put my head down, and scuttle away, wiping my chin.

I have just discovered love. The *real* thing, none of this Dave Anderson crap.

In the stairwell, I notice for the first time that outside the

window the ground is soaked and emerald-colored, jonquils lie supine in the rain, tulips are lolling their fat heads. I take the stairs three at a time, turning my miniskirt into a wide belt, race down the hall to Elizabeth's home-ec class and grab her as she's going in.

"Get sick," I tell her.

"We're making Rice Krispies treats," she says. "Wait 'til math."

"I *can't* wait, I'm *dying*," I say pleadingly, and then, because I know it's true: "*You'll* die too."

Fifteen minutes later we are reclining side by side on two narrow cots in the nurse's office. Elizabeth has a tremendous headache that requires a washcloth draped across her forehead, I have a tremendous stomachache that requires a metal bowl balanced on my chest.

I'm in love, it's serious, he's beyond what we've encountered before. He is like a *Beatle*, he's that cute. No kidding, honest to God, et cetera.

"He said 'my dear'?" she asks in a hoarse whisper. "He sounds like a queeb."

He's not a queeb, you had to be there. He made it sound *funny*. Not queebie at *all*, in fact, just the opposite. He's the opposite.

The nurse pokes her head in and we both groan. "No talking," she says.

"We weren't," we say in unison.

Elizabeth is willing to fall in love with him, too, but she needs to see him first, as a formality. We agree to meet after class at the fountain, in case he comes back for another drink. We go out and tell the nurse we're better. She sends Elizabeth back to home-ec but makes me go lie down again.

"You're still pale," she says shortly.

He doesn't show up at the drinking fountain again, but after

school we go to my house to pore over last year's yearbook. I have a feeling he's older than us, and it's true. We find him among last year's eighth-graders.

"Jeff Bach," I announce, and hand the yearbook over. We're in my living room eating Fritos and drinking pop. My sister hasn't gotten home from high school yet so we're safe, nobody's bugging us.

"He's got blond hair," she remarks, staring at the picture closely. She takes another handful of Fritos. "I thought you said he looked like a Beatle." She puts them in her mouth.

"I said he's as cute *as* a Beatle," I reply. "Not that he *was* a Beatle."

She stares at his face intently as she chews, and then comes to a conclusion. "Let's face it," she proclaims, "he's *cuter* than a Beatle."

We're both in love with Jeff Bach, ninth-grader extraordinaire.

The back door slams and my sister appears in the doorway to the living room. She is wearing a granny dress, her thick brown hair tucked into a crocheted snood at the nape of her neck. She arches her brows. "How's kindergarten?" she asks. She takes the bag of Fritos from Elizabeth's lap and heads upstairs with it. "Clean this house up," she says as she rounds the curve at the landing.

We leave and walk over to Elizabeth's house, where we tell Jinn about our new boyfriend. We get Elizabeth's yearbook and make her look at the picture. "Blond," she says politely, and turns her eyes back to the television. Pretty soon Elizabeth's stepdad comes home from work. We show him the picture. "How would you like it if I married *this* guy?" Elizabeth asks him rhetorically. He says he'd like it just fine and asks why the newspaper hasn't come yet.

"Who knows, that's why," Elizabeth replies. I get killed if

I'm not there when my mother gets home from work, so I leave and call up Elizabeth ten minutes later from two blocks over.

"What're you doing?" I ask.

There are four girls in our group, plus two best friends who hang around with another group approximately half the time. Besides Elizabeth and me there are Madelyn and Renee, and the two best friends, Carol and Janet. Renee is the oldest of six kids and we stay overnight at her house a lot because both her parents work nights at the post office and leave Renee in charge. They live in a big old house with three floors, and it never seems like there is any food except long loaves of sandwich bread, giant boxes of generic cereal, and powdered milk. If you're looking for mustard, or a bottle of pop, forget it. Renee is the only kid in the family with a room of her own and she keeps potato chips and Pop-tarts in her closet, which locks with a skeleton key. Each bedroom has a fire escape ladder in a metal box underneath the window.

Madelyn is destined to move away unexpectedly when we're in ninth grade, and all I can remember about her is that she was funny and mean, and that she threw a half pound of frozen hamburger at her mother once when she was told she couldn't go to a movie.

"Plus her dad slept in a coffin," Elizabeth reminds me. She has called me from her bathtub, the water is still running and she's talking loudly to compensate. "I saw him taking a nap in it once; it was a black box without a lid, and the headboard said *R.I.P.*"

"What a sicko," I say.

"No kidding," she agrees. The sound of water running stops abruptly, a splash is heard. "Wasn't there something suspicious about him?"

"That was Renee's dad." Renee's dad made everyone uncomfortable, he was very young, just like her mom, and he talked to us like we were adults. He flirted with us, except we didn't identify it as that, because he was a dad. We took on nervous smiles and sidled backward whenever he was around.

"There was more to *that* story than met the eye," she said, then, "hang on," and the sound of a giant lapping wave comes through the phone. "Jo Ann?" she says loudly. "*Jo Ann?* I dunked my head; now I've got water in my ears."

I feel cranky suddenly, and want to get off the phone. "Don't *call* me when you're in the bathtub," I say. "I don't want to listen to your personal hygiene. And I'm late for something."

"Buh-ruther," she says sarcastically. "What did I do? I dunked my head, big deal; how'm I supposed to wash my hair?"

"How about on your own time, that ever occur to you?"

"*How about if I smack your head off?*" and she slams her phone down with a huge noise.

We are thirty-eight years old. I wait fifteen minutes and call her back.

"Hi," she says. "Guess what I got in the mail?"

Divorce papers, with a smiley face on a Post-it note from her husband. "That was bugging me, you in the bathtub," I tell her. "Jim's the one who should get his head smacked off. Or Tina." Tina is Jim's receptionist, and the woman he left Elizabeth for.

"I'm not smacking anybody's head off," she replies dreamily. "Because I don't even care." When Jim first left her for Tina, Elizabeth made the mistake of asking why, and he told her. In the course of the conversation he mentioned a specific sex act that men tend to like a lot.

"You're kidding," I said.

"Not only am I not kidding," she replied. "But the thing is,

it's true. I mean, you hate to simplify these things, but he's the one who said it." She sighed hugely. "That's what they sit around doing."

Her voice had the same dreamy quality it has now, but a week later, when it had sunk in, she'd been ready to take out after him with a baseball bat. She'd tried to call him at work to tell him he was a dead man, but Tina wouldn't put her through. "Uh, I don't *think* so, Liz," she had said smugly, right before disconnecting her

So, any idea why Madelyn's dad slept in a coffin?

"He thought it was funny, of course," she said. "Men."

Jeff Bach, blond, the fifth Beatle, a student at our school. Lived below the hill and hung around with guys who were Mexican, which made him seem even more blond. Danny Garcia, one of his friends, yanks on my hair in science.

"Hey," he whispers. "You and Liz like Jeff."

I turn around and roll my eyes, trying for sarcasm. "I'm *sure*," I whisper back.

Forty minutes later, Elizabeth and I are side by side in the nurse's office. The next cot is occupied by someone who appears to be truly sick, not faking it. The nurse is excited by this and keeps poking her head in and staring at him.

News has been leaked, if Danny Garcia knows then everyone knows. If everyone knows, then Jeff must know. We think we could actually puke; we groan and stare at the paint on the ceiling. The nurse hears us and thinks she might have an epidemic on her hands.

"You should've said *Jeff who*," Elizabeth hisses.

I never thought of that. I start pretending like I'm beating myself up. We do our silent screaming routine. The guy on the other cot opens one eye. "I'm not really sick," he says.

"Us neither," we whisper back.

Pretty soon they both go back to class and I get kept for another hour and released at lunch.

"Eat some meat if you can," the nurse advises.

My own husband didn't have a receptionist, but he had a best friend, and the best friend had a wife. On a bitterly cold Sunday morning he went out to get doughnuts and didn't return for two hours. I took a bath, using my toes to turn the hot water on and off. Pretty soon my knees were brilliant pink, my forehead was sweating, and it came to me that I'd been in there a while. I wondered how come my doughnuts weren't back yet and then suddenly the answer hit me, the way a math problem can solve itself when you're not paying attention. *Oh,* I thought, *he's having an affair.* I stood up immediately, like the tub had ejected me, and began drying off.

When he came home I was dressed, standing in the middle of the living room with an ashtray in my hand, smoking a stale French cigarette I'd found in my desk. I hadn't smoked for four years but was quickly getting the hang of it again; only halfway through my first cigarette, and I already wanted another one. He was clattering around in the kitchen, putting breakfast on a blue plate, pouring a cup of coffee. I prepared a smoke ring and launched it in his direction as he walked into the living room.

He stopped. "What?" he said. His face turned into clay; on the blue plate were giant melting doughnuts, some with multicolored dots on top, some with white cream oozing from their back ends. "What?" he said again.

I told him and he didn't disagree. The only thing that happened was his face twitched, like a horse's hide, when I said the word. *Affair.* You are. And I am very. Upset. Actually I also

wailed, like a baby in its crib. That scared him and he set down the doughnuts and coffee, took a step toward me, a step back, then sat down on the edge of the couch. Unbelievably, he began to cry, which shut me up instantly.

Do I want to know who?

This from my husband Eric, who had held my hand when they lowered my mother into the ground, who put me in a bathtub once and poured cold water on me to break a fever, who whispered the names of the constellations again and again because I could never remember them. I guess I need to know who.

He tells me the name and the howling baby comes out again before I collect myself. *Kim?* She's a passive-aggressive *rat*, everyone knows that, *nobody* likes her. You like *her?*

Not really, he acknowledges. In some ways she's pathetic, the way she lets Bruce talk to her. He's no longer crying, he suddenly looks pious and overburdened. In as flat a voice as I can manage I suggest he go sit around somebody else's house for a while.

When the door closes behind him I stand in the center of the room and light another prehistoric cigarette. Off in the distance the phone rings. It's Bruce, wondering if Eric's around. I set the receiver back in the cradle without saying a word, and as I do so, the house settles over my shoulders like a stucco cape.

A spring night, one A.M., we have just escaped through the barricaded door of Elizabeth's bedroom into the inky darkness. We let our eyes adjust, breathing in the dusty smell of geraniums. A bridal wreath bush stands laden with tiny white bouquets, the sky is velvety beyond the branches of a sycamore, the stars are tiny pinpricks of light. We have six half-rolls of toilet paper borrowed from various gas stations and public toilets. We are on a mission.

"Let's go," I whisper and we move out silently, going from house to house, staying in the black shadows of the flowering bushes. Four blocks from her house we find ourselves trapped up against a garage while a man and a woman have an argument in the driveway. They've just pulled in and gotten out of the car, a station wagon with wood on the sides. The concrete driveway is ghostly blue in the moonlight, their faces are doughy.

"Why her?" the woman says over and over again. "Why her?"

The man tries to pet her head like she's a dog. "Honey, don't," he says each time she asks why her. *Honey, don't, honey, don't, honey, don't*. And then they kiss, staggering sideways. We seem to be standing in some unflowering rose bushes, absolutely still in the darkness, like a black and white photograph of two girls who have done this before. Something hits my arm and buzzes, I look down and see a June bug flapping around. Another one hits my cheek. I take Elizabeth's elbow and try to pull her away. She resists and glares at me, points one finger toward the people standing in a blue pool of moonlight twenty feet away. I grab her arm and yank her onto the driveway and run through the next yard and the next, her panting fast and loud behind me. We're laughing silently and hysterically. A ravine appears on the right and we run for it, diving down the hill, where we lay, gasping.

"You *queeb*," Elizabeth whispers. She punches me in the arm. "Why did you *do* that?"

I pause. "There were June bugs smacking into me," I tell her gently.

She immediately stops laughing and squeezes her eyes shut. A moan escapes from her lips. "I can't," she says without opening her eyes. "I can't keep going if there are June bugs."

"There aren't," I say. "It's not even June — those two are the only ones."

She still has her eyes closed. "No sir," she says in a small voice.

I try to think for a minute. Finally I say, "Don't wreck everything because of two June bugs."

She opens one eye and looks at me with it. "What about if there were *worms,* you wouldn't even walk in case one might *touch* you." I consider this a low blow and remain silent. "And you know it," she finishes.

A minute goes by, both of us staring through the ravine trees at the black sky. "You *know* it," she says once more. We get up slowly, like old people, readjust the toilet paper rolls that are tied around our waists on pieces of rope, and set out, subdued, to complete our mission.

A woman friend stops over to visit me one afternoon. She is lonely, melancholy, and at loose ends. Do you ever feel like this? she asks me. That's how the entire world feels, I say. Sit down, have some chips, have some dip. She's not one of my favorite people, but I'd rather talk to her than write, which is what I was doing when she dropped by. She's having husband troubles apparently, and winds up telling me she's thinking of having an affair.

"Have you ever done that?" she asks. Her head is tilted to the side quizzically, a trace of sour cream is adhered to her lower lip. I feel immensely warm and slightly guilty all of a sudden, and the walls of the room step in an inch or so, crowding me.

"Oh, Kim, it's not good to do that," I tell her. And I mention some lovely traits her husband Bruce has, not the least of which is that he's my own husband's best friend. She takes that for what it's worth and drifts back through the front door, gets in her little yellow car, and peels out.

Danny Garcia's house is on a cul-de-sac it takes us forever to find. By this time we are walking in the no-June-bug zone in the middle of the street, and talking in normal voices. As it turns out, his house has no trees, so we're momentarily at a loss. There are small bikes and wrecked toys in the front yard, and a sign that says *Koolade 4 Sale*. We caucus for a minute, crouched next to a blue sedan parked at the curb.

"Now what are we supposed to do?" I say. Elizabeth stares up at the split-level ranch house and thinks. She outlines a plan that involves only what we have available — if there are no trees, there are no trees. Simple, really.

Twenty minutes later we have draped giant strands of toilet paper over the roof of the house, seven of them, from one end to the other. We had to hurl them, unraveling whitely against the night sky, one of us in the backyard and one in the front. Our contingency plan was if a light came on or if anyone came out, we would run in two separate directions and meet at Renee's house, five blocks away. The strands are anchored on either side of the house with trikes and dump trucks. We meet in the shadow of the blue car to survey the situation.

"It needs more," I whisper.

"I'm too tired," she whispers back.

"We walked all the way over here and it only looks like about two *strands*," I insist. "Let's just get rid of the rolls." So we patiently unwind them, leaving pools of white against the pavement. We travel back up into the yard and, carefully holding the ends, throw the rolls over the roof, one after the other. The last two don't make it, our arms are too tired, and they land with a thud and roll back down the roof and into the bushes in front of the porch. In an instant a light goes on, the door bursts open, and Danny and Stuart Garcia are running

barefoot, sixty-five miles an hour. Elizabeth and I are half a block away by this time, and we veer off suddenly, one to the left, one to the right, like a dividing amoeba.

The yards are hard to navigate, there are things lying around everywhere, lawn mowers, rakes, bicycles, and, in one case, a tied-up dog who runs out to the end of his chain and stands up on his back legs, wagging his tail and pedaling his front paws. I can't tell which Garcia followed me, but I can hear him crashing around, one yard over. I stop and crouch under the awning of the dog's plywood house. The dog climbs in beside me happily and we both sit in the straw, me listening for the sounds of a Garcia, him biting a flea. There is a pale light burning in the kitchen of the house, illuminating an ornate clock and the corner of a fridge, harvest gold. Pots of African violets, a mound of spilled potting soil and a pair of gloves are sitting on a table by the back door. The dog, a beagle mix with long silky ears, leans up against me and yawns. I put one arm around him and we're buddies together, in the shade of his little abode. You can tell he doesn't get many visitors in here, but he's a good host. A gnawed-on bone is tucked in the corner. I hold it out and he tilts his head quizzically, then takes it only when he's sure I don't want it, and begins absentmindedly chewing.

From inside the plywood shelter we watch the night tick along. After fifteen minutes or so I hear voices, and I pull my legs farther inside and scrunch up into the black corner. Through the yard amble Danny and Stuart, wincing on their bare feet, talking in whispers and making little aggressive gestures toward imaginary enemies. The dog fades out into the night and stands on his hind legs again at the end of his chain. Stuart stops for a second and lets the dog rest his front paws against him. All I can see are their legs and hands, they can't see anything of me. Stuart lifts the dog's ear and touches the soft part inside. The dog stops wagging and holds himself very still, in paralyzed pleasure. They walk on, whispering, and the

dog gets a drink of water from a dishpan and then wanders back into his shelter. I'm sorry, but I have to go. He's pretty philosophical about it, following me to the end of his chain and then stretching out on the damp ground, back legs stuck out terrier-style, tail moving slowly back and forth.

I walk through backyards until I get to Renee's block and then I walk in the street. One time Elizabeth, Madelyn, and I walked around this block with our shirts off and tied around our waists. It was about three in the morning and the houses were dead and silent, the streetlights shone yellow spots on the pavement. We walked and walked, with our arms over our heads, letting the night air get on our skin. I'm not in the mood for any of that nonsense tonight. There she is, sitting on Renee's front porch.

"I thought they got you," Elizabeth whispers hoarsely. Her hair is going eight different ways and her cheeks are pink, her voice is croaky.

"I went in a doghouse with a dog," I say. "And they came right past me, and are they pissed." I tell her some of the words Danny and Stuart were whispering.

"Eek," she says.

Since there are no parents on the premises, we decide to wake Renee up and tell her what happened. Through the front window we can see the two littlest kids asleep on the floor in front of the snowy TV screen. Stacy has on a diaper and socks and has her head resting on a bed pillow without a case. Amy has on a T-shirt and no pants whatsoever, and has her head resting on a skanky stuffed dinosaur. Renee is asleep on the couch under an afghan, a book open across her chest. We tap on the window. Stacy stirs and puts a thumb in her mouth. Amy rolls over so her face is against the dinosaur's face.

"Seems like a shame to wake them up," I say, and then tap louder. Renee startles awake and the book falls off her chest.

"Don't wake the babies," she whispers as she lets us in. She

has drool on her from sleeping on the couch, and we don't want to point it out but we do anyway. "Oh," she says, wiping it off. We follow her out to the kitchen where she sits at the table, yawning. I sit on the counter and Elizabeth looks in the refrigerator.

"We would have been dead if they'd caught us," I tell Elizabeth. She concurs. We tell Renee what happened. She confirms what we already suspected: Stuart Garcia is dangerous. And she's in a position to know — she went steady with him in grade school.

"He wanted to drop me and go with Maria Valdez," she says sleepily. "So he threw a steak knife at me and it hit a tree. He got about forty swats with the wooden paddle from the principal." I repeat for her in great detail the words I heard him saying while I was jammed into the doghouse. It was an altogether stunning display of swearing, and we can't help but be impressed. Stuart and Danny have suddenly put themselves on the map.

"Those guys will say *any*thing," Elizabeth remarks. She's having a bowl of cereal, using milk that is thin and watery with a faint blue cast.

"How's that breast milk taste?" I ask her. She stares into the bowl for a second and then shrugs, takes another spoonful.

"What would you've done if they caught you?" Renee asks. In some ways Renee is the perfect friend, she's genuinely nice and asks you just exactly the questions you are prepared to answer. She is also pretty, with thin shiny hair and round brown eyes and a mouth that smiles even when she's just reading or listening to a teacher. The boys love her, too, and cluster around her, which works out well for her friends, who are neither nice nor friendly.

"I would've just started screaming," Elizabeth answers. And it's true, we all know it.

I make a slow-motion kicking gesture with my foot. "Right in the old codpiece," I say. Elizabeth makes a snorting noise and then has a nose attack right in Renee's kitchen. It's when she can't breathe through her mouth — she's still eating cereal — and her nostrils slam shut. She has to reach up and pry them open manually so she can get air.

I try to help her and we wake the babies up accidentally.

"Shit-fuck," Renee says wearily. The babies wander out to the kitchen, blinking their eyes in the brightness and whimpering. They both try to climb on Renee, who stares patiently at the ceiling for a second and then helps them up on her lap. They look at Elizabeth and me with blank, defensive eyes, Amy with her thumb jammed in her mouth, Stacy with her hand down her diaper.

"Do you have to go on the big-girl potty?" Renee asks her. She shakes her head no and closes her eyes. Suddenly we're all tired, even Elizabeth and me. We take the kids and Renee leads the way upstairs. She pokes her head in all the bedrooms: B.J. is asleep on Renee's bed, Alex is asleep on the rug beside his bed, Cindy is sleeping in B.J.'s bed. I have Amy, who's as heavy as a sandbag and smells like sour milk and baby shampoo. We finally put them on the king-size bed in the parents' room. There's no sheet so we cover them with the funky, crumpled-up bedspread and tiptoe out. B.J. is seven and weighs a ton so I take his feet and Elizabeth takes his arms and we carry him like a hammock between us and dump him into Cindy's bed so Renee can sleep alone. She whispers good night and we're gone, back into the cold spring air.

It takes about two blocks of freezing cold before we decide we have to ride instead of walk. We find a boy's bicycle with a long banana seat in somebody's backyard and take it; Elizabeth pedals standing up and I ride on back, with my legs stuck straight out on either side. When she gets winded I take over,

but I sit while I pedal, which scrunches her. I can't help it; I'm tired.

When we get to the big hill we leave the bike leaning against a tree and trudge ourselves straight up for one block and then it's two blocks of flat ground, and then we're at her house, sneaking back in.

I go first in case somebody's up; at least we know they won't throw a pop bottle at me. The coast is clear. Elizabeth steps into her bedroom and suddenly we're wide awake again. We debate about calling up the Garcias, and then, in an unusual display of restraint, don't. Instead, we go out to the kitchen and prepare a cake mix we find in the cupboard. We take it back into the bedroom and lie on the bed in the dark, eating cherry chip cake batter with big wooden spoons. We're wound up now, it's impossible to think about sleeping.

We discuss the Jeff Bach situation for a while. We come to the conclusion that it's hard to like someone so blond. "I like dark-haired guys, I think," Elizabeth says. I can see the shadow of her profile in the bed, she's gesturing with her wooden spoon.

"Me too," I say.

There is a long silence. It's late, four A.M. or something. We're finally getting tired again. She puts the batter on the floor next to the bed; I hand her my spoon and she drops it into the bowl. A few minutes pass.

"I might like Danny Garcia," she says tentatively. Another minute goes by.

"I might like Stuart," I say. She thinks this over. I turn on my side and she cuddles up right behind me; we sleep like two spoons whenever we're in the same bed.

"Stuart's dangerous," she whispers.

"I know it," I say softly, into the darkness, and then we're both asleep.

It's nineteen seventy-something, summer, nighttime, black country road running through rural Illinois, the sky is immense. Three miles ahead are train tracks that can be sailed over if you approach them right, all four tires will leave the ground at once. We're heading for our house, a two-story farm job with a big garden out back, a bunch of pigs that are not our responsibility, a summer kitchen with spiders and mice, and two dogs who wait patiently all day for us to get home so their lives can begin. I've thrown my lot in with the guy in the driver's seat, and he with me. We're both certain we'll never amount to anything, which only bothers us when we think about it. Right now we're high on dope and each other, and the night air smells like rain. The road is white where the headlights hit it, and everything else is pure black. The car is old and bumperless, with a plywood fender that has a dent where an agitated friend of ours karate-chopped it. The tape deck is not for the faint-hearted; the sound inside the car is huge and all-consuming. Right now it sounds like someone is playing a guitar using a razor blade for a pick, and the question being asked is Are you experienced? The answer is No, we aren't, but we're working on it.

Coming up on the long stretch before the giant Dip in Pavement and the subsequent railroad tracks, Eric glances over at me for an instant, assessing my mood, then pushes the lights off and we streak through the blackness down the center of the highway, dark moving inside of dark, our faces faint in the dashboard light. It sounds for a moment like the guitar player is saying Areyouanidiot? and then I decide to be into it.

I put one arm out my window, to feel the night air and create some drag. He presses harder on the gas. The sky is distinguishable from the ground only because it is blue-black, and

the land is black-black. There are stars. This is what they mean by barreling down the road. Not only could this be certain death, but we may take somebody else out, too, which is troubling. He isn't thinking of any of that; in fact, he's got his eyes closed, or else just the one I can see — he's trying to freak me out. That settles it. I put my foot on top of his and press it to the floor. I close my own eyes and imagine myself leaning into it, certain death. Darkness and his girlfriend, Darkness, are out for a ride through the countryside in the summer night. We hit the dip and are airborne for a breathless millisecond, then there's that long, terrible dope-inspired instant that stretches out forever, where you don't know if there'll be a train on the tracks or not, whether you'll get to continue living.

This time we do.

"They clean your room and cook your meals so you can write about Stuart *Garcia?*" Elizabeth asks incredulously. She's at her job in Chicago.

"Apparently," I reply. I'm in the wilds of upstate New York, at an artist's colony, sitting in a phone booth drawing pictures and talking to her while she formats something on her computer, which keeps beeping.

"You should say he was dangerous," she suggests.

I hate it here; why did I come here? All there is to do is write.

"You always go through this," she reminds me. There is the sound of a tiny bomb exploding, a ding, and she exhales loudly. "I just crashed my whole computer," she explains.

"I just crashed my whole life," I tell her mournfully. I'm afraid she's going to try to hang up. "Who even cares about the boys of my youth? There weren't any, it was all imaginary. I'm making it up as I go along." I draw a picture of a pit bull on the phone book in the phone booth. It has pointy ears, bowed

legs, and giant teeth. "Now I'm drawing a giant-toothed dog," I tell her.

"That's good," she says. "Remember that time you went to Florida to write and became troubled?"

"In the category of freak-out, *that* was the real thing." I draw a palm tree with coconuts hanging off it next to the pit bull.

"I made you eat a banana that time," she reminds me. We muse on that for a moment, until her computer comes back on line and says hello to her in a voice from outer space. We hang up.

As a matter of fact, there happens to be a banana in my lunch. Every day they give me a lunchbox with a sandwich, a piece of fruit, and a cookie in it. I eat the cookie, think about the sandwich, and put the fruit on my writing table, then I go back to staring out the window of my studio. This is how professional writers work.

I went to Florida once to work on a writing project. I borrowed a house on Key-something, with a million-mile view of the Atlantic, sliding glass doors, expensive furniture, and cockroaches the size of a man's big toe. My friend's sister, who was lending me the house, showed me how you had to spray Raid directly on the bug in order to make it die. At first it seemed unfazed, and then it wandered about a foot away and fell over. "They aren't cockroaches," she explained firmly.

"I'm not afraid of bugs," I told her. "I *like* bugs, actually." In fact, I'm married to one, is what I thought to myself. This was during a down phase in my marriage. I was there in Florida because he wouldn't stop seeing the wife of his best friend. "We're not *doing* anything," he would explain. "What are you — nuts?" The wife herself was miffed at me. "Why can't we still be friends?" she asked. I would speak to her only when cornered, and then only to call her names. She kept try-

ing though, calling my house at odd hours to ask me how I was doing in a concerned, schoolmarmish voice.

"Quit calling my house and quit screwing my husband," I'd reply evenly. She'd sigh; I'd hang up. Once I took the phone off the wall and threw it out the front door into a snowbank. Eric retrieved it wordlessly, dried it off, hung it back on the wall. "You suck," I told him. He stared at me for a long moment and then went back to whatever he was doing.

I was trying to make him miss me by going to Florida, but it wasn't working. On the way down, while driving in my car, I would have long imaginary arguments with him, where I hit every point square on the head and he was left speechless and remorseful. I had him apologizing to me left and right, every hundred miles or so. Between that and singing to the radio, it was a pretty productive trip down.

So, my friend's sister left and I wandered around her house, upstairs, downstairs, finally setting up my typewriter in front of a large glass door that opened onto a balcony with a view of the water and some boats. I organized all my writing paraphernalia, sharpened some pencils using a paring knife from the kitchen, and then sat down and began having a nervous breakdown.

Eventually the sun dropped into the water, leaving a fakey sunset, gaudy pink and yellow stripes along the horizon. The boats disappeared, one by one, and a group of long-legged storklike birds flew past the large glass door, out over the water, and then were gone. They weren't the kind of storks that carry babies, thank God; not bothering to have a baby being one of the things I deeply regretted the minute my marriage started unraveling. As soon as it got completely dark, the glass door turned into a giant black mirror, showing a ghostly image of me sitting in a wicker chair in the dimness. My hands were folded calmly in my lap. I looked like a dark painting of barely

controlled hysteria, surrounded by wicker and the long fronds of tropical plants. I felt like I was on an elevator that had burst through the top of the building and was still climbing. At some point I stood up creakily on my stiff legs and went looking for something to put me to sleep.

Three warm beers later I stretched out on the king-size bed and stared at the ceiling. I felt like myself as a six-year-old, lying in bed for hours, making up frightening stories in my head, waiting for my sister to wake up and torture me. Me as a kid: skinny and pale and jumpy, terrified of a particular cartoon character who was thin and wiry with a narrow, whiplike mustache. He wore a black outfit with a string tie and he tied girls to railroad tracks or to conveyor belts with buzz saws at the end. On the way to the bathroom, I heard the sound of a Frito crunching. It was a cockroach, stuck to my foot.

I began freaking out in earnest.

Heart pounding, I scraped the bug off, peed, and stared at myself in the dark mirror. I was spooked and looked it. I walked on my tiptoes back into the bedroom and jumped onto the bed. I pulled the sheet around me and curled into my usual sleeping position (fetal). I imagined everyone in my life abandoning me, all the while assuring me they weren't. I replayed a scene from several years ago: my mother in a hospital bed with Eric at her side, extracting a promise from him, he listening solemnly, speaking to her in a whisper, nodding, holding her hand; me in the hallway, exasperated and worn out, rolling my eyes, one last opportunity for defiance, sassing back even then.

I started a low-grade whimpering to keep myself company. It was dark and dark and dark and then it began to be light and light and then dawn showed up. I used a remote control to turn on the television and page through the channels. There was a religious program on, a Bullwinkle cartoon which was the last thing I needed, a worm's-eye view of a woman doing an aero-

bic workout, and CNN. I watched CNN intently, with the sound off and my eyes squinted almost shut.

I kept remembering some footage I'd seen of a plane crash that happened a few years back, where a seat with a passenger strapped to it was thrown hundreds of feet from the wreckage. The seat landed in an upright position, and the passenger, slightly charred, was sitting quietly with an arm on each armrest, deader than dead. I replayed the footage over and over, trying to make the passenger wake up, but to no avail.

At some point I went into the bathroom and threw up, then stared at myself again in the mirror, surveying the damage. My eyes looked like two red holes in a pink blanket. My stomach hurt.

I found the telephone, a cordless job, and carried it out onto the balcony with me. The Florida sun was climbing, the air felt like hot, wet lint. The same old boats were making their way back into view, chugging along silently, leaving trails of foam that leveled back out into flat blue. I sat with the phone in my hand until there was nothing left to do but dial it. I called my own number at home and a man answered. He said hello about five times and then hung up. It was my husband.

Everything was overwhelmingly bright, my eyes couldn't stand it. I went back in to the king-size bed. Suddenly the phone, still stuck to my hand, started ringing. I stared at it until it stopped. When the digital clock said 10 I called Chicago.

"Where *are* you?" Elizabeth says cheerfully. "I called you and Eric said you ran away from *home* or something."

"I'm in Florida, at Taylor's sister's house," I say. "I'm supposed to be writing."

"You sound weird," she says. "Jo Ann? You sound weird."

I am weird.

"Why are we not talking?" she asks gently. "Are we okay?"

No, unfortunately we're not. I swallow hard and stare at my clenched and hysterical feet. My stomach still hurts. I'm sitting in the center of a giant bed in a giant house on Key Nightmare.

"I'm freaking out," I tell her. "I'm ready to jump off a balcony into the sand or something."

She considers this for a long moment and then says, quietly, "Uh-oh, this is a marriage problem, right?" As far as she's concerned, her own marriage is as solid as a house, but the truth is, it's just about this time that her husband is beginning to notice what beautiful eyes his receptionist has, how the sound of her typing is like water rushing over a falls.

For about five minutes I can't talk, but instead nod or shake my head when she asks me questions. Her voice has taken on a soothing, reassuring tone I've never heard her use before. It makes me feel like crying. The bedroom is starting to really bother me so I close my eyes and grope my way out, still holding the phone to my ear.

"I'm walking," is what I finally say to her.

"*Good,*" she responds quickly. "If you're walking, then you're okay."

This is encouraging, so I walk some more. I walk out onto the balcony and stare at the phony boats on the horizon. I try to tell her what is happening to me — that my heart is beating so hard my T-shirt is moving, that I threw up because of some plane crash footage I saw two years ago, that I keep remembering being stalked by a cartoon guy with a whiplike mustache and a string tie.

"Well, I hate to break it to you," she says firmly, "but that sounds like *Eric*." Eric is pretty thin and so is his mustache.

"Well, *Eric's* certainly not stalking me," I tell her. I start to cry suddenly, which is a relief. "He's doing whatever the opposite of stalking me is." Now that I'm crying I can't stop. I'm

leaning over the balcony railing and tears are dropping into the sand below me. I tell Elizabeth this.

"Why don't you just *please* get off that balcony, and go back in the house?"

"I'm not going to *jump*," I say. "It's only about ten feet from the *ground*, for Chris'sakes."

"Oh," she says.

The problem is, whenever it occurs to me that he's leaving me, I start to feel like throwing up again. Also, I haven't slept for a couple of days. Or eaten. And it feels like there's an alien in my chest.

"You can't not eat," she says. "That's what we'll fix first." She sounds so confident that I feel myself relax a little. I'm still trapped in the elevator but I've lost that terrible zooming-upward vertigo feeling. I look at my feet. Under her direction, I walk downstairs with the telephone and stand in the kitchen. "Tell me everything there is to eat," she says.

One cupboard has rice cakes, spices, and vegetable oil, another has cans of things, boxes of cereal, and an envelope of mushroom soup, another has pots and pans, the refrigerator has mayonnaise and a jar of green olives. The sight of the pimientos makes me sick for a minute, I have to lean over and think of something else. When I say green olives to Elizabeth she immediately says, "Don't look at the pimientos." There is a basket in the middle of the kitchen table that holds two bananas, a paper clip, a packet of sugar substitute, a blue marble, and a ballpoint pen. "Perfect," she says.

She wants me to eat a banana.

"*Any*one can eat a banana," she says smoothly. "People give them to *babies*, they're so easy to eat."

"I'll throw up if I look at it," I tell her. My heart is pounding again.

"Oh no you won't," she tells me. "A *rice* cake would make

you throw up; bananas don't make people sick, else they wouldn't give them to babies." I can't argue with her logic, but I can't look at the bananas either. "I'm going to call you back in exactly half an hour. You take one bite every five minutes." I give her the phone number, set the telephone down on the kitchen table, and peel a banana without looking at it. Thirty minutes later the phone rings.

"I ate it," I tell her. Actually I ate half of it.

She has me take the phone in the bathroom and inventory the medicine cabinet. I do so obediently, the banana sitting in my stomach like a wad of clay. "Midol; emery board; Ramada Inn soap; Nyquil; unidentifiable pills way too big to take; sunscreen; sunscreen; eyeliner; generic aspirin; Bic razor, crusty." I sit down on the edge of the tub. The medicine cabinet has made me panicky again.

"Perfect," she says. "This is what you do now: put your swimming suit on and walk on the beach for one and a half hours, okay? Then come back and drink two doses of Nyquil and lie down on the couch. You don't have to sleep or anything, just lie down." She reiterates this. "In fact, it's actually better if you *don't* sleep." She's using reverse psychology on me.

The beach is empty, except for some old cans and a broken fishing pole. A bloated fish lies half buried in the sand, one tarnished eye staring placidly up at the sun. I step over it and make my way down the beach at the water's edge. Water is soothing, Elizabeth told me, water is soothing, water is soothing. I feel calm all of a sudden, looking at the water and the sky and the fins of sharks circling about two hundred yards out. "Those are dolphins," I say out loud. Each time I come across a bloated fish or a squashed something, I say, "That's not dead." When I feel like my legs are going to drop off I turn around and head back. By this time the sun is hanging about a quarter-inch above the part in my hair. My shoulders feel scorched and I'm

sort of hungry. Back at the house I eat a rice cake with a glass of water. It tastes like Styrofoam, which is somehow better than having it taste like food. I drink as much of the Nyquil as I can stand, stretch out on the couch, and count sheep with my eyes open.

Five hours later the phone rings off in the distance and I come to. I feel swampy and disoriented, stand up quickly, and then sit back down on the couch. It's hard to tell where the phone is located. Staggering through the house, I follow the noise into the bathroom.

"Guess who," she says cheerfully. I report to her on what I've accomplished — the walk, the rice cake, the Nyquil nap. "Whew," she says. "For a minute there I thought I was gonna have to come *rescue* you; I even called the airline."

I feel deeply touched by this, and begin weeping. I'm not completely out of the woods.

"Oh honey," she says quietly.

"He's dumping me," I wail. "For some pliant, rat-faced little nurse *practitioner* who doesn't have an unusual bone in her body."

"What's her husband think about all this?" she asks.

"Who knows. He's probably *relieved,* wouldn't you say?"

We ponder this for a while. "I called him a couple of days ago and asked him if he missed me," I say.

"Uh-oh," Elizabeth says.

"He had one of his honesty attacks."

"Why, that little fuck," she starts. "I'd like to get my hands around his skinny *neck*."

"He's already left me," I say, "he's just too chicken to take his body with him."

"I know you don't want to hear this," she says carefully. "But it seems to me that you wouldn't be this upset about him wanting to leave you. I think you're this upset because *you*

want to leave *him*." This makes my stomach lurch in a very sickening, grain-of-truth-to-it way.

"But I love him," I tell her. "He's the only man I've ever loved." Even I know how trite that sounds. I feel like a character in a Gothic novel.

"Keep in mind who you're talking to here," she says dryly.

"I can't believe I said 'He's the only man I've ever loved.' I'm supposed to be a *writer*, for God's sake." I might be starting to snap out of it.

"It's time for the other banana," she suggests. "And I'm gonna talk to you while you eat it."

Seventeenth summer, a farmhouse full of boys on the edge of town, a car full of girls heading toward it. It's Elizabeth's red convertible, prone to running out of gas and getting stuck in places that cars don't belong. As soon as we leave the city streets and hit the back roads, everyone except Elizabeth gets up and sits on the edge of the car instead of on the seats. When we go around curves there is a long moment where it feels like we might fall out and be run over by the back tires. We like this feeling. Because we're too young to die, we assume we won't. Also, alcohol is involved.

It's the year of Look Ma, No Bra, and extremely long blue jeans that drag on the ground and get caked with mud. Shoes are unheard of; hair is everything. We comb ours frantically as soon as the car stops. My own is long and lank, reaching just above my waist; it's useless to even try and restore order.

"Here." Renee takes my comb and starts working out the tangles gently, starting at the bottom. She raps me on the head with her knuckles when I tip my head back to finish my beer. "Stay still," she commands, in the voice she uses on the babies.

"Ouch," I say mildly.

Elizabeth assesses herself in the sideview mirror. She's trying to see if her rear end is sticking out. "Why do I have an egg-butt?" she asks. This is rhetorical.

Renee finishes my hair and asks if she should braid it. A vote is taken: two for the braid, two for leaving it down. I throw my vote in with leaving it, we do some last-minute adjustments, and then, making Janet go first because she has confidence, we step through the front door and into the farmhouse.

The living room walls are painted black and the furniture consists of a sprung couch with no cushions, an old dentist's chair, a black-light pole lamp, and a giant stereo system. Right now a guy named Dave is changing the album. Like a priest performing the sacrament, he kneels before the altar and removes the record from its sleeve. Holding the edges and blowing softly on it, he sets it on the turntable, moves the needle into place, and gently drops it. Deafening sound ensues.

Except for one guy named Bob, all the guys who live here are named either Steve or Dave, all have ponytails of varying lengths, and all worship Ted Nugent. They refer to him as Ted and speculate on his whereabouts constantly. They're a year or so older than us, high school graduates who are busy amounting to nothing. We all have crushes on one or another of them. Mine is in the kitchen right now, mixing up a concoction of lemonade and Everclear. He's a sweet-faced Steve with a charming personality and a massive drinking problem. He hardly ever notices me, but when he does I think I'm going to die. "Here," he says, handing me a plastic cup of potion. I take a sip and try not to shudder. It tastes like sugar-flavored eau de cologne. "Hey, that's good," I respond brightly. I'm working on having a better personality.

"Ted here yet?" he asks me.

"Uh, no," I reply. He wanders into the living room and I wait a second, then follow him.

Elizabeth and Janet are sitting on the funky couch reading album covers. Renee is on the floor, cross-legged, smoking a cigarette with her eyes closed. No sign of Carol. I look around. One of the Steves is missing as well. I drink some more of my medicine.

The music is so loud that the sound is distorted. I want to turn it down slightly, but I don't dare. It is an unspoken rule that girls don't touch stereo equipment. When the record ends there is a sudden leaden silence that rings almost as loudly as the music. Everyone looks startled and uncomfortable. A Dave gets up and pads over in his sock feet to put something else on. A different Dave loads a bong and passes it to his right. Someone switches off the regular light and switches on the black light. This is a relief for those of us who are worried about how we look; now everyone is equal, with velvety faces, lavender teeth and eyes.

The weed is laced with PCP; after two hits I feel like I'm in a hammock on the top deck of a gently rolling ocean liner. I stretch out on my back, using a stack of magazines for a pillow, and crawl inside the music. My head is an empty room, painted white, with high vaulted ceilings. There is a long beat of silence and then the sound of alarm clocks going off. I sit in a straight-backed chair in the middle of my head. Suddenly there is the pinging of a cash register and the sound of coins falling. I open my eyes briefly and see the rapt faces of the other revelers, the purple-toothed smile of a nodding Dave. I retreat back to the dark side of the moon. Money changes hands, guitars echo off the white walls.

When I come to it's some time later, there are more people around, blue-jeaned legs step over me from time to time. I like the party from this angle. Eventually my favorite Steve comes in and sits on the floor next to my head. He has another cup of poison for me. "You missed Ted," he hollers into my ear. In

honor of trying to have a better personality, I make a disappointed face.

Although there are girls present, none of them seem to be my friends. "Where's Elizabeth?" I mouth to him. He leans in and puts his lips, then his tongue, to my ear. I pull my head away. "She's occupied," he yells, and gestures toward a closed door. When I ask where everybody else is he shrugs. I truly hate it when this happens.

As it turns out, Renee is in the kitchen, very stoned, doing the dishes. Three guys are sitting at the kitchen table, one cleaning pot, the other two watching Renee like she's a TV show. When she runs out of dishes, one of them obediently picks up another stack off the floor and sets them in the water for her. This place is a pig sty. I pour myself another cup of whatever that crap is.

Renee looks at me foggily, trying to assess my mood. "Want to dry some dishes?" she asks.

"Not hardly, pal," I say. The guys at the table give me a long look and I give them one back. A Dave holds out his hand to me.

"C'mere," he says kindly, pulling me onto his lap. The Beatles are on the stereo. "The Long and Winding Road," a song that'll break your heart in about one minute, begins to play. I sit quietly on the Dave's lap and hum a few bars. He pets my hair awkwardly for a while and then puts his hand up the back of my shirt. The other two guys exchange a smirk.

I take Dave's ear by the lobe and whisper into it. His eyes open wide. He puts his hand across his chest protectively as I get up. "She's *fierce*," he says to the other two. Renee drops some crusty silverware into the brown dishwater. She struggles for a second to bring me into focus.

"Jo Ann doesn't like that kind of stuff," she explains to them.

"Well, man oh man," Dave says. "What did *I* do." The other two laugh.

Looks like my old personality is back.

In the phone booth in New York, I draw a picture of a girl with her fists on her hips, eyebrows converging, mouth set. She's wearing my clothes. I have one question to ask Elizabeth, but first she wants to tell me about her weekend.

"I went out with a guy who looks like the Artful Dodger," she says. "He's in a band *and* he wears a top hat. He couldn't wear it on the date, though, because we went to a movie."

"That's good," I say. I tell her I'm working on a party scene.

"Which party?" she asks suspiciously. "What am I doing at it?"

"It's sort of a composite of all parties, you know?" There's silence at the other end. "It's just a *party* party, is all, with those guys who all had the same names."

"The Ted Nugent guys?" she asks.

Well, yes.

"I never liked any of those guys, did I?" she says hopefully.

Uh, I think Dave Nelson would be hurt.

She probes her brain, comes up with a memory. "Oh." She thinks for a second. "Well, he was a nice guy," she says firmly. "Wasn't he?"

We ponder for a minute and finally both admit we can't remember. I say they all look alike to me, and then instantly regret it, because I'm going to hear a lecture. Here it comes.

"Your attitude towards men s-u-x," she begins. "Look at me. I got divorced, too, and I'm not bitter."

Well, I'm willing to be bitter on both our behalfs. In the meantime, the one question I have to ask is Why were you always with guys and I never was?

"Because you were mean, that's why," she says gently. "Remember how mean you used to get?" This makes me feel awful. I was a mean person.

"You weren't a mean *person,*" she says. "We were just weird back then. We were insecure."

But you weren't mean.

"Well, I had the exact opposite problem," she replies.

I light a cigarette illegally in the phone booth and try to blow the smoke into my coat pocket. The conversation goes on and on, more about the Artful Dodger. Meanwhile, back at the party, Renee shows me her pruny fingers.

"Exhibit A," she says. "This is exactly why you shouldn't take speed and go to a party." I pour her a cup of liquid nitrogen and she downs it quickly, the way she's doing everything else. "I keep thinking I want to clean the bathroom," she says.

"I'd steer clear if I were you," I advise her. "Five guys live here." She can see the wisdom in that.

Pretty soon Carol comes into the kitchen, blinking her eyes against the light. Her hair is a mess, her shirt is buttoned wrong, and she's been crying. He has hurt her feelings, which isn't hard to do. He forgot her name or something. "Let's go," she whispers. We rustle up Elizabeth and the three of us fade through the living room and out the door. The Steve I have a crush on is sitting on the front porch steps, smoking a joint, waiting for Ted. He reaches out and places his hand gently around my ankle. I stand there patiently until he lets go, and then continue down the steps. "See you," he says.

At the car, there is a moment of silence. Elizabeth tries to hand the keys off to me but I'm not in the mood. I climb in the back and hold on to my hair as we pull from the drive to the road. Carol stops crying and claims she's never going to another party. Elizabeth and I exchange a look in the rearview mirror. "In my whole entire *life,*" she says emphatically, "so

don't even try asking me to." The sky is full of diamonds, the moon is a narrow sliver, the road winds and curves, the drugs are wearing off. We left Renee and Janet at the party without a ride.

The voice of Motown comes on the radio and we sing quietly to ourselves. All the houses have their eyes closed as we sweep silently past them. Carol fixes her shirt, lights one cigarette off another, and I wave good-bye to them from the alley behind my house. Through the bushes, up the back walk, still humming. In the kitchen, two cookies and a long drink of water, up the stairs and into the bedroom. Across the hall my parents sleep peacefully behind their closed door, innocent as children.

On the way back from Florida I drive a hundred miles out of my way in order to visit my mother's grave. Small Illinois town where she grew up; the gas station, body shop, and ice cream parlor are owned by my uncles, on the edge of town a small barren cemetery is full of my dead relatives. My mother's tombstone is dark granite, on either side of it are pink geraniums, planted by my father. In front, beneath her name, is a coffee can full of wildflowers withering in the sun. Someone has been here before me, an aunt probably, driving past on her way into town from one of the nearby farms. The withering flowers prompt a maudlin scene in which I am both the actor and the audience. A red-tailed hawk circles overhead, a tractor chugs by on the highway, holding up a line of cars. A daughter weeps in the afternoon sunlight, a mother remains silent beneath a load of dirt.

Hours later my street appears in front of me, a tall catalpa tree, a child's scooter, and then the driveway where the husband stands, just off his bike, home from work. "Hi," he says

cordially, putting an arm across my shoulders. And then, "I have a meeting tonight." His hand looks as white as paste next to my Florida arm. Inside, he goes into the study and closes the door. I hear the long beep of the answering machine as he listens to the messages and then erases them.

In bed that night I remain stationary as he toils in the darkness. Afterward, there is silence and the sound of breathing. Next to the bed, my big collie whines in her sleep. Finally, he says quietly, with something in his voice I don't recognize, "It's good you're back."

Tick, tock. Breathe in, breathe out. There is no mercy at this hour of the night, and my own voice sounds strange in the darkness. *I'm not,* is what I tell him. He rolls over and puts his face in the pillow. Everywhere you turn these days there's someone crying.

Billboards, fence posts, and cows go by at seventy miles an hour, a van honks as we pass it and someone gives us the finger in a friendly manner. We're caravaning our way to the rock quarries for a swimming party. Three cars and two vans are full of people and beer; I'm riding on back of a motorcycle, driven by my unofficial date, a charming madman named Wally. Wally is already in the party mood and so am I, because it's my nineteenth birthday. I have on a microscopic swimming suit, a Rolling Stones T-shirt, and Wally's helmet. He has on cut-off blue jeans, sunglasses, and a baseball cap. Every once in a while he'll holler, "Hold on!" and then execute an amazing maneuver that involves other vehicles on the road. I'm absolutely terrified, and keep imagining what skin on pavement would feel like. Nevertheless, I can't quit egging him on.

The water is like cold silk when you first get in. Elizabeth and I float ourselves around on air mattresses until we see a wa-

ter snake swimming directly toward us with its head stuck up like a periscope. We take off for the beach and sun ourselves on an outcropping of rock. Somewhere in the vicinity, Wally is tapping the keg while others are running speaker wire. Eventually music comes forth and beer makes its way over to where we are. Guys start catapulting themselves into the water.

I get special treatment because it's my birthday. People keep calling me over to their cars and vans. "Here," they say generously. "Do some of this." In an effort to stay awake for my birthday, I decline almost everything. I'm a famous lightweight; even beer in the afternoon makes me sleepy. I stretch out on my rock and let the sun bake me while the others swim and get wasted. Elizabeth keeps up a running monologue next to me which I can tune in and tune out at will. Wally comes over to shake water on us from time to time; we bat him away like an insect.

Sometime during the early evening he produces three pills, one for each of us. "What are these?" I ask him. He looks at one of the pills closely, turning it over in his hand.

"'Lilly,'" he reads. "They're lilies, that's what. Red ones."

Down the hatch.

Within an hour I'm singing a medley of Beatles tunes to anyone who will listen. My legs are not working correctly. "Hey, Jude," I say to the guy sitting next to me. His name is Tom. "Did you have any of those red lilies?" He doesn't know what I'm talking about. Elizabeth is nowhere in sight but I can see Wally off in the distance, slapping his leg and laughing silently and hysterically. He squints over in my direction and motions me to come hither. I point to my legs and shake my head. We give each other the peace sign.

There's a fire going, and some people are roasting things over it. I hear my name being called. "Liz is looking for you," Tom tells me. He stands, stretches, and heads for the beer. She

comes tripping up, still in her swimming suit, with a man's workshirt over it. "Let's take a walk," she says. She's listing slightly to the right, but other than that, doing okay.

"I can't stand up," I tell her. I indicate the grass next to me. "You sit down."

We watch the other campers for a while, roasting their things, drinking their stuff, laughing and punching each other. "I can't stay here if you're going to sing," Elizabeth tells me. I stop singing.

Off in the distance the lizardy sound of Mick Jagger starts up, more cars arrive, people shout for no reason. The red lily has made me feel both weightless and heavy at the same time. The night air is cool against my sunburned arms. I can't remember what I did with my shoes. The only thing that would make me happier at this moment is if I could sing *Bang, bang, Maxwell's silver hammer,* but Liz won't let me. I try humming it softly but she starts to stand up so I have to cut it out. I wonder where Waldo is.

Renee and her boyfriend Pete emerge out of the darkness. She has my T-shirt and shoes. Even though my arms are balloon strings, I manage to get the shirt on and slip my swimming suit top off; the shoes I cannot even begin to contend with. Pete is short and very cool, with bedroom eyes, dark curly hair, and an uncivilized manner. Renee is working on taming him. He likes it that I took my swimming suit top off even though he didn't get a glimpse of anything. "Nice tits," he says generously. We send him to get beers but right before he leaves he bestows a big, fat birthday kiss on me. I dry my face on my T-shirt.

Here comes Janet, so tan her blond hair looks fake. She's got a concerned look on her face. Well, there's bad news. Wally's fiancée, Leeann, has just arrived unexpectedly. It was a surprise; she blew in from the north like bad weather, and now my

birthday is wrecked. Everyone groans, including Tom and Pete, who like it when I'm in a good mood. *Bang bang Maxwell's silver hammer came down upon her head.* I shrug and put a decent face on it. I can't think of anything to sing.

At some point during the evening Wally catches my eye. Leeann is standing with her back to me, looking wifely and cruel. He holds his hands palms-up in the age-old gesture of *Hey, this is not my fault.* I look away with no expression on my face. Tom brings me a roasted marshmallow that burns the roof of my mouth. I lean my head on his knee and he pats my sunburned shoulder. It's my nineteenth birthday and here I am, Eleanor Rigby.

"She married him right out from under me," I say. We're back to the phone booth. All I have to do is close my eyes and I can see his long, pipe-cleaner legs, his hazel madman's eyes. He still remains the legendary good kisser.

She wants to know what made it legendary. I don't know; it was almost twenty years ago. Probably the fiancée in the background. "He was nuts," she says. Yeah, that didn't hurt either.

All the sweet, absent boys. Smoking jays like they were cigarettes. Playing their air guitars. Doling out their legendary kisses. We have a moment of long-distance silence for ourselves, perpetually the back-up singers.

"Hey, man," Elizabeth says, "speak for yourself."

It's 1976 or thereabouts. Feminism strikes suddenly, leaving destruction in its path. I've always had a tendency to be mean to men; now there's a reason for it. I'm learning to keep my hands in my pockets, so they won't see my fists.

Someone's living room, floor pillows, chamomile tea, soft-

voiced women in painter's pants and big hoop earrings. Consciousness-raising. We learned why Susan B. Anthony should get her face on a coin. We learned that the speculum can be our friend. Some of us learned that the word *orgasm* actually described a real phenomenon.

"Hey," we said in unison.

I'm here to tell you that sisterhood is a powerful thing. We worked on constructing egos for ourselves; we tried to convince each other that our lives were worth inhabiting. We stopped shaving our armpits and gave ourselves wash-and-wear hairdos called shags. Occasionally, one of us would lob a beer can at the head of a deserving male. Feminism. The only down side I can remember is that the shags were hard to grow out.

The separate-but-equal principle held sway for a brief time. The guys who used to remove our clothes with their sliding glances dressed us right back up again when they saw our armpits. Women stalked out of the room when men accidentally called them honey. Eventually, though, we all calmed down a little and attempted to harmonize. Some lean-torsoed men tried to even the odds by putting on glittery eyeshadow and climbing up on platform heels to play their guitars. With the advent of cocaine, parties suddenly got livelier and longer.

Across the room, a guy navigates his way through the smoky throng to play with the equalizer. From there he goes to the front porch, where he adjusts a slide projector. This is his party, apparently. He's projecting slides of a David Bowie/Iggy Pop concert on the house across the street. There's a rivet punched through his ear lobe, a silver star, a small tribute to androgyny. He's simultaneously mellow and wired but he speaks thoughtfully and listens carefully. At some point, while one of us is talking, he presses his hand against the small of my back and doesn't move it. It stays there for more than a decade.

Some highlights. Early days: long evenings in the country house, I make drawings and smoke cigarettes, drink cups of tea. He stokes up the blue glass bong, plugs in an electric guitar, and plays "Secret Agent Man" over and over. We populate our house with dogs and have long, monotonous discussions about how to make them behave better. We go in the bedroom sometimes and close the door to get away from them, then feel sorry and open it again and let them boil up onto the bed and stick their noses in our faces. We do a wavery but heartfelt rendition of "Good Night, Irene" as we're driving, late, back from friends' houses. On a beach in South Carolina we lie on our backs and stare at the night sky and congratulate ourselves on getting along so well. Months later we discover grains of sand in the cuffs of his trousers, remember, and give each other secret, sappy looks.

We're pretty nice people for the most part, although neither of us ever sands off the edges we started out with. I am prone to my usual fits of melancholy and self-doubt; he has a tendency toward a manic energy that is enervating for anyone who beholds it. I have long ago lost all interest in drugs and alcohol but each evening he disappears inside a plume of smoke and emerges mellowed and distant. Rock and roll, of course, never dies. Sometimes very late at night we sit in the dark living room listening to the voices of various dead guys — Tommy Bolin, Jimi Hendrix, Bob Marley — while studiously ignoring each other. I observe that he isn't fully present past eight o'clock each night, and surprise myself by feeling grateful. I am left free to traipse around in my own psychic landscape. When we have fights he has a tendency to reply in baby-talk, which causes me to go berserk. I rant, then I rave, berating him in such florid terms that no one can keep a straight face. We get sheepish, we make up. The years tick by.

My lifelong addiction to books wanes, leaving me feeling

bored and bereft. Some time later I discover that I've left off reading them because I've decided to write them instead. He thinks this is a fine idea and supports it unconditionally, but finds that he is unable to read what I write because drowsiness overtakes him. I watch him several nights running as he nods and dozes, tries with an enormous effort to focus, and finally gives up. We agree without much discussion that it isn't necessary for him to read my writing. His own work is too consuming, he doesn't need one more task piled on top of the others. The match stops flaring, the bong stops bubbling, the old familiar chords of "Secret Agent Man" no longer bounce like tennis balls around the room. The dogs skulk into their corners.

His own work. Political organizing that begins on a power-to-the-people grassroots level and gradually works its way up to power-to-the-person. He educates the sheep and then becomes the shepherd. It's a rush to have them all listening, paying attention, laying down their votes. Another case where reefer has led to the hard stuff.

We're on the slippery slope now, it's only a matter of time. It's women galore. He begins to look at me with an appraising eye. Familiarity, that good friend of contempt, makes me seem plain as dishwater. Once when we fight over something and apologize later, he admits that he might have been a bit stern with me. For hours the word hangs in the air above my head like a grand piano. *Stern*. He might have been stern with me. I realize that one of the reasons he doesn't want children is that he thinks he already has one. I start listening to how he talks to others compared to how he talks to me. In a crowded room one night I catch myself getting ready to take him by the necktie and heave him up against the wall. I feel like a rabid dog, but I smile placidly and make idle chat with the wife of his best friend, the future chiseler. In the car on the way home I say to him in the most dangerous tone I can come up with, "*You have*

got to treat me like an equal." The wiper blades clock back and forth, car lights bear down and then pass. He says, looking straight ahead through the glistening windshield, simply and sadly, "I can't."

An update on the Artful Dodger. Turns out he's our age and has a day job, besides playing the drums.

"Well, you've gotta love a guy in a band," I say encouragingly.

"I agree," she says. "I just wish he played the *guitar*."

A woman walks by the phone booth in a nightgown, carrying a coffee cup and a cigarette. It's early afternoon. I knock on the glass and wave hello. There are any number of eccentrics around here. She's a painter.

Here's a good one: After the divorce I was on my way somewhere early one morning and saw Eric's brand-new girlfriend walking from his house to her own, wearing nothing but a pale lavender nightgown and a pair of Birkenstock sandals. Her hair was stuffed into a rubber band and hung down her back like a horse's tail, she was holding a sheaf of papers and a long leash, at the end of which was her dog, a big black biter. The nightgown was one of those Indian-style jobs, with embroidery along the bodice. It's the sort of thing you could convince yourself didn't look *totally* like a nightgown if you only had three blocks to walk and it was too early for anyone to be out driving around. Except I was. Out driving around. I spent the rest of the morning draped over someone's couch, sobbing and eating cinnamon toast.

I tell Elizabeth about this. Yeah, yeah, she remembers. Well, never again, I vow. Thank God *that's* in my past. Who *needs* it. Blah blah blah. The boys of my youth give me the malaise.

"Oh brother," she says.

Don't oh brother me. And I gotta go, I'm late for my nap.

The truth is, I'm weary of all that men stuff. It's either so boring that I'd rather hang around with my girlfriends or it's like gunfire to the chest. I actually *like* it inside the bell jar — I don't have to breathe anyone's air but my own and I still get a view of the landscape. There's a woman here at the colony, Stasia, a filmmaker who went to a workshop to learn how to walk over a bed of hot coals. She tells me about it postnap, as we're waiting for the dinner bell, having drinks on the terrace. The thing is, why would anyone want to walk over a bed of hot coals?

"I saw a flyer for it on a lamppost," she explains.

They spent an afternoon in the presence of a short charismatic man, talking about their feelings and consulting various higher powers. At about four-thirty they took their shoes off and performed the miracle. So, what did it feel like?

"It felt like hot coals," she says.

I knew it would.

The door to the terrace swings open and out walks our friend Frank. Right behind him is a new guy. Frank immediately starts filling us in on how much work he got done during the day. I feel vaguely guilty about the magnitude of my afternoon nap. Somehow the quality of the light has changed on the terrace, there's a dangerous peach glow coming over the horizon. The new guy is introducing himself to a group of people. There are handshakes around. Today Frank finished a painting and started two new ones. Stasia says that you don't burn your feet because the coals are too light. The new guy looks over in this direction. It's like when you put your hand in a hot oven; the coals are almost light as air, they're hot but have very little density so they don't burn you. I can feel the frayed edge of his denim jacket and he's standing all the way over there. I look at my hand. Frank asks me how the boys of my youth are doing.

"They're boring," I say absently. Here he comes.

Pertinent details. Blond poet. A slightly jaded and weary air about him. Something recognizable in the sideways glance, the set of the shoulders. He's sober now, but from what I can tell the former bad boy is buried in a shallow grave. The color of his eyes escapes me but not the quality of the gaze. He appears to be fully and alarmingly present at all times. I have to get out of here.

He leaves me a note on the mail table, full of charming misspellings. We meet and walk, describe our lives. He puts his hand on my arm as we cross a street and continues listening, offering kindness and advice. I have a sudden overwhelming desire to touch his face. I put my hands in the pockets of my jeans. It feels crowded inside my bell jar; condensation forms and I begin weeping. He watches calmly, one foot on the bumper of a car. At some point he reaches out, lightly touches my face.

I take to wearing a Walkman and earphones everywhere I go, piping music directly into my head. The phone booth is the only place it doesn't work.

"I can only talk for a minute," I tell her. My days are numbered here; I feel a longing for my empty living room, for the grizzled face of Sheba the dog. The blue enamel breakfast table, the rug with a picture of New Zealand on it, the bird's nest we found outside the country place years ago, made from hair shed by my old dead heroic-hearted collie. I'm tired of being here. I miss my stuff.

"I'm sick of *my* stuff," she says. "I want all new everything."

I want I want I want. I want to go home.

"What's going on?" she asks. After a short pause a lightbulb goes on over her head. "Uh-oh," she says.

Yeah.

"Heck," she says cheerfully. "That's *good*. Is he nice?"

I don't think I know what nice means these days. "Well, he hasn't pulled a gun on me," I tell her. She sighs.

I've spent my whole life in this phone booth. I want my circus footstool, my pink coffee table, my Albert Payson Terhune books. I want my Bruce Springsteen records. The Walkman lies dormant in my lap. I push the On button and the tiny voice of Van Morrison emanates from the earphones. "The thing is," I tell her, "he already has a brown-eyed girl. Back home." Thank God.

"Oh." She's thinking this over. "Hmmmm."

A pall settles over the conversation. I stare at my reflection, distorted in the chrome of the telephone. "This is still my youth," I finally tell her.

"Uh, whatever you say." She sounds skeptical.

I peer closer at the chrome mirror. My vertical wrinkle is still visible and it's afternoon. It's usually faded back into my face by mid-morning. Also, I might be getting jowls.

"I'm looking at my vertical wrinkle in the telephone," I say.

"Isn't it supposed to be gone by now?" she asks. "It's one o'-clock."

"I hate to break it to you, but it's two o'clock here," I inform her. "I need oil-of-old-ladies." I can't even bring myself to mention the jowls, for which there's no cure anyway. All the women in my family begin to look like bulldogs right around the age of thirty-eight; it's a legacy.

The Artful Dodger has taken a turn for the worse. "He's religious," Elizabeth says. "And not only that, but he thinks I'm going to church with him this Sunday." Oh boy. To my way of thinking, the problem isn't necessarily that he's religious; it's more that he doesn't have anything to counter it with, like a

drinking problem or weird sexual tastes. "Well, actually he is a little weird in that category," she admits. This livens up the conversation for a few minutes.

Before leaving the phone booth I plug the music back into my head. More hollering from Van. I notice as I set out on my walk that the New York landscape has taken on the blurred and sepia tones of a distant memory. I'm already back in Iowa, waiting for my body to join me.

Once home, I discover that I'm bored. Outside, long blank fields of corn and the blue midwestern sky. Inside, the same dustballs in the same corners. The cat carries tiny corpses up to the back step and arranges them in rows. The kid next door plays basketball with earphones on in his driveway, mouthing lyrics that would turn your hair white if you could hear them. Squint your eyes and he looks a little bit like Dave Anderson. Close your eyes altogether and the blond poet appears.

I perfect the art of brooding, gazing for hours at the paint on my living room ceiling, smoking and smoking. Elizabeth comes to visit me one weekend and we try on each other's clothes and paint our toenails maroon.

"I'll say one thing," she remarks. "I do happen to have decent *feet*." And she turns them this way and that, admiring.

My own feet look like they belong to a stranger with too much time on her hands. I stretch out on the couch and feed myself a potato chip. There is a long hair-sized crack running down the center of the ceiling.

"Don't brood in *front* of me," she says.

Mister Spider has built a web right above my giant, dying, phallic-looking cactus. It's a little trampoline and he's bouncing around in the center of it right now. Even the spiders are bored.

"It could be worse," she mentions. "We could be having to

entertain those two mopes." She means our ex-husbands, the Jim and Eric show.

If they were here, this is what they'd be doing: nothing, that's what. They'd be placidly sitting around, waiting for us to make something happen.

"So we'd still be bored," she concludes, "*and* we wouldn't even be able to paint our toenails, for fear of ridicule." It's true. Not only would it be boring but I'd have that old feeling back of constantly imagining myself as a widow wearing a great outfit. The phone rings.

"Who could be calling me here?" Elizabeth says.

We let it ring and ring until the answering machine kicks in and then we tiptoe over to listen. "This is what I do when you call," I tell her.

My answering machine voice lies about my whereabouts and then the beep comes on. Suddenly I'm standing on my circus footstool like a mouse has been let loose in the room. It's the guy.

"Hi, Jo Ann, this is X," he says and then leaves a long, rambling, totally coherent message and hangs up. Oh man. He's shimmering in my living room like a genie released from a bottle.

I don't know whether to faint or kill myself. Elizabeth laughs unbecomingly. I put both hands around my own neck. We do our silent screaming routine.

We are no longer bored.